973.92
MAy.

The Eisenhower Presidency and the 1950s

The Eisenhower Presidency and the 1950s

Edited and with an introduction by
Michael S. Mayer
The University of Montana

Houghton Mifflin Company   Boston   New York

Editor in Chief: *Jean Woy*
Senior Associate Editor: *Frances Gay*
Senior Project Editor: *Susan Westendorf*
Associate Production/Design Coordinator: *Deborah Frydman*
Manufacturing Coordinator: *Andrea Wagner*
Marketing Manager: *Sandra McGuire*

Cover design: Sarah Melhado
Cover image: Inauguration Day, January 20, 1953. Courtesy of
Dwight D. Eisenhower Library.

Printed in the U.S.A.

Library of Congress Catalog Card Number: 97-72519

ISBN: 0-669-41699-1

1   2   3   4   5   6   7   8   9-DOH   01   00   99   98   97

For Ruth, Victor, and Susan

The Editor

Michael S. Mayer

Born in Baltimore, Maryland, Michael S. Mayer earned a B.A. and an M.A. at Duke University and a Ph.D. at Princeton University. He has taught at Princeton University, St. Vincent College, the University of Alabama, Auckland University, and the University of Illinois. Mayer is now associate professor of History at the University of Montana. He is author of *Simon E. Soboloff* (1980), the *Instructor's Manual* to accompany *The American Nation* (7th ed., 1991; 8th ed., 1995; 9th ed., 1997), and the *Instructor's Manual* to accompany *A Short History of the American Nation* (6th ed., 1993; 7th ed., 1997). He also edited and wrote the introduction to Merrill Proudfoot, *Diary of a Sit-In* (1990). His articles have appeared in the *Journal of Southern History, Journal of Policy History, Congress and the Presidency, Australasian Journal of American Studies,* and *The New Zealand Journal of History.* He contributed essays to *Reexamining the Eisenhower Presidency* (1993), edited by Shirley Anne Warshaw; *Dwight D. Eisenhower: Soldier, President, Statesman* (1987), edited by Joann P. Krieg; *American Political Trials* (revised ed., 1994), edited by Michal R. Belknap; and *Law and the Great Plains* (1996), edited by John R. Wunder.

Preface

The fifties continue to fascinate and amuse Americans and historians of America. However, the attitude of Americans toward those years has changed markedly over time, from bemused contempt in the 1960s, to nostalgic longing in the 1970s, to a more sophisticated appreciation in the last fifteen years. Similarly, the historical reputation of Dwight D. Eisenhower, the president who occupied the White House during most of the decade, has evolved. Once regarded as an inept, if well-intentioned, figurehead, recent scholarship has portrayed him as an able leader. The essays in this collection reflect recent historians' understanding of the complexity of the era and the revised image of Eisenhower and his presidency.

The majority of the essays deal with politics and policies of the Eisenhower presidency. They reflect conflicting interpretations of Eisenhower's tenure in office and the policies he pursued. The last two chapters contain a brief sample of the brilliant work now being done on American culture and society in the postwar era. Studies of American culture during the period merit an entire collection devoted to that topic alone. Readers drawn to such subjects may consult the bibliographical essay at the end of this volume for a guide to that burgeoning literature.

This book is structured to help readers get the most from the various essays. Headnotes to each article place the essay in context and provide some information about the essay's author. The Chronology lists important dates and events. The bibliographical essay is organized by topic and offers additional reading on the issues raised by the essays in this collection.

I would like to thank the authors and publishers of the works reprinted in this volume for their cooperation. David Emmons of the University of Montana offered valuable comments on the introduction. Many other scholars read and commented on this work or parts of it. The book was improved by their suggestions, and I would like to thank them:

Richard M. Abrams, University of California, Berkeley
Numan V. Bartley, University of Georgia
Paul S. Boyer, University of Wisconsin, Madison
Richard C. Crepeau, University of Central Florida

William L. O'Neill, Rutgers University
F. Ross Peterson, Utah State University
Julian M. Pleasants, University of Florida
Michael Schaller, University of Arizona

Susan Mayer proofread parts of the manuscript.

Finally, the editors at D. C. Heath and Houghton Mifflin contributed greatly to the final product. James Miller, then the history editor at Heath, brought me to the project and got things under way. Lauren Johnson, a developmental editor at Heath, arranged for the first readers' reports. Jean L. Woy, Vice President and Editor in Chief for History and Political Science at Houghton Mifflin, guided the project during the transition from Heath to Houghton Mifflin and helped with the structure of this volume. Fran Gay, Editor for History and Political Science, listened, offered suggestions, and brought her enthusiasm and interest to the project. To all of them I owe a debt of gratitude.

M.S.M.

Contents

IV. Eisenhower and Foreign Policy

V. American Culture in the 1950s

VI. American Society in the 1950s

Introduction

The decade of the 1950s in America evokes many images: President Dwight Eisenhower's famous grin, Senator Joseph McCarthy's scowling visage, black leather jackets and ducktail haircuts, Marilyn Monroe's voluptuous curves and come-hither expression, the towering arc of a home run by Mickey Mantle, an over-the-shoulder catch by Willie Mays, suburban tract houses, young mothers strolling through suburban shopping centers with their children, Davy Crockett, Hula Hoops, Sputnik, the back seat of a '57 Chevy, Elvis Presley's curled lip, and a young Martin Luther King, Jr., leading the African American community of Montgomery, Alabama, in a boycott of the city's segregated buses. Indeed, the fifties serve as a kind of Rorschach test. What one imagines about the fifties often tells more about the person doing the imagining than it does about the fifties.

In the mid-1970s, America had just experienced the turmoil of the war in Vietnam, race riots, unrest on college campuses, and Watergate. The country was plagued with economic problems and an energy shortage. Faced with an uncomfortable present, Americans looked fondly back to the seemingly tranquil days of the Eisenhower era. The film *American Graffiti* and the television show *Happy Days* presented Americans of the seventies with a better image of themselves, or at least of their past. *American Graffiti* and *Happy Days* portrayed a prosperous America at peace with the world and with itself.

When examined on its own terms, however, rather than through the distorting lens of the sixties and seventies, the decade of the fifties takes on a different appearance. The reality of the fifties was only partly the world of *Happy Days*. The historian Carl Degler aptly summed up those years as a time of affluence and anxiety. Although the American economy was the most productive and the American standard of living was the highest in the history of the world, not all Americans shared in the wealth. Even if America was the most powerful nation in the world, Americans feared the Soviet Union, communism, and nuclear annihilation.

Everywhere one looks, the fifties present a more complex picture than a first glance would indicate. The American economy completed the transformation, begun in the 1920s, from a primary industrial economy to a consumer economy. The way people earned their livings, what they bought, and where they bought the new products all changed. The population shifted from the North and East to the South and West. Even as still more Americans moved to urban areas, about half of urban dwellers lived not in the cities, but in suburban peripheries. The migration to the suburbs stripped the cities of their tax bases, even as the demand for urban services increased. The baby boom taxed the resources of school systems, and progressive theories of education came under increasing and increasingly critical scrutiny. College campuses in the fifties were placid only in comparison with the turmoil of the sixties. The GI Bill opened the doors of higher education to millions of students who otherwise might never have considered college a possibility. The affluence of the period meant still more had the opportunity to go to college. In response to the increasing number of students, institutions grew in size and multiplied in number. Adding to the stress of rapid growth, the GI Bill changed the social composition of students—and eventually that of the professoriate. The country began, haltingly, to address the issue of racial inequality. A titanic struggle with the Soviet Union played itself out on an almost daily basis all over the world. Calm is a relative term.

Cultural critics, who had witnessed the horrors of Hitler's Germany and Stalin's Soviet Union, worried about the threat to the individual posed by mass society. The specter of totalitarianism provided the backdrop for virtually all intellectual endeavor of the decade. The sociology of David Riesman, William Whyte, and C. Wright Mills; the political theory of Hannah Arendt; the psychology of Harry Stack Sullivan; the theology of Reinhold Niebuhr; and the fiction of John Updike and J. D. Salinger all addressed the relationship of the individual to society and the threat that mass society posed to individuality. Some intellectuals saw in McCarthy the possibility of a totalitarian dictatorship emerging in the United States. Others worried that social pressures to conform, amplified by the mass media, could produce the same result without a dictatorship. The American people, they warned, might not need a Hitler or a Stalin; they might do it to themselves—voluntarily.

Only relatively recently have historians begun to explore the rich, complex, and sometimes contradictory experience of the

United States in the fifties. Historians in the 1970s who began to explore the Eisenhower era faced taunts from colleagues. How, the skeptics asked, could one write the history of an era when nothing happened? Those historians who ventured to write about Dwight Eisenhower and his administration faced even more pointed barbs. Snide comments about the bland leading the bland greeted historians and political scientists who indicated an interest in the thirty-fourth president.

The traditional image of Eisenhower was that of a detached, incompetent, genial former general who was utterly out of his depth as president. Jokes told of an Eisenhower doll (wind it up and it does nothing for eight years). This view was influenced at least in part by the fact that liberal Democrats dominated historical writing on the postwar era. The experience of the American involvement in Indochina and the domestic unrest of the 1960s prompted some to question the postwar liberal consensus. This, in turn, led some historians to re-examine the 1940s and 1950s from a different perspective. They found an appealing figure in Eisenhower, a president who ended one war and did not begin another, who cut defense spending and warned of the influence of the military-industrial complex. In addition, large collections of papers became available to historical researchers. New perspectives along with access to archives generated an active interest in the 1950s and in the president who presided over most of the decade.

The first of this new scholarship began to appear in the early 1970s. Explorations in the Eisenhower Library in Abilene, Kansas, led a number of scholars to conclude that Eisenhower was much more active, informed, and competent than had previously been assumed. Many also concluded that Eisenhower was more politically conservative than had generally been believed. In the mid-1970s, the Eisenhower Library opened several enormous collections of papers, including Eisenhower's own papers as president. The new material reinforced the perception of Eisenhower's involvement in his administration, his control over policy, his competence, and his ability to express himself clearly and forcefully with the written word. On the other hand, the new material called into question the image of Eisenhower as a hard-line conservative. The president's personal correspondence in particular revealed that although he was a fiscal conservative, his politics fell well within the consensus established by Franklin Roosevelt and the New Deal.

By the early 1980s, this wave of new scholarship became known as "Eisenhower revisionism." In one sense, Eisenhower revisionism has come to dominate scholarship on the Eisenhower presidency; at the same time, however, the term has become so broad as to be meaningless. Early revisionist scholars demolished the caricature of Eisenhower as a bumbling goofball. Virtually all scholars now accept, at least to some degree, the idea that Eisenhower was a capable politician and an engaged president. Once the old image of Eisenhower had been laid to rest, however, scholars began to debate the nature and wisdom of Eisenhower's policies. These debates dominate the first four chapters of this anthology.

The first chapter contains overall assessments of Eisenhower's presidency. James David Barber's account represents the older portrayal of Eisenhower as an uninformed, do-nothing, dithering grandfather. Fred Greenstein's early and important revisionist account posits that Eisenhower actively and successfully managed his administration from behind the scenes, while presenting himself to the public as a leader above politics and partisanship. Stephen E. Ambrose focuses on Eisenhower's policies and finds that, particularly in foreign affairs, those policies were wise and largely successful.

Senator Joseph McCarthy dominated the headlines, if not the administration, during Eisenhower's first two years in the White House. The second chapter presents two conflicting views of how Eisenhower dealt with McCarthy. Jeff Broadwater criticizes Eisenhower's approach to McCarthy and the "ism" to which the senator gave his name. Broadwater sees no evidence of Eisenhower's hand, hidden or not, in bringing down the junior senator from Wisconsin. In contrast, William Bragg Ewald, Jr., chronicles the administration's maneuvering behind the scenes, first to confront and then to destroy the demagogue from Wisconsin.

The third chapter examines Eisenhower's record on civil rights. Robert Fredrick Burk sees Eisenhower's response to emerging demands by African Americans for equality as minimal and largely symbolic. In the process, he argues, Eisenhower gave "both voice and official sanction to a new and more respectable kind of civil rights conservatism." Michael S. Mayer, while conceding that Eisenhower was moderate in his views and cautious in his actions, contends that Eisenhower and his administration made important, if limited, contributions to civil rights.

By his own calculation, Eisenhower spent most of his working hours as president on foreign policy. The fourth chapter turns its attention to Eisenhower's management of foreign affairs. Robert A. Divine's mildly revisionist overview of Eisenhower's foreign policy praises the president's restraint in the exercise of American power. Robert J. McMahon challenges the idea that Eisenhower was restrained in his use of power in the Third World.

The two selections in the fifth chapter consider various aspects of American culture in the 1950s. Richard H. Pells examines how intellectuals confronted issues of conformity and alienation during these years. Peter Biskind argues that concerns over science and the cold war permeated monster movies of the decade.

The last chapter surveys American society of the 1950s. J. Ronald Oakley provides a brief overview of the economy. Elaine Tyler May draws connections between cold-war ideology and domestic life; she concludes that the ideology of the cold war and the revival of domesticity were "two sides of the same coin."

Whether one looks at politics, culture, or society, one cannot help but be struck by the complexity and ambiguity of postwar America. These essays invite the reader to consider and to draw conclusions about key issues that continue to shape American life. Above all, they introduce readers to the wonderful richness of both American society in the 1950s and the scholarship that has attempted to make sense of it.

1950	David Riesman, *The Lonely Crowd*
	North Korea invades South Korea
	Alger Hiss convicted of perjury
	Klaus Fuchs arrested for spying
	Julius and Ethel Rosenberg arrested for spying
	Internal Security (McCarran) Act
	NSC-68
	Senator Joseph McCarthy charges there are communists in the State Department
1951	Twenty-second Amendment limits president to two terms
	Truman relieves MacArthur of command
	Supreme Court upholds Smith Act in *Dennis v. U.S.*
	J. D. Salinger, *Catcher in the Rye*
	C. Wright Mills, *White Collar*
1952	Dwight D. Eisenhower elected president
	Republicans win both houses of Congress
	Hollywood introduces three-dimensional (3-D) movies
	U.S. explodes first hydrogen bomb
	Norman Vincent Peale, *The Power of Positive Thinking*
	Ralph Ellison, *Invisible Man*
1953	CIA backs coup against Mohammed Mossadeq in Iran that reinstates Reza Shah Pahlavi
	Korean War armistice
	Earl Warren appointed Chief Justice of U.S. Supreme Court
	Marlon Brando stars in *The Wild One*
	Alfred Kinsey, *Sexual Behavior in the Human Female*
	Arthur Bestor, *Educational Wasteland*
	First issue of *Playboy*
	Joseph Stalin dies
1954	Supreme Court rules segregated schools unconstitutional in *Brown v. Board of Education*
	Vietminh force French to surrender at Dienbienphu
	Geneva Conference
	CIA backs coup against Jacobo Arabenz Guzman in Guatemala

Communist China bombards offshore islands of Quemoy and Matsu

Army-McCarthy hearings

"Shake, Rattle and Roll" by Bill Haley and His Comets becomes first rock 'n' roll song to break into top ten

1955 Jonas Salk's vaccine for polio approved for use

Supreme Court rules that schools must desegregate with "all deliberate speed"

Congress requires that "In God We Trust" appear on all U.S. currency

First McDonald's opens

James Dean stars in *Rebel without a Cause*

Elvis Presley has hits with "Blue Suede Shoes," "Heartbreak Hotel," and "Hound Dog"

AFL and CIO merge

Beginning of Montgomery bus boycott

Geneva Summit

Eisenhower suffers heart attack

1956 Eisenhower reelected

Montgomery bus boycott ends in victory when Supreme Court rules that segregated buses violate Constitution

One hundred and one southern members of Congress sign "Southern Manifesto" pledging to resist *Brown* decision by "all lawful means"

Suez crisis

Soviets crush uprising in Hungary

Federal Highway Act

William Whyte, *The Organization Man*

C. Wright Mills, *The Power Elite*

Alan Ginsberg, "Howl"

1957 Soviet Union launches Sputnik

Civil Rights Act of 1957

Founding of Southern Christian Leadership Conference

Eisenhower sends federal troops to enforce a court order to desegregate Little Rock's Central High School

Eisenhower Doctrine announced

Jack Kerouac, *On the Road*

Peak of baby boom (4.3 million births)

Quiz show scandals
1958 National Defense Education Act
Berlin crisis
U.S. Marines sent to Lebanon
Communist Chinese bombard Quemoy and Matsu
Sherman Adams resigns after accusations of improper use of official influence
U.S. launches *Explorer* (first American satellite)
National Aeronautics and Space Administration (NASA) founded
Berry Gordy, Jr., founds Motown Records
1959 Castro overthrows Batista in Cuba
Alaska and Hawaii become states
St. Lawrence Seaway opens
Vice President Richard Nixon's "kitchen debate" with Soviet Premier Nikita Khrushchev
Khrushchev visits the U.S.
1960 Soviets shoot down U-2 spy plane
Lunch counter sit-ins
Voting Rights Act of 1960
United States breaks diplomatic relations with Cuba
John F. Kennedy is elected president

I

Eisenhower as President

The official portrait of President Dwight D. Eisenhower. Eisenhower projected a paternal image, at once strong and kindly. This portrait captures his public image. (UPI/Corbis-Bettman)

James David Barber

EISENHOWER AS A "PASSIVE-NEGATIVE" PRESIDENT

From the 1950s well into the 1970s, most historians and political scientists regarded Eisenhower as, at best, a caretaker president. They contended that Eisenhower failed to exert forceful leadership and neglected major problems facing the nation. In his influential book *The Presidential Character,* James David Barber, a professor of political science at Duke University, followed this trend. Barber related personality traits to presidential performance and classified Eisenhower as a "passive-negative" president. Barber's was one of the most elegant scholarly treatments that portrayed Eisenhower as an ineffectual, uninformed, and disinterested president; perhaps it was the last.

The passive Presidents pose a different danger to the peace of the world and the progress of the nation: the danger of drift. Historically they mark breathing spells, times of recovery in our frantic political life. Their contribution can be restorative. They give ear to popular needs for reassurance or legitimacy; their elections represent a public sigh of relief after a period when the apparent aggressiveness or corruption of politics has worn down the people's political energies. The psychological pay-off is evident—but in an era of rapid social change the price of relaxation may be too high. The social problems do not disappear because a President neglects them. Sooner or later the accounting has to come. What passive Presidents ignore active Presidents inherit.

The passive Presidents may be a vanishing breed. By my estimation, there has been only one passive President since Calvin Coolidge, and his case is a mixed one. Possibly the public senses that rapid change requires an active President. But insofar as the popular needs for rest and moral restoration persist and accumulate, the psychological burden on the President will increase, and

Excerpted from James D. Barber, *The Presidential Character,* Fourth Edition (Upper Saddle River, N.J.: Prentice-Hall, 1992). Reprinted by permission of the author. Footnotes omitted.

eventually the people may once again call some Cincinnatus from the plow, not to get the nation moving again but to bind wounds and inspire faith.

The passive Presidents are puzzling. They hold the same place of ultimate power as Wilson, Hoover, and Johnson did, but they hold back from power's exercise. In terms of their own motives, one wonders why they take the job. In terms of political effect, one wonders how they protected the Presidency from collapse, or even significant modification, as they sidestepped positive commitments. In each case, the way they combined character, world view, and style helps make clear what it means for a man to be handed the Presidential sword only to spend much of his time trying to get it back in the scabbard.

The passive-*negative* type gives an impression of being reluctantly, unwillingly involved in his political work, in continual retreat from the demands office imposes on him. He tends to withdraw from the conflict and uncertainty of politics to an emphasis on vague principles and procedural arrangements. His presence in a political role can be explained primarily in terms of his sense of duty, which leads him to compensate for feelings of uselessness by becoming a guardian of the right and proper way, above the sordid politicking of lesser men. Calvin Coolidge was the clearest twentieth-century example. Dwight Eisenhower also showed these themes, but in a more complicated mix.

Calvin Coolidge complained that "One of the most appalling trials which confront a President is the perpetual clamor for public utterances." But this "foster-child of silence" was anything but quiet in public. In office 67 months, he held 520 press conferences, an average of 7.8 per month, compared with Franklin Roosevelt's 6.9. He gave radio addresses about once a month. He got off to an excellent start with the reporters, cracking jokes at this first conference; their "hearty applause" on that occasion made it "one of my most pleasant memories." They were "the boys" who came along on his vacations. Clearly he enjoyed their enjoyment, particularly when he could surprise or titillate them with Yankee humor. He carefully stage-managed his "I do not choose to run for President in nineteen twenty-eight" statement, releasing the news at noon on the fourth anniversary of taking office, grinning broadly. His wife was as surprised as the reporters were. He let himself be photographed in full Indian headdress, cowboy chaps and hat, overalls, and any number of other outfits; there is a picture of him presenting a sap bucket to Henry Ford. When a friend protested that his antics made people laugh, Coolidge said, "Well, it's good for people to laugh."

His formal addresses had a completely different tone. They were sermons from the church of New England idealism. "When the President speaks," he wrote, "it ought to be an event," by which he meant a serious and dignified and uplifting event. He spoke on "Education: the Cornerstone of Self-Government," "The High Place of Labor," "Ordered Liberty and World Peace," "Authority and Religious Liberty," "Religion and the Republic," "The Genius of America," "Destiny Is in You," "Do the Day's Work," "The Things of the Spirit Come First," and "The Chief Ideal of the American People Is Idealism"—this was Coolidge in the presidential pulpit. And he was quite serious. When Will Rogers imitated his nasal twang and penchant for clichés, he was much offended and refused Rogers' apology.

Coolidge sincerely believed in hard work. He felt busy, even rushed, but his constant routine included a daily nap and often eleven hours of sleep in twenty-four. Often tired and bored, he gradually abandoned all physical exercise except for brief walks and spent much time in silent contemplation, gazing out his office window. His strength was not effort but patience. "Let well enough alone," was his motto. He was the "provincial who refuses to become excited over events for which he has no direct responsibility." He kept Harding's cabinet, let former Attorney General Daugherty, who had been tried for conspiracy to defraud the government, hang on for a long time, tried to delay his friends' efforts to boost him in 1924. Asked how he kept fit he said, "By avoiding the big problems." Most of the time Coolidge simply did not want to be bothered.

Underneath these tactics, supporting and justifying them, was a strain of mystical resignation. "I am only in the clutch of forces that are greater than I am," he wrote, despite being "the most powerful man in the world." He bore his young son's death with Roman stoicism: "The ways of Providence are beyond our understanding." The dedicated man, he wrote in his newspaper column, "finds that in the time of need some power outside himself directs his course." Coolidge could wait, storing up his meager energies with a feeling of rightness in entrusting himself to fate. "Government is growth," he said, and added: "—slow growth." He and Providence presided while the rate slowed down.

Coolidge got rid of much work by giving it to others, and he believed in doing just that. "One rule of action more important than all others consists in never doing anything that some one else can do for you." He appointed or retained "men of sufficient ability so that they can solve all the problems that arise under their jurisdiction." He rarely interfered and he resented others interfering with him. His loyal helper Frank Stearns got repeated rebuffs for his trouble. Coolidge seldom discussed political matters with his wife. He complained of Hoover as Secretary of Commerce (Coolidge called him "the wonder boy" or "the miracle worker"): "That man has offered me unsolicited advice for six years, all of it bad!"

Eisenhower as President is, I think, best approximated in the passive-negative category, though his case presents certain difficulties. He carried over into the Presidency a rigorous schedule of activity, putting in longer hours than did Coolidge, at least until illness required him to slow down. He proves an exception to the simple idea that usually holds: that the relative expenditure of energy on Presidential tasks stands as a partial symptom of one's orientation to those tasks. Furthermore, Eisenhower often displayed optimism; he was certainly no gloomy gus in the White House, though he was often irritable and depressed. He comes as close as any President to being one who strays beyond our crude categories, enforcing the reminder that the forest can sometimes hide the trees. In the substance of his orientation, however, we can see pretty plainly themes much like those Coolidge played out more blatantly.

On a great many occasions in the biographies Eisenhower is found asserting himself by denying himself, taking a strong stand against the suggestion that he take a strong stand. No, he would not get down in the gutter with Joseph McCarthy, not stop the Cohn and Schine hijinks. Franklin Roosevelt has usurped Congressional powers, he thought, and he would not do that: "I want to say with all the emphasis at my command that this Administration has absolutely *no* personal choice for a new Majority Leader. *We* are not going to get into *their* business." When "those damn monkeys on the Hill" acted up, he would stay out of it. Was he under attack in the press? "Listen!" Eisenhower said. "Anyone who has time to listen to commentators or read columnists obviously doesn't have enough work to do." Should he engage in personal summitry on the international front? "This idea of the President of the United States going personally abroad to negotiate—it's just damn stupid." With a new Cabinet, wouldn't it make sense to oversee them rather carefully? To George Humphrey, the President said, "I guess you know about as much about the job as I do." And his friend Arthur Larson writes that the President found patronage "nauseating" and "partisan political effect was not only at the bottom of the list—indeed, it did not exist as a motive at all." In 1958 the President said, "Frankly, I don't care too much about the congressional elections."

Pressed to appear on television, Eisenhower said, "I keep telling you fellows I don't like to do this sort of thing. I can think of nothing more boring, for the American public, than to have to sit in their living rooms for a whole half hour looking at my face on their television screens." Furthermore, he did not want to get into traditional political speechmaking: "I don't think the people *want* to be listening to a Roosevelt, sounding as if he were one of the Apostles, or the partisan yipping of a Truman." Asked to make a speech, he would respond with irritation: "What is it that needs to be said? I am not going out there just to listen to my tongue clatter!" Sometimes he would agree reluctantly: "Well, all right, but not over twenty minutes." And for all his cheerfulness in the midst of applauding crowds, he expressed a strong distaste in private for the "killing motorcades" and "another yowling mob" and the "unattractive lot" of local politicians he encountered. For whatever reasons (he had once been struck by lightning while delivering a lecture), Eisenhower "the man—and the President—was never more decisive than when he held to a steely resolve *not* to do something that he sincerely believed wrong in itself or alien to his office."

Sherman Adams explained that Eisenhower "focused his mind completely on the big and important aspects of the questions we discussed, shutting out with a strongly self-disciplined firmness the smaller and petty side issues when they crept into the conversation." In other words, he did not so much select problems upon which to concentrate as he selected an *aspect* of all problems—the aspect of principle.

When someone aggravated Eisenhower, his practice was, he said, to "write his name on a piece of paper, put it in my lower desk drawer and shut the drawer." When it came time to end his four-pack-a-day cigarette habit, "I found that the easiest way was just to put it out of your mind."

Eisenhower's tendency to move away from involvements, to avoid personal commitments, was supported by belief: "My personal convictions, no matter how strong, cannot be the final answer," he said, and the definition of democracy he liked best was "simply the opportunity for self-discipline." As a military man he had detested and avoided politics at least since, in his first command, he was pressed by a Congressman for a favor. His beliefs were carved into epigrams:

> He that conquereth his own soul is greater than he who taketh a city.
>
> Forget yourself and personal fortunes.
>
> Belligerence is the hallmark of insecurity.
>
> Never lose your temper, except intentionally.

It is the tone, the flavor, the aura of self-denial and refusal that counts in these comments. Eisenhower is not attacking or rejecting others, he is simply turning away from them, leaving them alone, refusing to interfere with them.

His character is further illuminated in his complaints, which are concentrated around the theme of being bothered. His temper flared when he felt he was being imposed upon, interfered with on matters that he wanted others to handle. From the beginning of his Presidency he resented the heavy schedule—much of it trivial—and being constantly asked to involve himself in unnecessary detail. He "heatedly gave the Cabinet to understand that he was sick and tired of being bothered about patronage." "When does anybody get any time to think around here?" he complained to Adams.

"Nothing gets him out of sorts faster," writes Robert Donovan, "than for a subordinate to come in and start to hem and haw about a decision. He wants the decision and not the thinking out loud." Leaving the White House for a ten-day Christmas vacation in 1953, he remarked, "Nothing can get me mad today. Anything that will get me away from *this* place!" His heart attack in September 1955 was triggered, Eisenhower said, when he was repeatedly interrupted on the golf links by unnecessary phone calls from the State Department. Long before that his reluctance about being bothered with politics was evident. Back in 1943 when an American Legion post suggested he run for President, Ike burst out, "Baloney! Why can't a simple soldier be left alone to follow out his orders. And I furiously object to the word 'candidate'—I ain't and won't." When he finally managed to stop the boomlet for his nomination in 1948, he said he felt "as if I've had an abscessed tooth pulled" and in 1950 he said, "I don't know why people are always nagging me to run for President. I think I've gotten too old." "Look, son," he told a persistent reporter as the 1948 speculations continued, "I cannot conceive of any circumstance that could drag out of me permission to consider me for any political post from dogcatcher to Grand High Supreme King of the Universe." Campaigning in 1952 and "told of the scheduling of yet another speech or, worse still, another motorcade, he would grate his teeth in wrath and grind out the cry: 'Those fools on the National Committee! Are they trying to perform the feat of electing a dead man?'" And, he said, "You know, once in a while I get to the point, with everybody staring at me, where I want to go back indoors and pull down the curtain."

Why then did Eisenhower bother to become President? Why did he answer those phone calls on the golf links? Because he thought he ought to. He was a sucker for duty, and he always had been. Dutiful sentiments which would sound false coming from most political leaders ring true from Eisenhower.

My only satisfaction in life is to hope that my effort means something to the other fellow. What can I do to repay society for the wonderful opportunities it has given me?

. . . a decision that I have never recanted or regretted. The decision was to perform every duty given me in the Army to the best of my ability and to do the best I could to make a creditable record, no matter what the nature of the duty.

> . . . in trying to explain to you a situation that has been tossed in my teeth more than once (my lack of extended troop duty in recent years), all I accomplished was to pass up something I *wanted* to do, in favor of something I thought I *ought* to do, and then . . . find myself not even doing the latter.

Eisenhower did not feel a duty to save the world or to become a great hero, but simply to contribute what he could the best he was able. Throughout his life—from the family Bible readings, from the sportsmanship of a boy who wanted nothing more than to be a first-rate athlete (and risked his life to save his leg for that), from the West Point creed—Eisenhower felt amid the questions about many things that duty was a certainty:

> His intimates have learned that no appeal will move him more deeply than "This is a duty you owe the American people." When he was being pressed to run for the Presidency, one aide recalls that every possible argument and pressure was employed upon him, "but the only one that made any difference was that it was his duty."

Another aide remembered that Eisenhower "never lost his view of himself as standing apart from politics generally and from his own party in particular"—he never saw himself as personally dominating political forces. "He has taken on a third-person attitude toward life," another observer wrote. " 'The President feels—' and 'It seems to the President—' have become standard marks of his speech, supplanting the widespread and overworked 'I'. The impression he gives is of standing aside, as employer, and viewing himself as employee."

Yet Eisenhower very much wanted to make a contribution. Once while laboring over a speech he said, "You know, it is *so* difficult. You come up to face these terrible issues, and you know that what is in almost everyone's heart is a wish for peace, and you want so much to do *something*. And then you wonder . . . if there really *is* anything you can do . . . by words and promises. . . . You wonder and you wonder. . . ."

In all these respects, and also in his personal comradeliness, Eisenhower fits the character of the passive-negative type. The key orientation is toward performing duty with modesty and the political adaptation is characterized by protective retreats to principle, ritual, and personal virtue. The political strength of this character is its legitimacy. It inspires trust in the incorruptibility and the good intentions of the man. Its political weakness is its inability to produce, though it may contribute by preventing. Typically, the passive-negative character presides over drift and confusion, partially concealed by the apparent orderliness of the formalities. Sam Lubell caught the crux of this character when he saw in Eisenhower "one man's struggle between a passion for active duty and a dream of quiet retirement." And Eisenhower himself displayed the essential passiveness of his political character when he told Walter Cronkite in 1961, "The President has to be concerned with everything that happens to any human in the United States and often abroad and that is—that happens to be brought to his notice." "He once told the Cabinet," Adams reports, "that if he was able to do nothing as President except balance the budget he would feel that his time in the White House had been well spent."

Eisenhower's beliefs about the world were, in many ways, as vague as Coolidge's, with the same highly general mode of expression in epigram. He rejected extremism, radical or reactionary, and came out for the middle of the road. In policy terms perhaps the most important Eisenhower contribution to domestic politics was his readiness, as the first Republican President since Hoover, to accept the broad dimensions of the welfare state rather than following some of his right-wing critics who wanted the New Deal repealed. Eisenhower invoked principles, but he refused to interpret them rigidly. Eisenhower had purposes, but he stopped short of pursuing them by mobilizing fully, behind his leadership, the political forces which had thrust him into office.

President Eisenhower's style centered in the organization of interpersonal relations. His remarkable rhetorical success seems to have happened without either great skill or great energy on his part. By the 1956 election voters had, by and large, forgotten all the reasons they had offered for his election in 1952 except "I like Ike." He won almost casually what so many other candidates and Presidents have sought so intensely through artifice: popular confidence in himself as man and President. Ike's very bumbling appears to have made him seem more "sincere," to use one of the

favorite human qualities of the 1950s. Not above letting professional advertising men tell him what to do in his campaigns, Eisenhower as President kept editing warm words out of his speeches. In
1957 Doris Fleeson parodied his speech style with a version of the
Gettysburg Address translated into Eisenhowerese, beginning:

> I haven't checked these figures, but 87 years ago, I think it was, a
> number of individuals organized a governmental set-up here in this
> country. I believe it covered certain Eastern areas, with this idea
> they were following up based on a sort of national independence
> arrangement and the program that every individual is just as good as
> every other individual.

He much preferred—and developed an effective style in—speaking
conservatively, especially about such large themes as peace and
prosperity. The Washington cognoscenti might ridicule him, but
he came across to the country. Walter Johnson summarizes his
contribution.

> Without Eisenhower as head of the Republican party, the venom that
> disgraced democratic politics in the closing years of Truman's presi-
> dency would have been rife in the nation. He purged national life of
> rancor. And by presenting himself continuously as standing at the
> moderate and reasonable center of American life, he was able to tune
> in on the deepest instincts of the people, who, at this stage in their
> history, desired pause, comfort and repose; a mood which reflected
> the spectacular expansion of the middle class base of American life.

This man, who had little use for inspirational blather, whose
speeches would not be long remembered for their eloquence, and
who continually resisted demands that he lecture his fellow citizens, revitalized national confidence almost in spite of himself. He
is a puzzling case. *His* political habits never stressed rhetoric, yet
that is where he excelled.

Eisenhower liked to deal with problems at a high level of policy. He resisted detail, resisted involvement in the niggling issues
that so often make the difference in politics. By a kind of role levi-
tation, he could rise above any number of low-level issues, as he
tried to do in the matter of Joseph McCarthy. Inevitably this sometimes left him out of touch with his responsibilities. In early 1957
Eisenhower presented his administration's budget—and promptly
invited Congress, much to the amazement of his supporters there,

to suggest "sensible reductions" in it. He submitted a civil rights bill and then told the press he did not himself agree with all aspects of it. *Life* magazine commented that "the fiasco of his program is in some part due to his own indecision and seeming unsureness in support of it." With painful honesty, Eisenhower would admit in press conferences that he had "never heard of" significant Administration activities. Sam Lubell [a noted political analysist in the 1950s] found increased speculation among voters as to who was actually running the country.

Eisenhower's stylistic bent was for organizing officialdom into a smooth-running machine—a structuring version of his personal relations style. He set about this quite deliberately:

> For years I had been in frequent contact with the Executive Office of the White House and I had certain ideas about the system, or lack of system, under which it operated. With my training in problems involving organization it was inconceivable to me that the work of the White House could not be better systematized than it had been during the years I had observed it.

In *The President's Men,* Patrick Anderson gives a cogent account of how Ike went about this reform. "The essence of Eisenhower's system of administration," Anderson writes, "was his belief in the delegation of authority." Retaining the basic staff offices he had inherited (Press Secretary, Congressional Relations Office, Special Counsel's Office, Appointments Secretary), the President added "The Assistant to the President" (Sherman Adams), a Special Assistant for National Security Affairs to work with a more formal National Security Council system, a Staff Secretary and a Secretary to the Cabinet (to turn that body into a regular instrument of Presidential decision-making), plus a number of Special Assistants to the President to advise him on particular policy areas. The overriding purpose of all these new elaborations was to simplify the President's task—to make sure he could save all his energies for the uttermost strategic considerations, undistracted by the litter of tactics. "A President who doesn't know how to decentralize will be weighed down with details and won't have time to deal with the big issues," Eisenhower said.

When Secretary of Defense Charles E. Wilson bothered him too often with details, Ike was blunt: "Look here, Charlie, I want *you* to run Defense. We *both* can't run it, and I *won't* run it. I was elected to worry about a lot of things other than the day-to-day operations of a department."

Eisenhower's carefully charted system did save him from immersion in trivia; decisions were so thoroughly staffed that by the time they got to him a great deal of extraneous matter had been sliced away and he could say yes or no. He was thus able, he felt, to ride herd on the immense variety and complexity of modern government. The President became the Supreme Coordinator, a coach of coaches, the master steersman keeping the craft moving steadily down the middle of the stream. But the system had its costs. To his natural disinclination to be "bothered" was added, as a result of extreme delegations, his staff's disinclination to "bother" him. "But the less he was bothered," as Richard Neustadt noted, "the less he knew, and the less he knew, the less confidence he felt in his own judgment. He let himself grow stale"—and thus all the more dependent on his advisors. Proposals which finally reached him were too often bland and superficial, bled white by the processes of compromise.

"The misfortune of Eisenhower's presidency," Anderson concludes,

> is that a man of such immense popularity and good will did not accomplish more. All the domestic problems which confronted the nation in the 1960s—the unrest of the Negro, the decay of the cities, the mediocrity of the schools, the permanence of poverty— were bubbling beneath the surface in the 1950s, but the President never seemed quite sure that they existed or, if they did, that they were problems with which he should not concern himself.

A character attracted by duty but repelled by politics, with a commonsensical, centrist view of the world, using a style stressing central coordination (though succeeding better on the rhetorical level), Eisenhower presided high over the nether regions of policy. Down there, much of the time, the "rich, full life" grew richer and fuller, sheltered by world peace, fed by an expanding economy. What was missing was a sensitivity at the highest level of government to the brittleness of social and political accommodations and a readiness to use power, where necessary, to stimulate creative tension. . . .

What Coolidge and Eisenhower shared was a political character and, to a degree, similar views of the world. Their styles were quite different, Coolidge primarily a rhetorician, Eisenhower primarily an interpersonal coordinator. But both shared with other passive-negative people in politics a propensity for withdrawal, for moving away from conflict and detail. Their stance toward political life was one of irritated resignation. They were performing duty under duress, not crusading after some political Holy Grail. Each felt that he ought to serve, ought to contribute, ought to do what he could to make things better for America. But one senses in their attitude an assumption that merely occupying the office of President provided justification enough, and that all expenditures of energy beyond that point were extra, not required. In any case, men of this type convey a resistance to intrusion, to being bothered by demands that they perform. Beneath the surface, they seem to be saying that they should not have to initiate, that problems should come to them rather than they to the problems, and that their responsibilities were limited primarily to preserving the fundamental values by applying them to disagreements no one else in the system could resolve.

The elements in the passive-negative orientation are consistent: the man does as little as he can of what he does not like to do. Psychologically, one suspects the demands of conscience are met in part by maintaining the feeling of sacrifice—the person confirms that he is doing his duty by the fact that he does not enjoy it. Thus reluctance is a defense. Low self-esteem is counteracted by the observation that others continually turn to one for help, for useful action.

Coolidge restored confidence in the legitimacy of his office after the scandals of the Harding administration; Eisenhower did the same following Truman's "mess in Washington." Each was valued for "character" in the sense of old-fashioned personal virtue and stability, and especially for his antipolitical honesty, for his apparent disdain for the calculated ploy. Perhaps the rhetoric of politics erodes, over time, as activists press for achievement and for those vigorous verbal banners which stretch so thinly over conglomerations of compromise. Eventually the people's hunger for straight talk comes through and produces a candidate who, whatever else he may be, seems honest.

The trouble with the passive-negative type in the Presidency is that he leaves vacant the energizing, initiating, stimulating possibilities of the role. He is a responder; issues are "brought to his attention"—and there are too damned many of them. Under the flag of legitimacy, the nation unites—and drifts. Presidential dignity is restored at the cost of Presidential leadership. As long as we have no king, this type may be necessary from time to time. But while we are restoring the national spirit in this way, the body politic lapses into laxness and the social order deteriorates as neglected tensions build up. Eventually some leader ready to shove as well as to stand fast, someone who enjoys the great game of politics, will have to pick up the pieces.

Fred Greenstein

EISENHOWER AS HIDDEN-HAND PRESIDENT

Fred Greenstein, a professor of politics at Princeton University, argued in an early and important revisionist article that conventional portrayals of Eisenhower's presidency (such as James David Barber's) were badly mistaken. According to Greenstein, Eisenhower did not delegate away the authority of the presidency, was not lazy or uninformed, and was not uninterested in politics. Rather, Greenstein argued, Eisenhower operated behind the scenes while maintaining a public image of the nonpartisan, genial former general. According to Greenstein, this "hidden hand" style of leadership enabled Eisenhower to maintain his popularity while actively and effectively pursuing his political and policy objectives. Writing at the end of Jimmy Carter's administration, Greenstein addressed himself to a growing sense that the modern presidency was an unmanageable office. At the time when Greenstein wrote, Eisenhower was the only president since Franklin D. Roosevelt to have won election to and served two full terms.

From Fred Greenstein, "Eisenhower as an Activist President: A Look at New Evidence" from *Political Science Quarterly*, vol. 94, no. 4 (1979–1980), pp. 575–580, 581–592, 596–599, footnotes omitted. Reprinted with permission.

The administration of Dwight D. Eisenhower is commonly thought to be devoid of interest to those who seek insight into the range of feasible ways to conduct the presidency in the era since the responsibilities and demands of that office mushroomed under Franklin D. Roosevelt. Most of the scholarly and serious journalistic commentators on Eisenhower as president have characterized him as an aging hero who reigned more than he ruled and who lacked the energy, motivation, and political skill to have a significant impact on events. If Eisenhower was an exemplar, to their minds, it was the negative sense of showing how one ought *not* to be president.

In recent years, however, there has been a slowly but steadily rising tide of Eisenhower revisionism. Some of the new interest in Eisenhower stems from nostalgia for the alleged placid, uncomplicated nature of the 1950s. Other interest derives from "postliberal" attraction to the kinds of policies he espoused—for example, curbs on defense spending, mildly incremental approaches to expanding welfare policies, and efforts to hold down inflation. A third category of revisionism, which might be called "instrumental revisionism," arises from reassessments of Eisenhower's performance as a political practitioner. In view of the debacles of his successors, the conduct in office of the only post-Twenty-second Amendment president to be elected to and complete two terms (and with continuingly high levels of public support at that) seems worthy of reconsideration on that ground alone.

Instrumental revisionist reexamination of Eisenhower's performance has to date been largely deductive. The two writers who have argued most forcefully that Eisenhower was not inept but instead a skilled politician who practiced the art of ruling in a deceptively veiled fashion are journalists who have relied heavily on close readings of the published record. Both have ingeniously reconstructed what seems to them the logic of Eisenhower's actions in various widely publicized events. They also have drawn on passages from writings of his contemporaries, such as the following by Richard Nixon in his 1962 memoir:

> [Eisenhower] was a far more complex and devious man than most people realized, and in the best sense of these words. Not shackled to a one-track mind, he always applied two, three or four lines of

reasoning to a single problem and he usually preferred the indirect approach where it would serve him better than the direct attack on a problem.

The observations on Eisenhower's presidential style adduced in this article differ from those of previous instrumental revisionists in that they are inductive rather than deductive. They are based mainly on one of the many newly available primary sources on his presidency, namely the collection of several thousand documents in the Whitman File at the Eisenhower Library. This archival trove, which is named after Eisenhower's personal secretary, Ann Whitman, was opened for scholarly perusal in the mid-1970s. The Whitman File provides far more thorough documentation of Eisenhower's day-to-day activities than has been preserved for other presidencies, including: daily lists of the president's appointments; detailed minutes of formal meeting such as those of the cabinet, National Security Council (NSC), and legislative leaders; extensive notes and numerous transcripts of informal meetings between the president and other political figures; transcripts or summaries of his face-to-face and telephone conversations; texts of pre-press conference briefings; and many observations by Mrs. Whitman of comings and goings in the White House, of offhand remarks by the president, and even of fluctuations in his mood and temper.

The Whitman File also contains Eisenhower's copious comments on and interpolations in the numerous drafts of his speeches; his memoranda and notes to colleagues; an extraordinary number of "personal and confidential" letters he dictated to correspondents; and his private diary, which reaches back to Eisenhower's service in the 1930s as aide to General Douglas MacArthur in the Philippines and extends forward into his late retirement years. The Eisenhower presidency is further illuminated by the unpublished diaries and oral histories of his personal associates, many of whom are now more disposed to be interviewed than would have been the case shortly after the end of his administration.

The conclusions I draw from an extensive reading of the archival materials are more consistent with the inferences of the instrumental revisionists than with the traditional lore deprecating Eisenhower's leadership skills and efforts. Eisenhower was politically astute and informed, actively engaged in putting his personal stamp on public policy, and applied a carefully thought-out conception of leadership to the conduct of his presidency.

The Nature and Style of Eisenhower's Activism

The term activism is commonly used to refer to three presidential attributes that in fact may vary independently of one another: sheer extent of activity; commitment to use the office so as to have an impact on public policy; and actual success in affecting policy. Despite the widespread belief that Eisenhower was not an activist president in any of these respects, he worked hard and both intended to and did have an impact on policy. Moreover, as will be illustrated throughout this essay, his activism has not been evident to many observers of his presidency due to the "low-profile" nature of his leadership style. I shall begin by considering the extent of activity of this president who often was portrayed as being more attentive to golf than to government.

Extent of Activity

The extent of Eisenhower's activity can be assessed by examining the lists of his appointments and meetings for each official day. The lists for some days can be supplemented by taking account of the prodigious amount of correspondence he dictated and other paper work he engaged in along with his numerous telephone conversations. Furthermore, oral histories and interviews with people who worked with him provide information on Eisenhower's activities during the time not covered by the appointment lists—between appointments and before and after his official day.

The appointment list for October 13, 1960, which falls at about the median in number of appointments, is quite instructive, because in addition to demonstrating the sheer extent of his activity, it suggests the distinctive nature and style of certain aspects of Eisenhower's activism. The conventional view of him as an inactive president is manifestly inaccurate. He arrived at his office at 8:12 A.M., but his work had begun much earlier. Before leaving the White House residential quarters, Eisenhower often held 7:30 meetings over breakfast. On many days, moreover, he chatted with his closest confidant, his brother Milton, who regularly spent three-day weekends living in Washington and using an office in the

Executive Office Building. And by the time Milton Eisenhower, Press Secretary James Hagerty, and the staff members who each morning briefed President Eisenhower on intelligence matters saw him, he had closely read several newspapers—papers to which he paid particular attention were the *New York Times, New York Herald-Tribune,* and the *Christian Science Monitor.*

The October 13 log lists seventeen meetings during the morning and afternoon, ranging from brief exchanges with his appointments secretary to the weekly meeting of the National Security Council. The first part of the log continues from 8:12 A.M. to 5:13 P.M., with a forty-five minute preluncheon break for the rest and exercise prescribed by Eisenhower's doctors. Ordinarily, his work day would have continued for perhaps another hour, and there probably would have been a predinner hour session of informal business conducted over cocktails in the official residence. This last hour was when Eisenhower met with his major friendly adversaries, House Speaker Sam Rayburn and Senate Majority Leader Lyndon Johnson, and it often was an occasion for reflective discussion with John Foster Dulles or Milton Eisenhower.

But on this evening, Head of State ceremonies were scheduled. President and Mrs. Eisenhower attended a dinner given for them by King Frederick and Queen Ingrid of Denmark at the Danish embassy, along with a performance of the Danish Royal Ballet (with reception of guests during the intermission). The Eisenhowers dropped off the king and queen at Blair House at 11:32 P.M. and arrived at the Executive Mansion at 11:37 P.M.

If Eisenhower typically was as busy as the log of activities on October 13, 1960, suggests, how did the misimpression of his lassitude arise? For one thing, the administration did not release to the press full lists of Eisenhower's meetings. For another, it was not deemed appropriate that some of the meetings be announced—indeed this was the case with three of those held on the day under consideration, which are listed as officially "off-the-record." The nature of these meetings helps to alter the impression of Eisenhower as a passive, apolitical president who "delegated away" authority to make decisions on major issues.

The first of these three off-the-record meetings was with business leaders working with a group called "Vote Getters for

Nixon and Lodge." (The 1960 presidential campaign, of course, was well under way.) The second and considerably longer meeting also pertained to the election. It was an hour-and-a-half luncheon attended by forty-eight dignitaries of the Republican Finance Group. Among those present were the current and immediately preceding GOP chairmen and a panoply of major figures in industry and finance—men with such names as Harvey S. Firestone, Jr., Laurence S. Rockefeller, Lamont du Pont Copeland, and Paul Mellon.

These GOP fund-raising activities were part of Eisenhower's continued efforts to broaden, unify, strengthen, and modify the Republican party, notwithstanding his simultaneous efforts to convey the impression of nonpartisanship. But, even when his party-related labors were not so conspicuously open to polemical assertions about GOP business ties and wealthy fat cats as were these two gatherings, Eisenhower avoided publicizing the extent of his participation in party leadership. There was, moreover, a deliberate method in his practice of not publicizing these endeavors. First, visible partisanship was eschewed, for it would interfere with Eisenhower's attempts to muster the bipartisan congressional coalitions necessary to pass his programs. Second, his efforts were directed toward strengthening the support of centrist groups in the party; these efforts, if widely publicized, would tend to provoke factional conflict within the GOP, between the right wing and the center. Finally, Eisenhower comported himself in a manner consistent with his view that the presidency as an institution, and hence he personally, should be perceived as representing the entire American population, not just one party. This hidden rationale for not publicizing an important array of his goals and actions is a distinguishing mark of Eisenhower's style of presidential activism. Furthermore, it is not difficult to see why unpublicized activism was misinterpreted as presidential passivism. . . .

Delegation of Authority

Decision making by the president after vigorous debate among advisers was not a product of the so-called new Eisenhower of 1959–60; rather, this procedure was followed throughout his first six years in office as well. During those years, Eisenhower still had in his employ Sherman Adams and John Foster Dulles, to each of whom he is commonly believed to have abdicated fundamental policymaking powers. Eisenhower did strongly hold that the ability to delegate power and to utilize staff support was a necessary condition for effective leadership of large, complex organizations. . . .

Eisenhower did entrust important responsibilities to Adams and Dulles. He prized the service of both men, but he was not awed by them. In his view, both were overly gruff and insensitive to their abrasive effect on others, but these shortcomings were more than compensated for by the high quality and prodigious quantity of their work. . . .

The evidence required for close, if not definitive, analysis of the Eisenhower-Dulles and Eisenhower-Adams relationships is now accessible. It includes not only the Eisenhower Library sources enumerated above, but also the several hundred oral histories in the Columbia University Eisenhower Administration collection, the papers and oral histories in the Princeton University John Foster Dulles collection, and Adams's papers in the library of Dartmouth College.

Richard Immerman has reported preliminary findings of a study of how Eisenhower and Dulles worked together. The evidence overwhelmingly indicates that their relationship was collaborative. The two men agreed in their basic policy goals as well as their assessments of the political realities of the time and the strategies appropriate to deal with them, although they differed from time to time on matters of tactics. Their common beliefs and perceptions were reinforced by daily contact—direct meetings when Dulles was in Washington, electronic communication when he was traveling. . . .

Eisenhower and Dulles practiced a division of labor resembling that of a client with his attorney—a client who has firm overall purposes and an attorney who is expected to help him devise ways to accomplish those purposes and to argue his case. The public impression that emanated from the quite different personal styles of these men—Dulles the austere cold warrior, Eisenhower the warm champion of peace—contributed to a further division of labor. Dulles was assigned the "get tough" side of foreign-policy enunciation, thus placating the fervently anti-Communist wing of the Republican party. Meanwhile, amiable Ike made gestures toward peace and international humanitarianism—for example, Atoms for Peace, Open Skies, and summitry at Geneva.

As a cabinet official, Dulles was in the formal line of policy-making command. Adams, albeit *"The* Assistant to the President" and the first staff member listed in the *Government Organization Manual,* nonetheless was a staff aide. Formally, therefore, he was not a policymaker, but of course it is well known that important staff aides invariably have an impact on policy. In the popular lore of the 1950s, Adams was thought to be the man who made the domestic policy decisions that the apolitical Eisenhower then ratified. . . .

How does the lore square with the reality of the Eisenhower-Adams relationship? In a word, poorly. While Adams did conduct daily staff meetings, their purpose was not to shape administration policy but to disseminate it. Although Eisenhower allowed Adams's role to evolve (as Adams put it, the president "never specifically defined my responsibilities or outlined their limits"), he guided Adams in much the fashion he had guided his military staff deputies. Adams was encouraged to be present at as many of Eisenhower's meetings as possible, but since Adams himself made countless phone calls daily and conducted numerous "fire fighting" meetings in his office, he simply could not be present at all of them. Even when he missed Eisenhower's meetings, Adams could learn what had transpired, because they were usually summarized by a staff aide in a memorandum for record. Attending meetings and reading summaries served to attune Adams to Eisenhower's decisions and thinking.

Adams was expected to be so well aware of Eisenhower's views that he could make decisions consistent with them. And it was incumbent upon him to know enough to be able to keep out of the Oval Office problems and people the president wanted dealt with by aides. Adams learned what he was to do and not to do not only through osmosis but also more directly. Frequently Eisenhower wrote notes to him or called him into his office to indicate an action that was needed or a policy that should be implemented. If Adams felt he could not act for the president, he was expected to step into the latter's office for a decision.

Was Adams an all-powerful gatekeeper who controlled the flow of information to Eisenhower and who presented him with briefly worded consensus policy recommendations for his ratification? The evidence is decidedly to the contrary. All cabinet members could see Eisenhower individually, if they considered it necessary, and were encouraged to speak freely at cabinet meetings. The weekly meetings with legislative leaders were another source of information to the president, as were a number of senior White House aides besides Adams. Furthermore, Eisenhower, not Adams, had selected the most important members of the staff Adams nominally headed, and several of these men had direct access to Eisenhower without "clearing with Sherm."

In addition to the regular meetings with the cabinet and legislative leaders, the newspaper reading, conversations with his brother Milton, and intelligence briefings, Eisenhower had many other ways of seeking and receiving information. He read an extraordinary volume of official documents and maintained a voluminous "personal and confidential" correspondence with his extensive network of friends in the business and military communities and in other walks of life. His periodic stag dinners with carefully selected national figures were still another source of knowledge. Finally, it is instructive to note that although Adams had the impression that Eisenhower rarely used the telephone, the telephone logs for some days contain as many as a dozen calls in which Eisenhower sought information, gave instructions, rallied support, and made policy decisions.

Adams, in short, was an expediter of the president's policies and a like-minded agent, not a prime policy mover—this notwithstanding the not uncommon view that "O.K., S.A." was tantamount to adoption of a given course of action by "D.D.E." In this connection, the matter of "O.K., S.A." sheds light on a way that Adams's services had some of the same effect for Eisenhower as did Dulles's. The major policy papers and correspondence that went to the president did *not* bear this inscription. Rather, it was largely to be found on recommendations for minor patronage positions. Apart from being time consuming, such decisions are a notorious source of recrimination. It was much to Eisenhower's advantage that Adams take the blame for the bulk of them. (Eisenhower was able to benefit from those he informally arranged and then instructed Adams to implement.) More broadly, Adams's reputation as "abominable no man," like Dulles's as grim cold warrior, preserved Eisenhower's ability to appear as a benevolent national and international leader.

Stephen Hess has described Eisenhower's general approach to delegation of authority as one that "artfully constructed . . . an elaborate maze of buffer zones." Hess adds that "Eisenhower gave himself considerable freedom of action by giving his subordinates considerable latitude to act." It should be emphasized that Eisenhower's buffering practices did not consist exclusively of allowing subordinates to carry out the more controversial components of administration policy. But the division of labor in which the subordinate protected the president's ability to be perceived as being above the fray was in some instances a conscious strategy. For example, Press Secretary James Hagerty (one of the staff members who had regular, direct access to the president) once reminisced:

> President Eisenhower would say, "Do it this way." I would say, "If I go to that press conference and say what you want me to say, I would get hell." With that, he would smile, get up and walk around the desk, pat me on the back and say, "My boy, better you than me."

The uses by Eisenhower and subordinates of this type of strategy are better described as acts of "pseudo-delegation" than of true delegation. In these cases the policy was Eisenhower's, but in its promulgation Eisenhower's hand was hidden. There is much further evidence of a variety of ways in which Eisenhower practiced what I shall designate as "hidden hand leadership."

Hidden Hand Leadership

Covert or hidden hand leadership is an alternative political tactic to seeking to enhance one's professional reputation. Neustadt, it will be recalled, argues that the principal sources of presidential influence are the president's "professional reputation" among other politicians as a skilled leader, his prestige with the general public, and his use of formal powers. Eisenhower was prepared to sacrifice the first for the second. Further, he preferred informal to formal means of influence.

One type of hidden hand leadership Eisenhower practiced involved working through intermediaries. An example is provided by the following rough notes summarizing a telephone conversation in which Eisenhower charged Treasury Secretary Humphrey with the task of urging Eisenhower's friend, the Texas oil millionaire, Sid Richardson, to persuade Lyndon Johnson to be more cooperative.

Called Secy. Humphrey—asking him to speak to Sid Richardson (who was really the angel for Johnson when he came in). Ask him what it is that Tex wants. We help out in drought, take tidelands matter on their side, & tax bill. But question is, how much influence has Sid got with Johnson? He tells Sid he's supporting us, then comes up here & disproves it (yesterday for instance). Perhaps Sid could get him into right channel, or threaten to get Shivers into primary & beat him for Senate. Humphrey says this is exactly the time to do it, too; & if he talks to Sid, it can't be said that DDE is taking advantage of long-time friendship. DDE admits Sid himself has helped us; but can't let Johnson do as he pleases. He nagged George on Bricker, now on this one. If Sid is friend of fine conservative govt., he'd better pull away from Johnson. Humphrey said Johnson's alibi to Sid this time was, "They wait until we are committed; then they come after us." But we just can't tell them things in advance—they always give it to the press. Sid understands rough language; Humphrey can use it, & will!

Another element of Eisenhower's deliberately unpublicized kind of activism consisted of exploitation of his putative lack of political skill. This is illustrated by an episode described in his private diary in which he took the blame for a diplomatic error on the part of Secretary of State Dulles. The diary entry was stimulated by a meeting with the retiring ambassador to the Court of St. James, "my good friend, Walter Gifford."

While Eisenhower was still at Supreme Headquarters Allied Powers Europe (SHAPE), he had learned of Gifford's plan to retire as soon as the next administration was in office. "With this knowledge, I of course was interested in the task of selecting a completely acceptable and useful successor. We started this job shortly after election in early November and it was not long before we determined that all things considered Winthrop Aldrich would be our best bet. This selection was made on the most confidential basis, but to our consternation it was soon public knowledge." Because Dulles felt the situation embarrassing and in need of public announcement, Eisenhower authorized this, but "put in my word of caution that Walter Gifford would have to be protected in every possible way."

In the haste to act quickly, Gifford's planned resignation and Aldrich's intended appointment were announced promptly, without clearing the matter with the British. Eisenhower continues:

This upset the British government very badly—and I must say most understandably. As Anthony Eden pointed out in his informal protest to Walter Gifford, this meant that Britain was being subjected to pretty rough treatment when there was no effort made to get the usual "agreement." He said that with this precedent, any small nation could pursue the same tactics and if Britain should protest, they could argue that since the United States had done this and Britain had accepted it, no real objection could be made. To guard against any such development as this, I am going to advise Anthony, when I see him next month, to lay the blame for this whole unfortunate occurrence squarely on me. He will have the logical explanation that my lack of formal experience in the political world was the reason for the blunder. Actually, I was the one who cautioned against anything like this happening, but manifestly I can take the blame without hurting anything or anybody, whereas if the Secretary of State would have to shoulder it his position would be badly damaged.

Perhaps the most striking example of hidden hand leadership, at least in domestic politics, was Eisenhower's extensive behind-the-scenes participation in the sequence of events that culminated in the Senate's censure of Joseph McCarthy in December 1954. Working most closely with Press Secretary Hagerty, Eisenhower conducted a virtual day-to-day campaign via the media and congressional allies to end McCarthy's political effectiveness. The overall strategy was to avoid *direct mention* of McCarthy in the president's public statements, lest McCarthy win sympathy as a spunky David battling against the presidential Goliath. Instead Eisenhower systematically condemned the *types* of actions in which McCarthy engaged.

Hagerty arranged with sympathetic newspaper reporters, publishers, and broadcasters for coverage that underscored the president's implicit condemnation of McCarthy. In addition, an arrangement was made whereby an administration spokesman rather than McCarthy received network air-time on an occasion when Adlai Stevenson castigated the Republican party for McCarthyism. Finally, much attention was given to persuading congressional leaders to conduct the hearings evaluating McCarthy's conduct in a fashion that would vitiate McCarthy's usual means of defending himself against counterattack. Eisenhower's orchestration of the covert aspects of the events that led to McCarthy's censure even now have not been documented in the published literature on the period.

Rhetorical and Cognitive Style

Eisenhower's published discourse was a principal source of the many deprecations of his fitness for presidential leadership. His unpublished discourse—both writings and transcripts of discussions—leads to an impression quite different from that conveyed by the published record. Eisenhower's critics derided his apparent inability to think and express himself clearly along with his seeming lack of knowledge. The evidence that gave rise to their view was the fuzzy and tangled prose in his answers at press conferences; his frequent professions of ignorance in response to reporters' questions about issues one would expect any self-respecting president to discuss knowledgeably; and the middle-brow, middle-America rhetoric of a large portion of his speeches.

Three kinds of evidence in the Whitman File make necessary a reevaluation of Eisenhower's level of knowledge and his rhetorical and cognitive styles: the transcripts of Eisenhower's conversations and conferences; his markups and insertions in the numerous drafts through which all of his major speeches went; and his personal correspondence. These sources reveal a skilled, sophisticated use of language on Eisenhower's part and extend my description of the nature and style of his activism.

Conversations and Conferences

A large number of the papers preserved in the Whitman File are transcripts or paraphrases of Eisenhower's conversations and conferences dealing with specifics of policy, in numerous instances matters that many people believed Eisenhower was neither interested in nor attentive to. An example is a transcribed paraphrase of a meeting with the chairman of the Council of Economic Advisers, in which the president requested a shift of emphasis in a passage of a draft of the 1959 Annual Economic Report. This document reveals the man who allegedly read only simplified one-page memos both reading and commenting upon a good many pages of complex subject matter.

The President called Dr. Saulnier in and said that he had read the first two chapters of the proposed economic report. He liked them, but felt there was one very definite omission. He felt that in these two chapters there would be some account of the history of the weakness of the automobile market. He thinks it very important to say what caused this weakness—and he listed the causes as (1) lack of statesmanship in the search for market and (2) overextension in the use of credit terms. This latter had the effect of encouraging buying and unusual wage demands.

The transcripts of conversations and conferences also include minutes of pre-press conference briefings. Some of these explain one verbal regularity that led president-watchers to take it for granted that Eisenhower was poorly informed—his frequent statements in press conferences that he was unfamiliar with an issue. Eisenhower made such claims when he preferred not to discuss a matter. For example, in the July 31, 1957, briefing, Eisenhower was reminded that Egyptian President Nasser had made a series of speeches criticizing the United States and that the "Egyptians are trying to say [these speeches] have disturbed us." Eisenhower replied that if asked about Nasser's speeches he would state that he had not read them, whereas in fact hypothetical questions and answers on the topic were present in that session's briefing papers. It turned out, as was often the case with topics discussed in the preliminary conferences, that no journalist asked a question about Nasser's speeches.

Numerous similar assertions of Eisenhower's intention to deny knowledge of a sticky issue about which he was informed, or to say that he had not kept up with the technicalities of a matter, can be found in the pre-press conference transcripts. These assertions are borne out by abundant examples of follow-through. Virtually all of Eisenhower's press conferences include remarks such as "Well, this is the first I have heard about that," "You cannot expect me to know the legal complexities of that issue," and so on. No doubt all presidents have feigned ignorance or "stonewalled" occasionally, but out-and-out denials of knowledge are far more common in Eisenhower's press conferences than in those of the other modern presidents.

Insight into Eisenhower's confusing prose in press conferences is provided by the report, in his memoirs, of the following

incident. In March 1955, two months after the passage of the Formosa Straits Resolution, reporters were still seeking unequivocal
answers to such questions as whether, under what circumstances,
and with what kinds of weapons the United States would defend
the Nationalist Chinese-held islands of Quemoy and Matsu, if they
were attacked from the mainland. In the March 16 conference,
Eisenhower warned that in the event of a "general war" in Asia, the
United States was prepared to use tactical nuclear weapons "on
strictly military targets and for strictly military purposes." Just before the next week's conference, the State Department urgently requested, through Press Secretary James Hagerty, that the president
refuse to discuss this delicate matter further.

> "Don't worry, Jim," I told him as we went out the door of my of-
> fice, "if that question comes up, I'll just confuse them."
>
> One question on this subject came that morning from Joseph
> C. Harsch, of the *Christian Science Monitor*: "If we got into an issue
> with the Chinese, say, over Matsu and Quemoy, that we wanted to
> keep limited, do you conceive of using [atomic weapons] in that sit-
> uation or not?"
>
> I said that I could not answer that question in advance. The
> only thing I knew about war was two things: the most unpredictable
> factor in war was human nature, but the only unchanging factor in
> war was human nature.
>
> "And the next thing," I said in answer to Mr. Harsch, "is that
> every war is going to astonish you in the way it occurred, and in the
> way it is carried out.
>
> "So that for a man to predict, particularly if he has the respon-
> sibility for making the decision, to predict what he is going to use,
> how he is going to do it, would I think exhibit his ignorance of war;
> that is what I believe.
>
> "So I think you just have to wait; and that is the kind of
> prayerful decision that may some day face a President."

The July 17, 1957, pre-press conference briefing is illuminat-
ing on both the vagueness of his press conference statements and
the nature of the Eisenhower-Dulles relationship. Eisenhower expressed to his staff annoyance that on the previous day the secre-

tary of state, in his own press conference, had "wandered" into a discussion of a national security matter that Eisenhower felt should not have been commented upon at all, namely the disposition of American missiles in Europe. After checking by telephone with Dulles about precisely what had been said, Eisenhower informed his associates that if this matter were to arise in that day's press conference, "I will be evasive," as he in fact was.

Not only Eisenhower's claims of ignorance and ambiguous language, but also his fractured syntax led 1950s observers to deprecate his professional skills and, for that matter, his intelligence. Prudential calculation and personal style conspired to produce the garbled phrases quoted in so many writings drawing on Eisenhower's press conference utterances. The element of calculation is portrayed by Eisenhower in his memoirs, where he discusses the intra-administration objection to his decisions to release transcripts and later tapes on the ground that "an inadvertent misstatement in public would be a calamity." He explains that, "by consistently focusing on ideas rather than on phrasing, I was able to avoid causing the nation a serious setback through anything I said in many hours, over eight years, of intensive questioning."

The element of style involved a personal trait Eisenhower was well aware of, namely his tendency in spontaneous discourse to ramble and to stop and start. This trait derived from his tendency to have more ideas than he could readily convert into orderly sentences. Interestingly, in the absence of an audience waiting to seize upon controversial misstatements, he could dictate lengthy letters of noteworthy clarity. In press conferences, wary of misstatement and prone to a conversational mode of sputtering, he continually edited his discourse while talking. Overall, both the calculated and unintentional aspects of Eisenhower's press conference style had the same effect as his approach to delegation of authority: they damaged his reputation among the political cognoscenti, but protected his options as a decision maker and insulated him from blame by the wider public for controversial or potentially controversial utterances and actions.

Speech Drafts

Speech writing and editing were hardly novel experiences to Eisenhower when he entered partisan politics. For a number of the interwar years he had been speech writer for none other than Douglas MacArthur. His post-V-E Day Guild Hall speech in London had received wide acclaim for its eloquence. In view of this background, it should come as no surprise that as president, Eisenhower devoted great attention to his speeches. Mrs. Whitman estimates that twenty to thirty hours of the president's time, with much intervening response by speech writers, was spent on any speech of consequence.

The president's comments on the first draft of his 1954 State of the Union Message, of which thirty-eight were specific and four overarching, will serve to demonstrate his markups and insertions. The specific comments included two kinds of word changes and instructions to insert new paragraphs (which he dictated). The major purpose of one kind of Eisenhower's changes was to simplify language, striving to make the speeches more persuasive to the segment of the population to which he thought the Republican party ought to extend its appeal—members of normally Democratic population groups, such as white-collar workers and people who had completed high school but had not gone to college. To this end, Eisenhower eliminated phrases such as "substantial reductions in size and cost of Federal government" and "attacks on deficit financing," on the ground that the "man we are trying to reach" understands usages such as "purchasing power of the dollar" and stability "in the size of his market basket." Hence it was neither an accident nor an indicator of Eisenhower's own verbal limitations that when contrasted with the high-culture rhetoric of the principal Democratic spokesman of the time, Adlai Stevenson, Eisenhower's utterances seemed banal.

The second kind of change, editing with a view to perfecting diction and step-by-step progression of the exposition, probably was not necessary for rhetorical effectiveness with the general public. It was consistent with an enduring aspect of Eisenhower's cognitive style, namely intellectual precision. His demand for logical, carefully organized presentations is exemplified in the overarching recommendations concerning his 1954 message that he made to speech writer Bryce Harlow. They are the sort of recommendations one expects from experienced teachers of English composition: "Use blue pencil"; reexamine the structure of presentation by thinking through the sequence in which the paragraphs are put; "sections need to be more distinctly marked. Do not be afraid to say 'I come now to so-and-so.' . . . you cannot take the human mind from subject to subject . . . as quickly [as the present draft of this speech has attempted to do]." An illustration of the many suggestions for more precise diction is the instruction, accompanied by its rationale, to change a statement from "confidence has developed" to "constantly increasing confidence" in order to make clear that a "continuing action" is being described. (Eisenhower ranked tenth in his West Point class in English composition.)

Personal Correspondence

Eisenhower's correspondence ranges from "personal and confidential" letters, many of which are quite long, to brief memoranda to aides and administration officials. In the long, confidential communications, the prose is crisp, the phrasing elaborate, and the reasoning logical and clear. It is remarkable that these highly focused letters were usually dictated in one draft that required little editing. . . .

Lessons of Eisenhower's Leadership

By the end of the 1970s, eight men had served in the presidency that expanded so greatly during Franklin D. Roosevelt's administration. Not only Roosevelt, but also Truman, Eisenhower, Kennedy, Johnson, Nixon, Ford, and Carter in various ways have exercised executive leadership within the constraints and opportunities provided by their environment in seeking to ride the presidential tiger.

On reexamination, Eisenhower's approach to presidential leadership, emerges as distinctive and consciously thought-out, rather than an unfortunate example of artless drift and unthinking application of military organizational principles to civilian leadership. . . .

Eisenhower's delegations of responsibility were substantial. But they were designed to avoid abdication of power, notably by making certain so far as possible that the "competent assistants" were cognizant of their chief's policy goals. Relevant as his stress on delegation was to mid-century governance, it is even more germane to presidential leadership in the far more complex and pervasive government of the final decades of the century. . . .

Eisenhower by all testimony was remarkably successful in commanding the loyalty of his governmental subordinates. As a consequence, he did not in fact invariably have to accept the blame for their "real or apparent" errors; in many cases they were willing lightning rods. . . .

In his private assertions and actions, Eisenhower consistently preferred results to publicity when strategic and tactical maneuvering was required. He deliberately cultivated the impression that he was not involved even in the most successful of the maneuvers in which he directly participated. Presidents like Kennedy (for example, in the campaign early in his administration to expand the House Rules Committee and his assault on the steel industry) and Johnson (for example, in his highly visible mediation of the railroad strike, early in 1964) deliberately sought to enhance their professional reputations as political operators. Eisenhower seems to have had neither a need nor a desire to do so. He employed his skills to achieve his ends by inconspicuous means and was aware that a reputation as a tough political operator could be inconsistent with acquiring and maintaining another source of presidential influence, namely public prestige. . . .

Other presidents will not be able to imitate Eisenhower slavishly, even if they wish to. Not only do few men become chief executive with so great a reservoir of public esteem, but also many will consider it necessary to seek more substantial and hence more controversial policy innovations than Eisenhower deemed desirable. Whether one likes what Ike liked or not, aspects of the distinctive approach to conducting the presidency he devised will bear examination as future options.

Stephen E. Ambrose

THE EISENHOWER PRESIDENCY: AN ASSESSMENT

The author of a highly acclaimed two-volume biography of Eisenhower, Stephen Ambrose finds much to praise and much to criticize in Eisenhower's presidency. Near the end of the second volume, Ambrose attempts an assessment. Ambrose believes that Eisenhower's "greatest successes came in foreign policy and the related area of national defense spending" and that in spite of some significant failures, America was "damned lucky to have him." Ambrose concentrates more on specific policies than on methods of governance. In doing so, he anticipates the subsequent direction of scholarship on the Eisenhower presidency.

Any attempt to assess Eisenhower's eight years as President inevitably reveals more about the person doing the assessing than it does about Eisenhower. Assessment requires passing a judgment on the decisions Eisenhower made on the issues of his time, and every issue was political and controversial. Further, all the major and most of the minor issues of the 1950s continued to divide the nation's political parties and people in the decades that followed. To declare, therefore, that Eisenhower was right or wrong on this or that issue tends to be little more than a declaration of the current politics and prejudices of the author. The temptation to judge, however, is well-nigh irresistible, and most of the authors who write about the 1950s give in to it.

Thus William Ewald, in *Eisenhower the President,* concludes "that many terrible things that could have happened, didn't. Dwight Eisenhower's presidency gave America eight good years—I believe the best in memory." There were no wars, no riots, no inflation—just peace and prosperity. Most white middle-class and middle-aged Republicans would heartily agree with Ewald. But a black American could point out that among the things that did not happen were progress in civil rights or school desegregation. People concerned about the Cold War and the nuclear arms race could point out that no progress was made in reducing tensions or achieving disarmament. People concerned about the Communist menace could point out that no Communist regimes were eliminated, and that in fact Communism expanded into Vietnam and Cuba. On these and every issue, in short, there are at least two legitimate points of view. What did not happen brought joy to one man, gloom to another.

One of the first serious attempts at assessment was by Murray Kempton in a famous article in *Esquire* magazine in September 1967. Kempton called the piece "The Underestimation of Dwight D. Eisenhower," and in it he admitted that Eisenhower was much shrewder and more in control of events than he, or other reporters, had ever imagined during the fifties. Eisenhower was "the great tortoise upon whose back the world sat for eight years," never recognizing "the cunning beneath the shell." Garry Wills took up the same theme in his 1970 book *Nixon Agonistes*. Such judgments were little more than confessions on the part of the reporters, and they shed little light on the Eisenhower Presidency.

Members of the academic community also confessed. Thus Arthur Schlesinger, Jr., who wrote speeches for Stevenson during the presidential campaigns of 1952 and 1956, was—at that time— critical of Eisenhower for failing to exercise vigorous executive leadership, as Schlesinger's heroes, Andrew Jackson, Franklin Roosevelt, and Harry Truman, had done. Later, after Watergate, Schlesinger wrote *The Imperial Presidency.* In that book, Schlesinger's major criticism of Eisenhower was that Eisenhower went too far in his use of executive powers, especially in his proclamation of the principle of executive privilege when he refused to turn over documents or personnel to McCarthy's investigating committee, and in his insistence on exclusive executive responsibility during foreign-policy crises.

To repeat, then: To say that Eisenhower was right about this or wrong about that is to do little more than announce one's own political position. A more fruitful approach is to examine his years in the White House in his own terms, to make an assessment on the basis of how well he did in achieving the tasks and goals he set for himself at the time he took office.

By that standard, there were many disappointments, domestic and foreign. Eisenhower had wanted to achieve unity within the Republican Party, on the basis of bringing the Old Guard into the modern world and the mainstream of American politics. In addition, he wanted to develop within the Republican Party some young, dynamic, trustworthy, and popular leaders. He never achieved either goal, as evidenced by the 1964 Republican Convention, where the Old Guard took control of the party, nominating a candidate and writing a platform that would have delighted Warren Harding, or even William McKinley. Franklin Roosevelt did a much better job of curbing the left wing of the Democratic Party than Eisenhower did of curbing the right wing of the Republican Party.

Eisenhower wanted to see Senator McCarthy eliminated from national public life, and he wanted it done without making America's record and image on civil-liberties issues worse than it already was. But because Eisenhower would not denounce McCarthy by name, or otherwise stand up to the senator from Wisconsin, McCarthy was able to do much damage to civil liberties, the Republican Party, numerous individuals, the U.S. Army, and the Executive Branch before he finally destroyed himself. Eisenhower's only significant contribution to McCarthy's downfall was the purely negative act of denying him access to executive records and personnel. Eisenhower's cautious, hesitant approach—or nonapproach—to the McCarthy issue did the President's reputation no good, and much harm.

Eisenhower had wanted, in January of 1953, to provide a moral leadership that would both draw on and illuminate America's spiritual superiority to the Soviet Union, indeed to all the world. But on one of the great moral issues of the day, the struggle to eliminate racial segregation from American life, he provided almost no leadership at all. His failure to speak out, to indicate personal approval of *Brown* v. *Topeka,* did incalculable harm to the civil-rights crusade and to America's image.

Eisenhower had hoped to find a long-term solution for American agriculture that would get the government out of the farming business while strengthening the family farm. In this area, he and Secretary Benson suffered abject failure. The rich grew richer thanks to huge government payments for the Soil Bank, the government in 1961 was more closely and decisively involved in agriculture than it had been in 1953, and the number of family farms had dropped precipitously.

In 1953 Eisenhower had entertained wildly optimistic hopes for the peaceful uses of nuclear power. Electricity too cheap to meter, he believed, was just around the corner, as soon as nuclear power plants went into operation. New transocean canals would be blasted open, artificial harbors created, enormous strides in medicine taken, the world's fertilizer problems solved, the energy for the industrialization of the Third World created. But as he left office in 1961, there had not been any such significant application of nuclear power to civilian purposes.

In foreign affairs, Eisenhower's greatest failure, in his own judgment, which he expressed on innumerable occasions, was the failure to achieve peace. When he left office, the tensions and dangers and costs of the Cold War were higher than they had ever been. In large part, this was no fault of his. He had tried to reach out to the Russians, with Atoms for Peace, Open Skies, and other proposals, only to be rebuffed by Khrushchev. But his own deeply rooted anti-Communism was certainly a contributing factor to the failure. Eisenhower refused to trust the Russians to even the slightest degree. He continued and expanded the economic, political, diplomatic, and covert-operations pressure on the Kremlin for his entire two terms. This was good policy for winning votes, and may even have been good for achieving limited victories in the Cold War, but it was damaging to the cause of world peace.

Allied with the failure to achieve peace was the failure to set a limit on the arms race (never mind actual disarmament, another of his goals). Better than any other world leader, Eisenhower spoke of the cost of the arms race, and its dangers, and its madness. But he could not even slow it down, much less stop it. The great tragedy here is opportunity lost. Eisenhower not only recognized better than anyone else the futility of an arms race; he was in a better position than anyone else to end it. His prestige, especially as a military man, was so overwhelming that he could have made a test ban with the Russians merely on his own assurance that the agreement was good for the United States. But until his last months in office, he accepted the risk of an expanding arms race over the risk of trusting the Russians.

When finally he was ready to make an attempt to control the arms race by accepting an unsupervised comprehensive test ban, the U-2 incident intervened. Fittingly, the flight that Powers made was one Eisenhower instinctively wanted to call off, but one that his technologists insisted was necessary. In this case, as in the case of building more nuclear weapons, holding more tests, or building more rockets, he allowed the advice of his technical people to override his own common sense. That this could happen to Eisenhower illustrates vividly the tyranny of technology in the nuclear/missile age.

Another area of failure came in the Third World, which Eisenhower had hoped to line up with the Western democracies in the struggle against Russia. In large part, this failure was caused by Eisenhower's anti-Communism coupled with his penchant for seeing Communists wherever a social reform movement or a struggle for national liberation was under way. His overthrow of popularly elected governments in Iran and Guatemala, his hostility toward Nassar, his refusal to seek any form of accommodation with Castro, his extreme overreaction to events in the Congo, were one result. Another was a profound mistrust of the United States by millions of residents of the Third World. A third result of his oversimplifications was an overcommitment in Indochina, based on an obsession with falling dominoes.

In Central and Eastern Europe, Eisenhower had hoped to take the offensive against Communism. But his unrealistic and ineffective belligerency, combined with his party's irresponsible advocacy of uprisings and liberation within a police state, produced the tragedy of Hungary in 1956, which will stand forever as a blot on Eisenhower's record. In his Administration, "roll back" never got started, as "stand pat" became the watchword. But the free world was not even able to stand pat, as Eisenhower accepted an armistice in Korea that left the Communists in control in the north, another in Vietnam that did the same, and the presence of Castro in Cuba.

These failures, taken together, make at first glance a damning indictment. According to Eisenhower's critics, they came about because of the greatest shortcoming of all, the failure to exert leadership. In contrast to FDR and Truman, Eisenhower seemed to be no leader at all, but only a chairman of the board, or even a figurehead, a Whig President in a time that demanded dramatic exercise of executive power. Eisenhower was sensitive about this charge, which he had heard so many times. When Henry Luce made it, in an August 1960 *Life* editorial, Eisenhower took time to provide Luce with a private explanation of his methods—"not to defend," Eisenhower insisted, "merely to explain."

He realized, he told Luce, that many people thought "I have been too easy a boss." What such people did not realize, he pointed out, was that except for his "skimpy majority" in his first two years, "I have had to deal with a Congress controlled by the opposition and whose partisan antagonism to the Executive Branch has often been blatantly displayed." To make any progress at all, he had to use methods "calculated to attract cooperation," and could not afford "to lash out at partisan charges and publicity-seeking demagogues." In addition, the government of the United States had become "too big, too complex, and too pervasive in its influence for one individual to pretend to direct the details of its important and critical programming." Nothing could be accomplished without competent assistants; to command their loyalty, the President had to be willing to show patience, understanding, a readiness to delegate authority, and an acceptance of responsibility for honest errors.

Finally, Eisenhower concluded, "In war and in peace I've had no respect for the desk-pounder, and have despised the loud and slick talker. If my own ideas and practices in this matter have sprung from weakness, I do not know. But they were and are deliberate or, rather, natural to me. They are not accidental."

Shortly after Eisenhower left office, his successor suffered an embarrassing defeat at the Bay of Pigs. In passing his own judgment on the event, Eisenhower concentrated his criticism on Kennedy's failure to consult with the NSC before deciding to act. He chided Kennedy for not gathering together in one room representatives of every point of view, so that he could hear both the pros and cons. Since Eisenhower made such a major point of this failure to consult, it is only fair to apply the same standard to Eisenhower's own Administration. How well did he listen to every point of view before acting?

In some cases, fully. In other cases, hardly at all. In the various Far East crises that began with Korea in 1952 and continued through Dien Bien Phu, the Geneva Conference of 1954, and Formosa, he consulted with every appropriate department and agency, listened carefully to every point of view, and acted only after he was satisfied he had taken everything into consideration and was prepared for all possible consequences. But in other areas, he was surprisingly remiss. He did not give the anti-McCarthy people a full hearing, for example, and only once met with Negro leaders on civil-rights issues. Until 1958, he allowed himself to be isolated from the nuclear scientists opposed to testing. On national defense, he gave the proponents of more spending every opportunity to express their views, but except for one meeting with Senator Taft in 1953 he never listened to those who urged dramatic cuts. Advocates of more spending for domestic social programs or for tax cuts seldom got near Eisenhower. He kept the U-2 such a closely guarded secret that only insiders who were proponents of the program ever gave him advice on how to utilize the spy plane.

But on major questions involving the European allies, he consulted with the heads of government in Paris, Bonn, and London before acting (except at Suez, and the failure to consult there was no fault of his). His record, in short, was mixed, and hardly pure enough to justify his extreme indignation at Kennedy for Kennedy's failure to consult the NSC before acting at the Bay of Pigs.

How effective, if not dramatic, Eisenhower's leadership techniques were can be seen in a brief assessment of his accomplishments as President, an assessment once again based on his own goals and aspirations. First and foremost, he presided over eight years of prosperity, marred only by two minor recessions. By later standards, it was a decade of nearly full employment and no inflation.

Indeed by almost every standard—GNP, personal income and savings, home buying, auto purchases, capital investment, highway construction, and so forth—it was the best decade of the century. Surely Eisenhower's fiscal policies, his refusal to cut taxes or increase defense spending, his insistence on a balanced budget, played some role in creating this happy situation.

Under Eisenhower, the nation enjoyed domestic peace and tranquillity—at least as measured against the sixties. One of Eisenhower's major goals in 1953 was to lower the excesses of political rhetoric and partisanship. He managed to achieve that goal, in a negative way, by not dismantling the New Deal, as the Old Guard wanted to do. Under Eisenhower, the number of people covered by Social Security doubled as benefits went up. The New Deal's regulatory commissions stayed in place. Expenditures for public works were actually greater under Eisenhower than they had been under FDR or Truman. Nor were Eisenhower's public works of the boondoggle variety—the St. Lawrence Seaway and the Interstate Highway System made an enormous contribution to the economy. Eisenhower, in effect, put a Republican stamp of approval on twenty years of Democratic legislation, by itself a major step toward bringing the two parties closer together.

Eisenhower's positive contribution to domestic peace and tranquillity was to avoid partisanship himself. His close alliance with the southern Democrats, his refusal to ever denounce the Democratic Party as a whole (he attacked only the "spender" wing), his insistence on a bipartisan foreign policy, his careful cultivation of the Democratic leaders in Congress, all helped tone down the level of partisan excess. When Eisenhower came into the White House, his party was accusing the other party of "twenty years of treason." The Democrats in turn were charging that the Republicans were the party of Depression. When Eisenhower left office, such ridiculous charges were seldom heard.

In 1953, Eisenhower had also set as a major goal the restoration of dignity to the office of the President. He felt, strongly, that Truman had demeaned the office. Whether Truman was guilty of so doing depended on one's perception, of course, but few would argue against the claim that in his bearing, his actions, his private and social life, and his official duties as head of state, Eisenhower maintained his dignity. He looked, acted, and sounded like a President.

He was a good steward. He did not sell off the public lands, or open the National Wilderness Areas or National Parks to commercial or mineral exploitation. He retained and expanded TVA.

He stopped nuclear testing in the atmosphere, the first world statesman to do so, because of the dangers of radiation to the people who had chosen him as their leader.

In the field of civil rights, he felt he had done as well as could be done. His greatest contribution (albeit one that he had grown increasingly unhappy about) was the appointment of Earl Warren as Chief Justice. In addition, he had completed the desegregation of the armed forces, and of the city of Washington, D.C., as well as all federal property. He had sponsored and signed the first civil-rights legislation since Reconstruction. When he had to, he acted decisively, in Little Rock in 1957. These were all positive, if limited, gains. Eisenhower's boast was that they were made without riots, and without driving the white South to acts of total desperation. Progress in desegregation, especially in the schools, was painfully slow during the Eisenhower years, but he was convinced that anything faster would have produced a much greater and more violent white southern resistance.

In 1952, when he accepted the Republican nomination for the Presidency, Eisenhower called the party to join him in a "crusade." Its purpose was to clean the crooks and the Commies (really, the Democrats) out of Washington. Once those tasks had been accomplished, Eisenhower's critics found it difficult to discover what his crusade was aiming at. There was no stirring call to arms, no great moral cause, no idealistic pursuit of some overriding national goal. Eisenhower, seemingly, was quite content to preside over a fat, happy, satisfied nation that devoted itself to enjoying life, and especially the material benefits available in the greatest industrial power in the world. There was truth in the charge. Eisenhower's rebuttal also contained an elementary truth. The Declaration of Independence stated that one of man's inalienable rights was the pursuit of happiness. Eisenhower tried, with much success, to create a climate in the 1950s in which American citizens could fully exercise that right.

His greatest successes came in foreign policy, and the related area of national defense spending. By making peace in Korea, and avoiding war thereafter for the next seven and one-half years, and by holding down, almost single-handedly, the pace of the arms race, he achieved his major accomplishments. No one knows how much money he saved the United States, as he rebuffed Symington and the Pentagon and the JCS and the AEC and the military-industrial complex. And no one knows how many lives he saved by ending the war in Korea and refusing to enter any others, despite a half-dozen and more virtually unanimous recommendations that he go to war. He made peace, and he kept the peace. Whether any other man could have led the country through that decade without going to war cannot be known. What we do know is that Eisenhower did it. Eisenhower boasted that "the United States never lost a soldier or a foot of ground in my administration. We kept the peace. People asked how it happened—by God, it didn't just happen, I'll tell you that."

Beyond keeping the peace, Eisenhower could claim that at the end of his eight years, the NATO alliance, that bedrock of American foreign policy, was stronger than ever. Relations with the Arab states, considering the American moral commitment to Israel, were as good as could be expected. Except for Cuba, the Latin-American republics remained friendly to the United States. In the Far East, relations with America's partners, South Korea, Japan, and Formosa, were excellent (they were still nonexistent with the Chinese). South Vietnam seemed well on the road to becoming a viable nation. Laos was admittedly in trouble, but it appeared to be the only immediate danger spot.

What Eisenhower had done best was managing crises. The crisis with Syngman Rhee in early 1953, and the simultaneous crisis with the Chinese Communists over the POW issue and the armistice; the crisis over Dien Bien Phu in 1954, and over Quemoy and Matsu in 1955; the Hungarian and Suez crises of 1956; the Sputnik and Little Rock crises of 1957; the Formosa Resolution crisis of 1958; the Berlin crisis of 1959; the U-2 crisis of 1960—Eisenhower managed each one without overreacting, without going to war, without increasing defense spending, without frightening people half out of their wits. He downplayed each one, insisted that a solution could be found, and then found one. It was a magnificent performance.

His place in history is, of course, a relative matter. He has to be judged against other Presidents, which means that no judgment can be fair, because he did not have the opportunities, nor face the dangers, that other Presidents did. We cannot know how great a leader he might have been, because he ruled in a time that required him, at least in his own view, to adopt a moderate course, to stay in the middle of the road, to avoid calling on his fellow citizens for some great national effort. He did not face the challenges that Washington did, or Lincoln, or Franklin Roosevelt. How he would have responded to setting precedents, rather than following them, or to a Civil War, or to a Depression, or to a world war, we cannot know. What we do know is that he guided his country safely and securely through a dangerous decade.

Shortly after Eisenhower left office, a national poll of American historians placed him nearly at the bottom of the list of Presidents. By the early 1980s, a new poll placed him ninth. His reputation is likely to continue to rise, perhaps even to the point that he will be ranked just below Washington, Jefferson, Jackson, Lincoln, Wilson, and Franklin Roosevelt.

In attempting to assess the Eisenhower Presidency, certain comparisons must be made. Since Andrew Jackson's time, only five men have served eight consecutive years or more in the White House—Grant, Wilson, Franklin D. Roosevelt, Eisenhower, and Ronald Reagan. Of these five, only two—Grant and Eisenhower—were world figures before they became President. Of the five, only two—Eisenhower and Roosevelt—were more popular when they left office than when they entered. In contrast, to his Democratic predecessors and successors, Eisenhower kept the peace; in contrast to his Republican successors, Eisenhower both balanced the budget and stopped inflation.

Eisenhower gave the nation eight years of peace and prosperity. No other President in the twentieth century could make that claim. No wonder that millions of Americans felt that the country was damned lucky to have him.

II

Eisenhower and McCarthy

The Army-McCarthy hearings. Senator Joe McCarthy of Wisconsin uses a chart to illustrate the Communist Party organization in the United States. The army's counsel, Joseph Welch, looks bored and a bit pained. (UPI/Corbis-Bettman).

Jeff Broadwater

EISENHOWER AND THE ANTI-COMMUNIST CRUSADE

Senator Joseph R. McCarthy, the red-baiting junior senator from Wisconsin, was one of the most vexing problems Eisenhower faced during his presidency. Jeff Broadwater, a professor of history at Barton College, argues that by not publicly confronting McCarthy, Eisenhower failed to exert leadership. He concludes that Eisenhower made, at most, a modest contribution to bringing down the demagogue from Wisconsin. Broadwater further contends that for all his basic decency, Eisenhower shared many assumptions of the Republican right. This observation may be well taken, but it fails to consider that the same observation might be made of most Democrats and liberals of the era; they too agreed that communism was a threat and that the way to meet that threat was through repression. Hubert Humphrey and Herbert Lehman, two of the leading Democratic liberals at midcentury, were sponsors of the Communist Control Act of 1954, a repressive measure that the Eisenhower administration opposed. Finally, Broadwater takes Eisenhower to task for failing to remake the Republican party in his own, moderate, image. Without doubt, Eisenhower failed in that task. However, given the ideological divisions within the party and the strength of the Republican right, it remains open to question whether Eisenhower, or anyone else, could have wrought such a transformation.

Throughout its first year in office, the Eisenhower administration had repeatedly sparred with Joseph R. McCarthy, but as 1953 came to a close, it had avoided an open break with the Wisconsin senator. Hoping to preserve its uneasy alliance with Republican conservatives, the White House had vacillated before McCarthy's onslaughts against alleged Communist influence within the executive branch of the federal government, in particular his assaults on the International Information Agency and the Voice of America. It

From *Eisenhower and the Anti-Communist Crusade* by Jeff Broadwater. Copyright © 1992 by the University of North Carolina Press. Used by permission of the publisher.

was this policy of appeasement that guided Secretary of the Army Robert T. Stevens when McCarthy later turned his fire on the U.S. Army, which, he claimed, had been infiltrated by Communists and Communist sympathizers. Even then, the administration tried to come to terms with McCarthy; President Eisenhower acted decisively to check his formidable opponent only when the army-McCarthy controversy threatened to spread its political fallout into the White House itself. Faced with a worsening political crisis, the president responded with a sweeping assertion of executive privilege, denying McCarthy—and the rest of the nation—access to a broad range of information about the workings of the national government. In a sense, the timidity of the White House probably helped to ruin McCarthy by encouraging him to pursue an increasingly reckless and self-destructive course, but the senator's fall came at the expense of something approaching a national trauma. As a political battle between Eisenhower and the Republican Right, the affair ended in stalemate. Although McCarthy, behind whom party conservatives hoped to expand their influence, was ultimately discredited, Eisenhower proved unable to establish his unquestioned control of the GOP's future. The events leading to McCarthy's downfall can now be detailed.

In August 1953, McCarthy announced his intention to investigate the U.S. Army Signal Corps Engineering Laboratories at Fort Monmouth, New Jersey. McCarthy offered as evidence of subversion at the post little more than what came to be known as the "purloined letter," a letter, supposedly written by J. Edgar Hoover, that purported to identify thirty-five Fort Monmouth employees as security risks. Despite the paucity of evidence, however, the installation offered congressional witch-hunters an inviting target. The atomic spy Julius Rosenberg had once worked for the Signal Corps and had known many of the scientists at Fort Monmouth. Most of the concern about Communist infiltration at the facility was unfounded, but the army had been abysmally slow in processing security cases there; one employee about whom derogatory information was received in 1948 continued to work on classified projects until he was suspended in September 1953. As late as that October, nineteen employees with access to confidential information remained under investigation. Secretary Stevens, perhaps mindful of the weakness of his position, and certainly aware of the conciliatory stance the administration had taken thus far in its dealings with McCarthy, pledged to cooperate with the Senate probe. Indeed, Stevens took McCarthy and his staff on a guided tour of the Signal Corps facility. By the end of October, General Kirke Lawton, the commander at Fort Monmouth, had suspended thirty-three employees.

The army refused to accede, however, to McCarthy's demands for the security files of the employees in question. Nor would the army make available for interrogation the army loyalty board members who had previously cleared certain Fort Monmouth employees. In the spring of 1953, Assistant Attorney General J. Lee Rankin had advised H. Struve Hensel, then a consultant to the secretary of defense, "that the presidency was a continuing office" and that, accordingly, the army should consider itself bound by the Truman administration's policy against the release of loyalty files and the interrogation of loyalty board members. To be sure, Harry S. Truman, in an April 3, 1952, letter, had instructed Secretary of State Dean Acheson not to provide Congress with personnel files, the names of employees under investigation, or the names of loyalty board members. Beyond that, the legal basis for the army's position appeared murky, at best. From a political standpoint, Stevens's reliance on the precedent set by an embattled and unpopular Democrat seemed almost untenable. To bolster the army's position, army lawyer John G. Adams pressed the Justice Department for an executive order codifying the Truman policy. On December 12, Hensel and Adams met with [Attorney General] Herbert Brownell and [Deputy Attorney General] William Rogers. Brownell agreed that board members should not be subject to interrogation and promised to support the army in any confrontation with Congress. Yet despite repeated entreaties from Adams, no formal action affirming the army's right to withhold information from McCarthy's subcommittee on investigations was, for the moment, forthcoming.

The Fort Monmouth investigation would soon share the headlines with the budding military career of G. David Schine. The McCarthy aide had received notice in the summer of 1953 that he was soon to be inducted into the armed services. Almost immediately, Roy Cohn [Chief Counsel to McCarthy's Subcommittee on Investigations], with the apparent acquiescence of McCarthy, set about trying to secure a commission for Schine and a comfortable assignment in the New York City area. The youthful heir of a hotel magnate, Schine gave his associates ready access to fine restaurants and Broadway plays, but otherwise his value to the McCarthy subcommittee remains in question to this day, as do the motives behind Cohn's efforts on behalf of his friend. In any event, Schine, as a raw recruit in basic training, had a small cadre of senior army officers working to get him a commission. He eluded work details. He received weekend, holiday, and evening passes. On at least one occasion, he left his unit at Fort Dix, New Jersey, to return to his suite at New York's Waldorf Towers. And he went unpunished. Admittedly, the American defense establishment did not wholly surrender to Cohn and the young private. He did not receive a commission or special duties. . . .

Administration officials who were closer to the White House than Stevens and Adams still hoped to reach a rapprochement with McCarthy. Toward the end of 1953, Richard Nixon and William Rogers invited the senator to Key Biscayne, Florida, in yet another attempt to bring him under control. Urging McCarthy not to push the army investigation too far, Nixon warned him of the danger of becoming a "one-shot" senator. Nixon and Rogers wanted to channel McCarthy's investigative energies toward certain tax settlements that had been negotiated by the Truman administration. For the moment, the senator seemed to agree to take up the tax issue, but when press reports suggested that he would temper his crusade against communism, the senator called the story "a lie."

Indeed, Francis P. Carr, a lawyer on the staff of the McCarthy subcommittee, telephoned John Adams on January 19 to inform him that if the army did not produce its loyalty board members by January 22, they would be subpoenaed. Adams thought "the McCarthy group" had decided to increase its pressure on the army because it feared that Schine might shortly be sent overseas. With Stevens on a tour of the Far East, Adams contacted William Rogers and insisted, "I must have assistance from outside the Pentagon." The deputy attorney general agreed to arrange a meeting with Brownell.

When Adams arrived at the Justice Department on January 21, he was greeted not only by Brownell and Rogers but also by Sherman Adams, Henry Cabot Lodge, and presidential aide Gerald Morgan. The army lawyer told them of the pressures, among which he included the Fort Monmouth investigation, that McCarthy and Cohn had been applying to the army in an effort to secure favorable treatment for Schine. Sherman Adams suggested that John Adams begin compiling a record of the army's problems with Schine; Lodge and the White House chief of staff apparently agreed that such a document might profitably be leaked to the press and a few key senators. As to the specific issue at hand, Brownell indicated that an executive order safeguarding the confidentiality of the loyalty program would be presented to Eisenhower within "a couple of weeks." Nevertheless, the attorney general conceded that it might be impossible to keep loyalty board members away from the McCarthy subcommittee if they were subpoenaed to testify about official fraud or misconduct, as opposed to their own decisions in particular cases. Still, no one relished an open confrontation with McCarthy. Hoping that the GOP maverick could be persuaded by his fellow senators to withdraw his ultimatum, the group decided to dispatch John Adams and Gerald Morgan to Capitol Hill to seek support from McCarthy's Republican colleagues on the investigations subcommittee—Everett M. Dirksen, Karl E. Mundt, and Charles E. Potter. The strategy apparently worked; McCarthy announced on the following day that he would defer further action on the Fort Monmouth case until Secretary Stevens returned from the Orient.

Senator McCarthy had, in reality, only shifted his focus. He was now on the trail of an army dentist stationed at Camp Kilmer, New Jersey. Irving Peress, in filling out the paperwork before his induction into service in October 1952, had taken the Fifth Amendment when asked if he belonged to any organization that advocated the overthrow of the U.S. government. Apparently, the officials responsible for investigating the loyalty of recruits moved more slowly than did those in charge of inductions and promotions. Pursuant to Public Law 779, better known as the Doctors Draft Act, Peress received a commission as a captain and shortly thereafter a promotion to major. On January 30, 1954, McCarthy hauled Peress before a one-man subcommittee hearing in New York City, where the dentist again refused to answer questions about his political affiliations. The Wisconsin Republican demanded that Peress be court-martialed, but the army, looking for a quick way to dispose of a possible security risk and a definite political problem, gave the major an honorable discharge.

Few controversies could have engaged Dwight Eisenhower's attention, and emotions, as did McCarthy's forays against the service in which the president had spent most of his adult life. At a February 10 meeting at the White House, Eisenhower advised Stevens to admit the army's mishandling of the Peress case and to make a full disclosure of the relevant facts. Stevens should, Ike believed, explain the steps being taken to prevent the recurrence of similar episodes. And he should make plain his confidence in the army and his refusal to tolerate any "browbeating" of his subordinates. After meeting with the president, Stevens announced that he was instructing the inspector general of the army to initiate an "exhaustive investigation."

To McCarthy, this was "Communist jargon," a delaying tactic to protect Pentagon officials guilty of "coddling Communists." On February 18, the Wisconsin senator heard testimony from the commanding officer at Camp Kilmer, Brigadier General Ralph W. Zwicker, a combat veteran of World War II and a much-decorated hero of the Battle of the Bulge. Reluctant to disclose the details of the Peress case in light of the administration's policy of maintaining the confidentiality of personnel matters, Zwicker triggered a vitriolic outburst that exceeded even McCarthy's normal capacity for verbal abuse. Zwicker, the chairman stated, lacked "the brains of a five-year-old child" and, McCarthy went on, might not be "fit to wear the uniform" of the U.S. army.

After McCarthy finished with Zwicker, perhaps only Richard Nixon, among high-ranking administration officials, still retained hopes for a compromise with the senator. For his part, Secretary Stevens instructed General Zwicker to ignore further demands from McCarthy for additional testimony. With Eisenhower away on a golfing vacation, Nixon and the administration's congressional liaison, Jerry Persons, arranged a meeting in Nixon's Capitol Hill office with John Adams, Rogers, Dirksen, Senate Majority

Leader William F. Knowland, and I. Jack Martin of the White House staff. Eisenhower had hoped that, after the death of Robert A. Taft in 1953, Dirksen would become the Senate "champion" for the president's "middle-of-the-road" philosophy. The Illinois lawmaker now agreed to demand Cohn's dismissal and an end to McCarthy's arbitrary use of the subpoena power, his one-man subcommittee hearings, and his abuse of army witnesses. On each point, Dirksen failed to deliver; indeed, Adams believed that the purpose of the meeting was to persuade the army to capitulate to McCarthy and that Dirksen advised the subcommittee chairman to try to have the army lawyer fired. But Dirksen did make good on his promise to host a meeting between Stevens and McCarthy.

When Secretary Stevens, a former New Jersey textile manufacturer, went to Dirksen's office on February 24 for a luncheon meeting with McCarthy, he entered as a political innocent. He left as another casualty of the Communist controversy. At what would become known as the "chicken lunch"—for the menu and the army secretary's bungling—Stevens received from McCarthy, in the presence of Nixon and the Republican members of the subcommittee, the assurance that army personnel who appeared before the McCarthy panel in the future would receive fair and courteous treatment. In exchange, Stevens agreed to provide the names of those officials involved in Peress's promotion and discharge and to make them available to the subcommittee. Yet when Karl Mundt reduced the details of the meeting to a "memo of understanding" for distribution to the press, only the army's concessions to McCarthy were included.

With the release of the Mundt memorandum, the "McCarthy-Stevens row," in the words of James Hagerty, "broke wide open." Immediately perceived by the press as having surrendered to McCarthy, an almost hysterical Stevens called both Nixon and Hagerty on the evening of February 24 to discuss his resignation; they advised him against any rash action. Eisenhower's response to reports of the chicken lunch, he wrote later, "was not pleasant." Not only had Stevens demonstrated considerable political ineptitude, but Eisenhower's fellow Republicans, including the vice president, had embarrassed the administration and created a widespread, albeit erroneous, impression that someone in the White

House, if not the president personally, had instructed Stevens to settle his problems with McCarthy at any cost. . . .

Yet the president hesitated to bring the full force of his prestige to bear against the administration's congressional antagonists. To be sure, Eisenhower told James Hagerty that McCarthy apparently wanted to be president; Ike added, "He's the last guy in the world who'll ever get there, if I have anything to say." Nevertheless, Nixon persuaded Eisenhower not to issue a statement saying that congressional witch-hunters were as bad as the Communists they pursued. . . . Nixon, Sherman Adams, and several key aides prepared a more moderate statement setting forth Stevens's version of the chicken lunch. . . . Significantly, despite the urgings of Hagerty and White House counsel Bernard Shanley that Eisenhower make a personal appearance, Stevens was forced to issue his statement with only Hagerty and Roger Keyes, the acting secretary of defense, at his side. . . .

As he had done throughout his presidency, Eisenhower continued to resist pressure from his more liberal supporters to engage McCarthy in a verbal donnybrook, but the early spring of 1954 saw the budding of a new combativeness at the White House. At a press conference on March 3, Eisenhower assumed his most vigorous public posture to date, commending General Zwicker, calling on the GOP leadership to support "codes of fair procedure" for congressional committees, and regretting the turmoil caused by a "disregard of the standards of fair play." Still, the president's essentially temperate remarks, in the face of McCarthy's outrages, failed to satisfy much of the press.

Political necessity required that Eisenhower further distance himself from the Wisconsin senator. Delivering a well-received address to a Democratic fund-raising dinner in Miami on March 7, Adlai Stevenson charged, "A group of political plungers has persuaded the President that McCarthyism is the best Republican formula for success." The Republican party, the former Illinois governor continued, was "divided against itself, half McCarthy and half Eisenhower." The Eisenhower half quickly intervened to ensure that Vice President Nixon, not Senator McCarthy, would deliver the GOP's formal response to Stevenson. After Eisenhower made the appropriate arrangements with legislative leaders, Sherman Adams apparently telephoned the chairman of the Federal Communications Commission to guarantee that McCarthy would not receive network television time. Finally, on March 11, the army released John Adams's memorandum detailing the efforts made by McCarthy and Cohn to secure preferential treatment for David Schine. With the release of the Adams chronology, the junior senator from Wisconsin, Eisenhower later wrote, went "on the defensive for the first time." Along with such initiatives inevitably came increasing intraparty tensions. Fearful of losing the advantage of the Communist issue, many Republican members of Congress urged the White House not to attack McCarthy. . . .

The counterattack on their Wisconsin ally threatened hopes of Republican conservatives to gain control of their party. Henry Cabot Lodge and C. D. Jackson [Eisenhower's special assistant for psychological warfare] believed that McCarthy ultimately intended to destroy Eisenhower; Lodge thought it no coincidence that an attack had been launched on the organization with which Ike was so intimately linked. Eisenhower heeded such advice. Although he recognized that "Old Guardism and McCarthyism" were "not necessarily" synonymous, he also believed that a handful of Republican reactionaries were supporting McCarthy because they were "so anxious to seize on every possible embarrassment for the Administration." The GOP's Old Guard, the president thought, "hates and despises every thing for which I stand. . . ." For their part, many Republican conservatives undoubtedly shared Roy Cohn's later assessment that the controversy over subversion represented a "gut issue" capable of returning "a powerful right-wing bloc" to Congress.

In rallying to McCarthy's banner, Republican conservatives committed a tactical blunder. To be sure, the senator's popularity reached an all-time high in January 1954, with respondents in a Gallup survey rating him favorably by a margin of 50 to 29 percent. But even at his peak, the senator showed signs of political weakness. By pluralities, Americans disapproved of his "methods," believed he was hurting U.S. relations with allies, and purported to be less, rather than more, likely to vote for a Republican congressional candidate endorsed by McCarthy. Among one key group, the college-educated, the controversial legislator received an overall negative rating. Even before the start of the now famous army-McCarthy hearings, the senator's popularity had begun to erode.

By March 1954, McCarthy's positive standing in the Gallup Poll had dropped from 46 to 36 percent. Reports reaching the White House indicated a dramatic decline in his political clout. . . . The remaining McCarthyites were probably more zealous than the growing ranks of the disaffected, but for most Americans, a struggle between the senator and the president would be no contest at all.

* * *

On March 12, 1954, Senator McCarthy responded to the release of the Adams chronology with copies of eleven memoranda of dubious authenticity—the originals never surfaced—that conveniently purported to rebut the army's charges point by point. Denying that he had sought preferential treatment for David Schine, McCarthy charged at a midday news conference that Robert Stevens and John Adams had tried to use his former aide as a "hostage" to "blackmail" him into stopping his investigation of the army. . . .

The Senate could hardly allow the army's charges and McCarthy's countercharges to pass without a formal inquiry, a responsibility that fell, by default, to the permanent subcommittee on investigations. During a stormy executive session on March 16, the subcommittee decided that Karl Mundt, its second-ranking Republican, would assume the chairmanship pending a resolution of the army-McCarthy dispute. Mundt wanted to remove the controversy to the Armed Services Committee, but that body refused to accept it. Cohn was suspended, and the subcommittee agreed to seek new counsel. At the same time, the panel reached two critical procedural decisions. First, John L. McClellan of Arkansas, the senior Democrat on the subcommittee, won adoption of a resolution providing that the army-McCarthy investigation would proceed to the exclusion of all other business, thus minimizing McCarthy's ability to employ diversionary tactics. Second, the hearings would be open to the public and subject to live television coverage. Wanting to settle the matter quickly and quietly, Everett Dirksen proposed that the subcommittee conduct a closed hearing, to be followed by the resignation of a scapegoat from each side—Cohn for the McCarthyites and John Adams for the army. McCarthy, Charles E. Potter, and the Democrats joined together to defeat the

Dirksen proposal. It was as if all concerned, except the Wisconsin senator, knew that he could not withstand the scrutiny of the klieg lights.

When Eisenhower faced the press on March 17, he defended Stevens's "integrity and honesty" but conceded that the secretary might have made some mistakes. Privately, Ike believed that press coverage of the McCarthyites had "exaggerated, out of all proportion . . . , their importance to the nation as a whole." Nevertheless, the president displayed, as the investigations subcommittee prepared for the army-McCarthy hearings, a hitherto uncharacteristic interest in the affairs of the Senate. The day after his press conference, Eisenhower telephoned Karl Mundt to discuss the selection of a temporary replacement for Roy Cohn. Both men wanted a special counsel of unimpeachable stature; Eisenhower suggested the venerable John W. Davis, a former Democratic presidential nominee and a distinguished constitutional lawyer. Telling Mundt that nothing was "hurting our position more," the president admonished the South Dakota senator that the subcommittee was a "Republican committee" and that Mundt, Dirksen, and Potter could not afford to mishandle their responsibilities. On March 20, Eisenhower commended Senator Knowland for his pronouncement that McCarthy should not be allowed to vote as a subcommittee member during the course of the hearings or to question witnesses. "Everybody in the United States," Eisenhower told the majority leader, "will approve what you said." Over the heated objections of congressional liaison Jerry Persons, Eisenhower expressed the view at a March 24, 1954, press conference that McCarthy should not be allowed to sit as a judge in his own case. The White House had passed the point of considering a compromise with the McCarthyites. . . .

Within the confines of the subcommittee, however, certain compromises were possible. McCarthy agreed to resign, technically, from the panel, but he was allowed to name his own replacement, Idaho's Henry Dworshak, a quiet foot soldier in the McCarthy infantry. Moreover, McCarthy received the right to cross-examine witnesses. The loyalties of the subcommittee were confused and divided. Besides Dworshak, McCarthy could usually depend on the support of Mundt; the White House could not. When Eisenhower and his advisers debated the position the administration should take on McCarthy's right to sit on the subcommittee, Ike decided against expressing his opposition in a letter to Mundt. As Eisenhower told his staff: "You can't trust that fellow. He plays everything against the middle." So too did Everett Dirksen. Despite White House efforts to woo him, Dirksen wanted to protect McCarthy from the ordeal of a lengthy public investigation. . . . In the middle of the controversy fell a moderate Republican, Charles E. Potter of Michigan. Potter had lost both legs to a German artillery shell in the Colmar pocket. He would not be sympathetic to Schine's demands for a special assignment. Led by John McClellan, the subcommittee's Democrats lined up in solid opposition to the pro-McCarthy Republican majority. A crusty conservative with an impregnable political base, McClellan was not intimidated by McCarthy, or anyone else. . . . Next in seniority came W. Stuart Symington of Missouri. Formerly the secretary of the air force and a Pentagon loyalist, Symington emerged in the hearings as McCarthy's most fervent antagonist. The junior Democrat, Washington's Henry M. Jackson, was more reserved, but he would pursue McCarthy through the hearings with the earnest demeanor of a young district attorney.

Karl Mundt explored some strange leads in trying to find a temporary replacement for Roy Cohn as subcommittee counsel. It proved difficult to obtain a lawyer of the caliber Eisenhower desired. The position paid little, entailed considerable political risk, and required that a candidate have no public record on what was one of the two or three most controversial issues of the day. . . . Mundt finally selected Samuel P. Sears, a Massachusetts Republican, but Sears resigned almost immediately when it was learned that he had solicited funds for McCarthy in 1952. Ultimately Mundt, through the intercession of Everett Dirksen, located Ray H. Jenkins, a colorful and successful criminal lawyer from Knoxville, Tennessee. A Taft Republican, Jenkins admired McCarthy, but he had, thus far, kept his opinions to himself.

Robert Stevens, Milton Eisenhower advised his brother, would need "the best lawyer in the United States." Milton recommended Thurmond Arnold, the old New Dealer. On the suggestion of Brownell and Governor Thomas E. Dewey of New York, however, the army retained Joseph N. Welch, a liberal Republican hostile to McCarthy. A graduate of Harvard Law School and a self-made Brahmin, Welch headed the trial section of the old-line Boston law firm Hale and Dorr. Courtly and sixty-three years old, Welch, not Jenkins, would appear before the television camera as the proverbial folksy, small-town lawyer.

While the other players prepared for the hearings, McCarthy continued on his political descent. To be sure, the senator did embark on a speaking tour that demonstrated his ability to rally enthusiastic crowds of true believers. . . . Yet a Gallup survey taken after the release of the Adams chronology showed that Americans now disapproved of the nation's most outspoken anti-Communist by a margin of 46 to 38 percent. Old supporters started to abandon him. J. Edgar Hoover told Eisenhower that McCarthy had become an impediment in the war against subversion. Worse yet, McCarthy was deteriorating physically and, one must presume, mentally. Working virtually around the clock, he was drinking almost as steadily, seeming to draw strength not from food and rest but from tension and alcohol.

The hearings began on April 22, 1954, in an overflowing Senate caucus room before a network television audience. One of the first political spectaculars of the video age, the hearings . . . [became], in the words of columnist Walter Lippmann, "a national obsession.". . .

Secretary Stevens, who was on the stand for days, seemed ill-prepared and evasive. It became clear that the army, in its treatment of Schine, had gone to extraordinary lengths in attempting to appease McCarthy and, especially, Roy Cohn. Senator McCarthy fared miserably. First, the nation had an opportunity to see a red-baiter in action, not just the headlines he liked to create. Instead of bold-faced type declaring "Army Shields Reds, Senator Charges," Americans now saw a fading demagogue badgering witnesses, interrupting lawyers, upbraiding his fellow senators, and incessantly disrupting the proceedings with irrelevant "points of order." Second, Joseph Welch skillfully managed to mire McCarthy in what today would be called "the sleaze factor." There was the "purloined letter" supposedly written by J. Edgar Hoover about security risks at Fort Monmouth; if it was not a forgery, McCarthy had received it in violation of federal laws protecting government secrets. There were the eleven memos that McCarthy's secretary could not remember typing or filing. And there was a doctored photograph showing Stevens and Private Schine in an amicable pose. As journalist Drew Pearson assessed the hearings, "[The army] comes off badly—though McCarthy comes off a little worse."

Critics continued to urge Eisenhower to attack McCarthy publicly, but by April no need existed for the president to do so. McCarthy was destroying himself. On April 5, in a nationally broadcast address, Ike sought to assuage the fears that McCarthy and others—including the president himself at times—had aroused. American Communists, Eisenhower said, constituted only a tiny percentage of the nation's population. Unsubstantiated allegations made behind the shield of congressional immunity, he noted, could result in "grave offenses" against individual rights. Stopping short, however, of recommending concrete action to put an end to McCarthyism, the president instead reassured the nation that "public opinion" would ultimately "straighten this matter out." Eisenhower secretly followed the course of the hearings through Charles Potter. The Michigan Republican briefed Eisenhower on the first day of the hearings and again in early May. The president, according to Potter, initially thought that Stevens would perform well as a witness and that the hearings would be brief. Convinced that the White House had failed to support Stevens adequately, Potter feared that Eisenhower might not fully understand the situation on Capitol Hill. But Ike knew enough to "feel ashamed for the United States Senate," a sentiment he did not conceal at a May 5 press conference. The president hoped the benefits of the hearings, he told reporters, would at least be "comparable" to what the country had "suffered in loss of international prestige, and . . . self-respect."

Few Republican leaders could see any benefits in the army-McCarthy confrontation. . . . Beginning early in May, Everett Dirksen commenced his own campaign to bring the hearings to a close. As unveiled to the subcommittee on May 11, the Dirksen proposal provided that further public sessions would be limited to the testimony of McCarthy and Stevens, that any other testimony would be heard in executive session, and that Senator McCarthy would be allowed to resume his other investigations. Both John Adams and White House speechwriter William Bragg Ewald, Jr., later wrote that Fred A. Seaton, the deputy secretary of defense for legislative affairs and a politician with close ties to the White House, had pressured Stevens to agree to the Dirksen plan. Despite his disgust with the whole affair, however, Eisenhower would not order the army to compromise. Instead, the president sent word to Stevens, through Charles Wilson: "Do what you think is right." Believing that the hearings would clear his name and vindicate the army, Stevens refused to budge. Dirksen complained to the White House, but to no avail. On May 11, the Democrats and Chairman Mundt—who had promised not to terminate the proceedings without the agreement of all the principals—defeated the Dirksen compromise 4 to 3.

President Eisenhower might not have given Stevens such discretion if he had foreseen the next path the hearings would take, although there had been warning signs. On May 3 and again the next day, Roy Cohn, representing himself, repeatedly pressed Stevens for the legal basis of the army's refusal to make loyalty board members available to congressional investigators. On May 7, the army responded with a legal memorandum that was short on case law but stated that at a January 21, 1954, conference attended by "members of the White House executive Staff," William Rogers, John Adams, and the attorney general, "Mr. Brownell took the position that the success of the loyalty program required that security board members . . . be protected from the dangers inherent in the congressional review of their actions." The January 21 meeting surfaced again as Ray Jenkins questioned John Adams on May 12, the day after the subcommittee rejected the Dirksen compromise. Apparently, Adams believed the immunity of the loyalty boards derived from the traditional common-law rule that judges could not be summoned to give testimony about their decisions. "The boards are quasi-judicial in nature," he explained to the subcommittee. "They have somewhat the function of an appellate court." And Adams volunteered some details on the January 21 meeting: that Sherman Adams and Henry Cabot Lodge had been present, that they had discussed David Schine, and that it had been suggested that the army lawyer prepare a written summary of the Schine affair. Jenkins did not bore in on the particulars of the meeting, but Adams had implicated the White House. On the mention of Lodge's name especially, *Time* magazine reported, "the senators' political radarscopes blipped wildly." Obviously, the meeting possessed no relationship to Lodge's duties at the United Nations. Moreover, as the manager of Eisenhower's tough 1952 preconvention campaign, Lodge had attracted the political enmity of both Democrats and anti-Eisenhower Republicans.

Adams, as we have seen, had been trying since the fall of 1953 to force the Justice Department to clarify the administration's policy on the power of Congress to demand witnesses and documents from the executive branch. With regard to the ability of Congress to subpoena loyalty board members, Adams told the subcommittee that "two schools of thought" existed within the administration. Indeed, it was beginning to appear that one school existed for material embarrassing to the White House and another existed for everything else. Concerned about the release of the transcripts of telephone calls monitored by the Department of Defense, Herbert Brownell had advised Sherman Adams on May 2 that if the subcommittee sought to obtain "telephone conversations with the White House or the Department of Justice, the Administration should not allow them to be turned over." Along with Brownell's advice, the White House received a lengthy memorandum from William Rogers detailing numerous incidents in which presidents had withheld information from Congress. Fearful that he might be called to testify, Ambassador Lodge indicated to the president on May 7 that he would not honor a subpoena. Eisenhower replied three days later that the UN ambassador's position was "exactly correct." Yet as late as May 11, Eisenhower instructed Charles Wilson to provide Congress with all the facts relevant to the Peress case, except those touching on national security. The president did not, he told the defense secretary, want the army to appear guilty of a "cover-up."

Nevertheless, once John Adams offered the subcommittee an opportunity to pursue the army-McCarthy controversy into the Oval Office, the administration moved immediately to limit further disclosures. Sherman Adams ordered Seaton to collect for transmittal to the White House all records pertaining to "the inquiry before the subcommittee." On the same day, Eisenhower directed Wilson not to permit the disclosure before the Mundt panel of the substance of any conversations between employees of the executive branch that involved their official duties. Such confidentiality was essential, the president said, to the preservation of the separation of powers and the free exchange of advice.

Jenkins kept John Adams on the stand for all of May 13 without questioning him about his meeting with Sherman Adams and Lodge. The next day, a Friday, gave Stuart Symington a chance to cross-examine the army lawyer, and Symington went directly to the reason for Lodge's presence at the January 21 meeting. As Adams was conceding that no UN business had been under discussion, Welch, citing oral instructions from the Department of Defense, told Adams to say no more about the conference. The Democrats immediately objected, with Henry Jackson making the credible point that Adams, by disclosing the meeting and revealing some of its details, might legally be held to have waived any privilege. But on Welch's instructions, Adams dodged further questions about the meeting until the subcommittee recessed for the weekend.

When the hearings resumed on May 17, John Adams returned with a letter, freshly prepared by the White House staff, in which President Eisenhower instructed Charles Wilson that Defense Department witnesses were not to testify about conservations with other executive branch employees or to produce related documents. The army also submitted a memorandum incorporating Rogers's arguments in his earlier report to the White House. Eisenhower's directive stunned the subcommittee. Speaking for the Democrats, Senator McClellan charged, "The issuance of this Executive Order is a serious mistake." If it was to be issued, McClellan argued, it should have been done at the beginning of the hearings. Even the Republicans were taken aback; Charles Potter feared that Stevens and Adams were being "used as whipping boys" for the decisions of more senior administration officials. Confused and anxious to negotiate a modification of Eisenhower's order, the subcommittee voted to recess until the following week.

He had tried to "stay out of this damn business on the Hill," Eisenhower told the Republican leaders at their weekly meeting on May 17. Knowland and the House GOP leader Charles A. Halleck expressed reservations about the scope of the order, but Ike asserted that Sherman Adams and other executive aides, like military staff officers, possessed "no political existence" beyond the president. Ike admitted that he "couldn't tell the Senate its business," but he asserted, "A person like Governor Adams has no responsibility to the legislature." Eisenhower clung stubbornly to principle and, to be sure, expediency. He defended his order at a press conference two days later and, despite the personal intercession of Everett Dirksen, refused to modify his decision.

Eisenhower seemed personally offended at the possibility that two of his closest aides might be called to testify, as if the prospect threatened to invade his own privacy. As he told James Hagerty, "Any man who testified as to the advice he gave me won't be working for me that night." This was the other side of Eisenhower's rigid view of the separation of powers. Loath to involve himself ostentatiously in congressional affairs, he deeply resented legislative scrutiny of the upper reaches of the administration. Ironically, for so mild-mannered a chief executive, Eisenhower's instructions to Wilson represented an unprecedented assertion of presidential prerogative. No longer was the administration merely seeking to prevent the exposure of sensitive personnel files, the disruption of an administrative tribunal, or the abuse of a hapless general. Now the administration, through Attorney General Brownell, claimed that the president enjoyed an "uncontrolled discretion" over the release of information from the executive branch, although the attorney general quickly had to correct his statement that the courts had "uniformly" recognized such a right. In reality, the administration's argument rested on past incidents in which presidents had resisted Congress but avoided litigation. No definitive judicial decisions supported Eisenhower's claims. What soon became known as "executive privilege," wrote one constitutional scholar, was a "myth," an unwarranted assertion of executive supremacy "altogether without historical foundation."

Notwithstanding later criticisms, the order stood; it was widely perceived that the president, after months of public temporizing, had finally dealt a deadly blow to the nation's leading political rabble-rouser. McCarthy's startled reaction to the May 17 directive—"Mr. Chairman, I must admit that I am somewhat at a loss to know what to do at the moment"—contributed to that impression. Yet the senator's bewilderment was evidence more of his declining powers than it was of the efficacy of Eisenhower's action. At his peak, McCarthy had needed little to send Washington into turmoil—an ex-Communist willing to talk, a leaked document, a bald-faced lie. Now he seemed less resourceful, less intimidating. The hearings themselves, apart from their incalculable psychological damage, may have hurt McCarthy less than they did the Republican party. The senator's favorable rating slid to about a third of the population before the hearings began, and remained there. . . . But as David M. Oshinsky has perceptively noted, McCarthy's influence had long depended on "the *appearance* of mass support," and by the late spring of 1954, that appearance was dissolving. . . .

For his part, Eisenhower mixed restrained public denunciations of McCarthyism with a growing personal contempt. The president had earlier ridiculed the notion that McCarthy represented a menace to "our system of government." But McCarthy's call for government employees to ignore Ike's secrecy order of May 17 infuriated the president, who privately compared the senator to Adolf Hitler and labeled his plea "the most disloyal act . . . ever . . . by anyone in the government of the United States." In a well-received speech at Columbia University, Eisenhower warned against censorship, "hysteria, and intimidation" in the war against subversion. Near the end of the hearings in mid-June, Charles Potter, disgusted with his GOP colleagues' efforts to defend McCarthy, told Eisenhower that he might vote with the Democrats to deliver a report critical of the Wisconsin Republican. Frustrated himself, the president told James Hagerty, "That's all right with me."

* * *

Despite the attention, the army-McCarthy hearings, at least from a procedural standpoint, proved to be less important in McCarthy's ultimate downfall than did an earlier investigation by the Subcommittee on Privileges and Elections of the Senate Committee on Rules and Investigations. In February 1951, the subcommittee, then controlled by the Democrats, began questioning Senator McCarthy in a wide-ranging investigation that encompassed alleged financial misconduct and violation of state and federal election laws. Beset by partisan divisions and McCarthy's obstructionism, the panel's inquiry proved inconclusive. Then on June 11, 1954, Senator Ralph E. Flanders, a Vermont Republican, introduced a resolution calling on the Senate to strip McCarthy of his chairmanships unless he remedied his "contempt" of the Subcommittee on Privileges and Elections. . . .

Most Republicans resented Flanders's efforts to force their party to deal directly with the McCarthy issue. William Knowland denounced Flanders's resolution as "unfair and unprecedented." Knowland and Homer E. Ferguson of Michigan, another conservative Republican, pleaded with Flanders to withdraw it. . . . Vice President Nixon predicted that the resolution would not pass "in its present form" and perhaps not in any form. Secretary of the Treasury George M. Humphrey, widely regarded as one of the most influential figures in the administration, quietly went to Capitol Hill to urge Flanders to drop his attack on McCarthy.

The president, meanwhile, sent the Vermont senator a brief, and confidential, message of support. Privately, Eisenhower questioned the propriety of a censure motion lacking specific charges, as did Flanders's. Eisenhower refused publicly to endorse the anti-McCarthy initiative and, by all accounts, maintained his distance from the affair. Political scientist Fred Greenstein has depicted the president as the mastermind of a massive and surreptitious campaign to depose McCarthy, but much of his evidence consists of Ike's rather timid verbal assaults on blatantly paranoid anticommunism. Those statements impressed none of McCarthy's contemporary critics, even if they stung his supporters. In all fairness, the administration did contribute to McCarthy's destruction. Representatives of the White House, if not the president himself, plotted army strategy with Welch and his assistants. Yet few of Eisenhower's intimates, in the words of reporter Robert Donovan, believed "that the president followed any carefully planned, deliberate strategy toward McCarthy."

The divisions within the administration, along with the likelihood that presidential meddling in so delicate a Senate proceeding might trigger a pro-McCarthy backlash, counseled against White House intervention. To be sure, a few people on the "fringes of the administration," as William Knowland later recalled, assisted Senator Flanders. The Vermont senator received crucial legal and political support from the National Committee for an Effective Congress, which claimed the longtime Eisenhower supporter Paul Hoffman as its leading fund-raiser. Concerned that McCarthy was driving liberal and independent voters away from the GOP, Hoffman thought that the White House might be able to persuade Ferguson, Potter, and Eugene D. Millikin of Colorado to join in the Flanders motion. But the president, his contempt for McCarthy by now well known, left the Senate to its own devices.

On its own, the Senate moved deliberately. Faced with the virtually unanimous opposition of the Republican leadership, Senator Flanders modified his resolution to call simply for the censure of McCarthy. At the same time, demands were growing within the Senate for the inclusion in the resolution of a bill of particulars and for hearings on the Flanders resolution, both of which were seen as delaying tactics put forward by McCarthyites. Flanders and his supporters acceded to the demand for a set of specific allegations. Then, on August 2, 1954, the Senate voted 75 to 12 to refer the censure resolution to a select committee. As handpicked by Knowland and Texas Democrat Lyndon B. Johnson, the minority leader, the committee consisted of three Democrats and three Republicans, all respectable members of the Senate establishment. Utah's Arthur V. Watkins would head the panel. A Taft Republican and former member of the internal security subcommittee, Watkins boasted of having as much experience investigating Communists as did McCarthy. Unlike Karl Mundt, Watkins would manage his committee with a stern hand; the select committee hearings, which would not be televised, proceeded without the fanfare that accompanied the army-McCarthy confrontation.

The Watkins Committee hearings were played out against the background of the coming congressional elections—the first real political test of the administration's handling of the Communist controversy. As early as November 1953, Eisenhower had publicly disputed Leonard Hall's assertion that Communists in government would be the principal issue in 1954. Undoubtedly, the president feared turning the election into a referendum on McCarthyism, with the GOP taking the pro-McCarthy position. . . . Yet the senator retained significant pockets of support at the grass-roots level; throughout 1954, mail to the RNC was overwhelmingly pro-McCarthy. As former

Congressman O. K. Armstrong advised Hall after returning from a tour of the Midwest and West, McCarthy still possessed "a big following . . . one not to be antagonized needlessly." And even Lodge believed that anticommunism, minus McCarthy, represented "a marvelously popular issue."

Eisenhower responded to such advice with a little election year red-baiting of his own. As he had done before, the president sought to ignore, and to preempt, McCarthy. On June 10, Eisenhower told a national gathering of local party workers that the administration had been "intensifying legal action against the members and leaders of the Communist conspiracy." On August 30, the president, appearing before an American Legion convention in Washington, D.C., pledged to "wage a relentless battle against subversion and infiltration." Eisenhower said less about the issue during a fall campaign swing through the West, but he did assure a Republican rally in Denver that the government was "dealing decisively with 'the Communist menace.' " Ike also agreed to campaign in Illinois for the Republican Senate candidate, an archconservative McCarthyite who was challenging incumbent Democrat Paul H. Douglas. The president, however, insisted that the Republican nominee, Joseph T. Meek, not bring McCarthy into Illinois.

For the most part, however, President Eisenhower left the administration's anti-Communist crusading to Richard Nixon. On September 15, the vice president embarked on a tour designed to take him into thirty-one states over the next forty-eight days. All across the country, Nixon warned that a Democratic Congress would impede the war against communism and bragged that "thousands of Communists, fellow travelers, and security risks" had been "thrown out" of the government by the administration. . . . Both Eisenhower and the vice president later sensed a pervasive apathy among Republicans. Nixon attributed it to the divisions and embarrassment created within the party by the controversy surrounding Joseph McCarthy. The remedy, it seemed, was for the administration to take the initiative in the search for subversives.

Eisenhower believed that the survival of the Republican party depended on the rejection of its "dyed-in-the-wool reactionary fringe" but not, apparently, in the abandonment of the anti-Communist stance with which the conservatives were associated. He feared that a Republican defeat in November would encourage the "extreme right wing" to try to seize control of the organization. The actual results proved less menacing. Although the Republicans lost control of Congress, by a narrow margin, the results were especially disappointing for the Old Guard. . . . James Hagerty concluded that the party's association with McCarthy had hurt the GOP in New York and other large industrial states. But in most of the country, Communists in government seems not to have been a significant issue.

On September 27, 1954, the Watkins Committee had issued a report recommending that McCarthy be censured for his refusal to cooperate with the investigation of the Subcommittee on Privileges and Elections and for his harassment of General Zwicker. . . .

Eisenhower's refusal to attack McCarthy publicly, his support for a stringent employee loyalty program, and his own lapses into red-baiting could never placate the hard-core McCarthyites because the appeal of the Wisconsin senator transcended the narrow issue of Communists in government. To many conservatives at the Republican grass roots, New Deal liberalism had been indistinct from socialism, which, one pro-McCarthy correspondent wrote Kansas Senator Frank Carlson, was "the next step to communism." Since so many of them saw so little difference between a New Dealer and a Communist, McCarthy's supporters easily equated McCarthyism with a general conservative assault on the changes that had taken place in American politics and foreign policy in the last twenty years. Liberals had been dismayed by Eisenhower's public diffidence toward McCarthy, but Republican conservatives chafed at the president's failure to support McCarthy wholeheartedly and his affiliation with the eastern wing of the party. If Ike was not the conscious agent of an anti-McCarthy conspiracy, some McCarthyites thought, "the Republican New Dealers, pinks, intellectuals and liberals were taking him for a ride."

It was not surprising, then, that Eisenhower, according to James Hagerty, "hit the roof" when he learned that William Knowland would oppose censure as a threat to the investigative power of the Senate. In reality, Knowland feared alienating conservative support for his principal political objective, a strong U.S. commitment to the defense of Formosa. To be sure, Eisenhower publicly minimized the possibility that the censure issue might split the GOP. He showed no interest when, before the November elections, New

Jersey Senator H. Alexander Smith suggested a meeting between Attorney General Brownell and Senator McCarthy in another attempt to reconcile the senator and the administration. . . . Evidence exists that after the election, with McCarthy's influence clearly curbed, the administration may have considered some kind of compromise, which most senators would have welcomed. According to McCarthy's lawyer, Edward Bennett Williams, who reportedly discussed the issue with Bernard Shanley, the White House seemed eager to settle the controversy as quickly as possible. The Wisconsin senator, however, characteristically refused to apologize for his past behavior or to agree to anything less than a complete vindication by the Senate. On December 2, the Senate voted 67 to 22 to condemn McCarthy for contempt of the Subcommittee on Privileges and Elections and for contempt of the Watkins Committee.

Before the end of the week, Eisenhower broke his silence on the censure controversy by summoning Arthur Watkins to the White House. After a brief meeting—in which the president agreed once more to the release of the identities of those involved in promoting Peress—the White House issued a statement praising Watkins's handling of the select committee. . . .

Eisenhower made a modest contribution to the destruction of Joseph McCarthy, and thereby to the continuing vitality of the Republican party. But the president failed to win the Old Guard away from its favorite witch-hunter or to remake the GOP in the moderate image he had fashioned for himself. All of the twenty-two votes opposing censure came from Republicans, splitting the party's Senate membership in half. Except for Leverett Saltonstall of Massachusetts, all of the Republican leadership—Knowland, Dirksen, Millikin, and Styles Bridges—voted for McCarthy. . . .

* * *

Surely nothing in Dwight Eisenhower's record as president has garnered more criticism than his efforts, early in his administration, to appease Senator Joseph McCarthy. Ike's defenders can rightly note, however, that within a year and a half of Eisenhower's election in 1952, McCarthy found himself mortally wounded, politically and perhaps physically. The Eisenhower White House played a relatively modest role in McCarthy's downfall, but for so talented a demagogue, the Wisconsin anti-Communist demonstrated a remarkably brief shelf life once Eisenhower became president. Even some of those who, at the time, had urged the president publicly to confront McCarthy concluded in hindsight that Eisenhower's prudence may have been well-advised.

Yet Eisenhower's dealings with his principal Republican adversary suggest little about his handling of the Communist controversy; McCarthy could be separated too easily from McCarthyism. . . . President Eisenhower, despite his revulsion at McCarthy's "methods," found himself all too often caught up in the same kind of thoughtless hyperpatriotism.

At the outset of the cold war, General Eisenhower had demonstrated decidedly moderate instincts—defending McCarthyite targets like Philip S. Jessup, cooperating as NATO commander with European Socialist leaders, and expressing an interest in a rapprochement with Yugoslavia's maverick Communist strongman, Marshal Josip Tito. Under pressure from Republican conservatives, candidate Eisenhower moved steadily toward the Right in the heat of the 1952 presidential campaign. Once in the Oval Office, the old soldier seemed to embrace much of the agenda of the anti-Communists and to share many of their fears about the nation's internal security. Although Eisenhower eventually presided over an ebbing of the Communist controversy, it was not the result of a conscious commitment to bring the Red Scare to an end in the interest of free and unfettered political discourse. . . .

By subtly distancing himself from Senator McCarthy while otherwise subscribing to an anti-Communist cold war orthodoxy, Eisenhower managed to offer something to liberals and conservatives alike. More important, he successfully appealed to the broad, if indifferent, middle range of public opinion. By delegating authority—appearing to reign but not rule—Eisenhower minimized, in the public mind, his culpability for both the excesses and the lapses of his employee security program. In the course of the administration's quest for internal security, Eisenhower's ability to survive the Communist controversy with his popularity intact may have been his most impressive accomplishment. . . .

The administration had helped to exorcise Joseph McCarthy from the body politic, but the nation's postwar traumas left permanent scars. The principal crises of that generation of Americans who came after Eisenhower—the war in Vietnam and the Watergate scandal—had their roots in the 1950s. The growth of government secrecy, the abuse of intelligence agencies, and above all, a reflexive anticommunism all stemmed, at least in part, from the search for internal security. . . . The controversy over domestic communism, along with the question of civil rights for American blacks, represented the great moral issues of the day. On neither did Dwight Eisenhower demonstrate any particular sensitivity. He was a manager, not a moral leader.

William Bragg Ewald, Jr.

WHO KILLED JOE McCARTHY?

In contrast to Jeff Broadwater, Fred Greenstein has argued in *The Hidden-Hand Presidency* that Eisenhower pursued a deliberate policy of undermining rather than attacking McCarthy and that "it is difficult to see how . . . another technique would have worked faster and more decisively in the context of the time." Although William Bragg Ewald, Jr., agrees with Greenstein that Eisenhower was responsible for bringing down the demagogue from Wisconsin, he believes that "the President had no master plan . . . for carefully controlled action." Ewald, who earned a Ph.D. in English at Harvard, served as a member of the White House staff during Eisenhower's presidency. He also worked for Eisenhower's Secretary of the Interior, Fred Seaton. After Eisenhower left office, Ewald assisted in the preparation of Eisenhower's memoirs. Ewald set forth his position first in *Eisenhower the President* and then in more detail in *Who Killed Joe McCarthy?*, the conclusion of which is reprinted below.

The Eisenhower strategy against McCarthy was a strategy, exactly, to produce impotent isolation.

It was not a strategy that turned on McCarthy's issue of anticommunism. McCarthy and Eisenhower and indeed most of the

American people—given the evidence—saw the possibility of domestic Communist subversion as a significant problem. They saw it
as a problem in 1948 with the indictment of Alger Hiss; in 1950
with the revelation of the espionage of physicist Klaus Fuchs; in
1951 with the conviction of Julius and Ethel Rosenberg; in 1952
when Eisenhower won in a landslide as a man who would clean up
all the messes—including this one—in Washington.

And they saw it as a continuing problem in the late spring of
1954. In one study made during and just after the Army-McCarthy
hearings, only 7 percent of those polled said they believed no
Communists remained in government; and only 2 percent said
they would consider Communists in government no threat whatsoever. "Could the President," Governor Sherman Adams asked
reflectively years later, "have convinced the American people that
all of McCarthy's allegations were frauds? I doubt it."

The Eisenhower strategy against McCarthy was thus not a
strategy of flat denial of the existence of a problem of internal subversion. It was a strategy of detachment—of separating the decent
anti-Communist centrist followers from their indecent anti-Communist leader. It was a strategy that paralleled the one Eisenhower
had been following for more than a year in his attempt to get legislation through the Senate—the strategy, he confided to his diary
on April 1, 1953, of winning "away from the McCarthy-Malone
axis about five or six of their members," and thus reducing the
"splinter group . . . to impotence." By June of 1954, less than a
year and a half after Eisenhower entered office, that anti-McCarthy
strategy of isolation had largely succeeded.

The hearings ground on. McCarthy himself took the stand.
He denied he had ever sought favors for Schine. He dug in stubbornly as Senator Scoop Jackson of Washington, prompted by Bob
Kennedy, ridiculed a sweeping psychological warfare plan of David
Schine, a ridiculing that brought Cohn and Kennedy to a near fist-
fight right there in the conference room. And to the end McCarthy
maintained he had, sitting in New York City, dictated a memo to
Cohn and Carr, also in New York City, by long distance telephone
to his secretary Mrs. Driscoll, in Washington.

Frank Carr took the stand. Under avid grilling, he affirmed
and reaffirmed the authenticity of McCarthy's eleven memoranda.
He had indeed, he said, taken an elevator up three flights from his

first-floor office to dictate to Mrs. Driscoll on the fourth floor. He had indeed in one memo, he claimed, said that John Adams "came *down* [italics added] here" to Senate Office Building Room 101, through Carr was allegedly dictating in Mrs. Driscoll's office upstairs. McCarthy had one last name-calling clash with Senator Symington, and he had also one last round of wildly sprayed threats to probe the CIA, the Loyalty Security Board malefactors, and the perpetrators of the promotion of Peress. Then on June 17, at 6:32 P.M., after seventy-one half-day sessions, two million words of testimony, thirty-two witnesses, 187 hours of television time, and more than 100 thousand live attendees, the hearings sputtered to an end.

Still fuming with purple indignation on the sidelines, Struve Hensel [general counsel for the Defense Department] finally filed with the committee and then made public on June 20 his affidavit refuting in toto McCarthy's accusations against him. Hensel revealed McCarthy's admission in the May 17 executive session of the committee that he had no evidence whatsoever for his charge that Hensel had masterminded the Army attack in order to stop McCarthy's investigation of Hensel himself. He revealed McCarthy's offer to withdraw all his accusations against Hensel if in doing so he would not appear to be a "damn fool." And he revealed McCarthy's kick-below-the-belt Indian Charlie story.

On June 18, [John] Welch and [James] St. Clair [Welch's associate] for the first time went to the White House. "The President," Jim Hagerty wrote in his diary, "congratulated Welch for a very fine job. Welch told the President that he thought that if the hearings had accomplished nothing else, the Army had been able to keep McCarthy in front of the television sets for quite a while, long enough to permit the public to see how disgracefully he acted. He said he was sure this would be helpful in the long run. The President agreed with him. . . ." A few days later, on the evening of Friday, June 25, White House Chief-of-Staff Sherman Adams arrived at the home of Fred Seaton for a relaxed buffet supper of the Friendly Sons and Daughters of Franklin Pierce.

The attention of the nation, held mesmerized all those weeks by the spectacle on the tube, began to turn elsewhere. By late August and early September the Congress at last was passing Eisenhower's legislative requests—the biggest volume in his entire eight years. By October the President was campaigning coast to coast for the election of Republican senators and congressmen, campaigning on a scale and with an intensity unmatched by any other President in American history in an off-year election. By November, though the Republicans lost control of the Senate and House, they lost it by an eyelash, in an election in which the issues of McCarthy and McCarthyism and domestic communism had virtually disappeared.

Finally, on December 2, in response to a resolution introduced by Ralph Flanders of Vermont and reported out by a committee headed by conservative Republican Arthur V. Watkins of Utah, the United States Senate—in the third such action in its entire 165 years—voted to condemn McCarthy for "conduct contrary to Senatorial traditions." The vote was 67–22 (all the negative votes were Republicans, including majority leader William Knowland). The conduct condemned was McCarthy's abuse of a Senate subcommittee on privileges and elections that had been looking into his financial activities; and his abuse of the Watkins censure committee itself—a committee McCarthy had branded the "unwitting handmaiden" of the Communist party. These Senate charges had no direct connection whatsoever with the Army-McCarthy controversy. Two days after the censure vote, Eisenhower invited Chairman Watkins to the White House and—in words eagerly released to the press by Jim Hagerty—praised him for "a very splendid job."

So Joseph McCarthy, senator from Wisconsin, was politically dead. He had been brought down by many people and many forces, including the force of fortuitous accident. But above all he had been defeated by Dwight Eisenhower.

It is wrong, of course, to ascribe the political demise of McCarthy to a grand strategy furtively and flawlessly masterminded in the Oval Office by Eisenhower himself. The President had no master plan, no week-by-week, month-by-month blueprint for carefully controlled action. After the McCarthy browbeating of Zwicker, for example, while one of his top lieutenants—Cabot Lodge—was urging, with the President's enthusiastic approval, a fighting denunciation by Stevens in an open hearing, another top

Eisenhower lieutenant—Jerry Persons—was setting up the fried chicken lunch. Eisenhower did not convene, with keen foresight, the January 21 meeting in Brownell's office; he did not order the writing of the Adams chronology; he did not supervise its leakage to the press to put McCarthy on the defensive; and he did not plan the hearings as a means of exposing the loathsome foe to the TV viewing public, thus destroying him. Indeed, Eisenhower expected the hearings to last only a few days. And at the end of the first week, disgusted, he wanted them stopped.

Moreover, Eisenhower did not issue his May 17 directive to Charlie Wilson as a grand stroke to help the Army in its argumentation with McCarthy. Welch and St. Clair had no idea the directive was coming. In complete independence and isolation, Herbert Brownell and Bill Rogers had devised it as a constitutional answer to a constitutional problem. The time had come, in their view and that of the President, to shut off an endless trail of inquiry which was beginning to lead away from the Pentagon and into the Justice Department and the White House.

Eisenhower, nevertheless, did win. He won because, first, he and his administration took the anti-Communist issue away from McCarthy. Truman had tried to do the same thing. He had established an elaborate mechanism of boards to test and decide the loyalty of government employees. Some of the most conspicuous departures from the State Department—particularly among the old China hands—occurred not under Eisenhower and Dulles but under Truman and Acheson. For example, by the time Eisenhower took over, O. Edmund Clubb had left. So had the first of the three Johns—John Stewart Service. A second John, John Carter Vincent, had been looked into again and again and again. Perhaps, if Acheson had remained Secretary of State, Vincent would have been cleared. Perhaps he would have been found, once again, a man of dubious loyalty. In any event, Foster Dulles permitted him to resign with a full pension, and McCarthy howled. The third John, John Paton Davies, did depart in 1954, two years into Dulles's term as Secretary of State, but only after Dulles had taken a searing from McCarthy on nationwide television for having kept this perfidious holdover so long.

But despite his loyalty apparatus, Truman had failed to appropriate the antisubversion issue. By the time Truman left office, despite the State Department purges, McCarthy as a symbol of anti-Communist cleanup was galloping faster than ever. In contrast to Truman, Eisenhower succeeded. By the time the hearings ended, Eisenhower had on his side of the sharp line separating him from McCarthy the three most salient anti-Communists in America: Richard Nixon, who had got Alger Hiss; Herbert Brownell, who had devised the administration's toughened loyalty-security procedures and exposed Harry Dexter White; and the greatest prize of all, J. Edgar Hoover. All three had declared themselves, in the spotlight of public attention, allies of the President.

Eisenhower won, next, because he never engaged in a personal vituperative attack on McCarthy as an individual, which might have swelled McCarthy's press coverage and forced his followers to rally behind a man they saw as a martyr. Truman and Acheson had engaged in such personal attack. And after three long years, they had helped produce millions of words for McCarthy in headlines and front-page news. And the more they tried to slug it out, the more suspicion of stonewalling and complicity they brought down on their own heads, the more inviting targets of attack they became, and the more lustily the demagogue's followers would bellow: "McCarthy is my leader, I shall not be moved. . . ." Ike from the start saw this trap and evaded it. "I really believe," he wrote in his diary April 1, 1953, "that nothing will be so effective in combatting [McCarthy's] particular kind of troublemaking as to ignore him. This he cannot stand."

Eisenhower won, further, because he never engaged in an attack on McCarthy as a member of Congress, thus forcing senators and representatives—ever touchy about their powers in an independent branch of government—to coalesce in an institutional defense of an injured fellow member. Though at least one citizen wrote in urging Eisenhower to "fire McCarthy," Eisenhower could not. He could not deprive a congressional committee of its constitutional right to investigate the executive branch. He could insist on a measure of courtesy. But he had no power to stop vigorous inquiry. "Only the United States Senate," the President told his brother Milton, "can deal with McCarthy." And "only the people of Wisconsin," he told Jim Hagerty, "can get rid of him."

Given these limitations, Eisenhower won because through a devoted, canny, and streetwise organization—notably Sherman

Adams, Jim Hagerty, Struve Hensel, and Fred Seaton, an organization that forthrightly improvised much of its own way—he chipped and sliced and cut at the detested foe until the combined forces—including, memorably, the forces of Justice under Brownell and Rogers—finally brought him down.

As this process came to its climax, Eisenhower won because his cohorts, most visible on nationwide television, became convincing and believable symbols of simple human decency. By the time the hearings ended, the American people had indelibly in their consciousness the stark distinction between Stevens (patently honest, bumbling, good-hearted, guileless), John Adams (meticulous with fact, scrupulous, sincere, impressive in testimony) and, supremely, Joe Welch (dapper, courtly, and kind), and the barracudas ranged against them, from McCarthy and Cohn to the backroom boys with their cropped photos and their memos of questionable authenticity.

And Eisenhower won, above all, because he constantly held up before his fellow countrymen a standard to which—in the words of his great hero, George Washington—wise and good men, weary of niggling negative controversy, could repair: a standard of abstract principles of freedom of the mind, fidelity to the Constitution, fair play, honesty, magnanimity; of legislation to be passed and work to be done to move the country forward.

"The militarists in Berlin, Rome and Tokyo started this war," Franklin Roosevelt declared in a magnificent utterance at the heart of the great worldwide conflict, "but the massed, angered forces of common humanity will finish it." Led by the President of the United States, the massive awakened forces of common humanity also ended McCarthyism.

III

Eisenhower and Civil Rights

When a federal court ordered the admission of nine black students to Little Rock's Central High School, Governor Orval Faubus used the National Guard to prevent the black students from entering the school. In this photo, a mob of angry white students shout abuse at Elizabeth Eckford, one of the black students. To enforce the court's order, Eisenhower federalized the Arkansas National Guard and sent one thousand paratroopers from the 101st Airborne Division. (AP/Wide World Photos)

Robert Fredrick Burk

EISENHOWER AND CIVIL RIGHTS CONSERVATISM

Eisenhower confronted numerous contentious issues during his presidency, but perhaps none of his policies has generated so much criticism
from historians as his approach to civil rights. Robert F. Burk, a professor
of history at Muskingum College, argues that Eisenhower pursued only
symbolic equality and in doing so promulgated "a new and more respectable kind of civil rights conservatism." It is worth considering,
however, the extent to which Eisenhower's policies and attitudes differed from those of liberals of his era. The main issue on which liberals
differed from Eisenhower on civil rights reflected a larger disagreement
about the proper role of the federal government in American life. At the
end of the following excerpt, Burk seems to indicate that liberals, even
in the 1960s, engaged in symbolic policies similar to those of the Eisenhower administration.

The beginning of 1960 marked a new phase in the civil rights
movement in the South, one spurred by the activity of a new generation of black activists. Increasingly aware of the federal government's reluctance to intervene with police power to protect citizenship rights, black college students in the South turned to new
strategies to force public confrontations with the practitioners of
Jim Crow. Before 1960, civil rights protest primarily had featured
techniques, including court suits and local black boycotts, that had
not forced face-to-face confrontation between segregationists and
their black victims. Only on rare occasions, as with the successful sit-
ins at Wichita, Kansas, and Oklahoma City, Oklahoma, outlets of the
Katz drugstore chain, had the confrontational tactics of "direct action" been employed. But on February 1, 1960, a new era began
when Joseph McNeill, a freshman at North Carolina Agricultural
and Technical College, started a student sit-in at a Woolworth variety store cafeteria in Greensboro, North Carolina. Four days later,
protests spread to the city's S.H. Kress store. With community

tensions rising and members of the Ku Klux Klan offering assistance to segregationists, Greensboro black protestors assented to withdraw from the stores for two weeks to allow local business leaders to reevaluate their service policies.

Receiving aid and volunteers from the newly formed Student Nonviolent Coordinating Committee (SNCC), the sit-in movement soon extended to a host of other Upper South cities, including Richmond, Hampton, Portsmouth, Nashville, and Chattanooga. From his observation post in Washington, E. Frederic Morrow [administrative assistant to the president and the first African American to hold an executive position in the White House] noted the importance of the emerging organized black activity. In his internal memorandum on the "Student Protest Movement in the South," Morrow described it as a "new trend . . . adding to legal suits economic pressures and direct action." President Eisenhower and his other advisers, however, were uncertain whether the rise of black civil disobedience and direct action was a positive development or not. Adoption by Southern blacks of nonviolent confrontation as a strategy to force negotiation with segregationists did represent a form of direct black resolution of racial disputes not reliant upon federal sponsorship. On the other hand, any official attempts by Southern governments through their police power vigorously to suppress the demonstrators opened up additional dangers of police brutality, civil rights violations, and federal-state confrontations.

The administration's fears that the sit-in movement might not fail to release it from intervention but actually make involvement more likely were underlined in early March. Martin Luther King, Jr., and A. Philip Randolph issued calls to the White House for federal intervention to restrain Alabama police violence against demonstrators. A week later, on March 16, 1960, the President refused to offer any "sweeping" opinion on the merits of the sit-in movement. Although he expressed general sympathy with the aims of the protestors, Eisenhower suggested that the government's responsibility was limited to preventing discrimination in areas of "public charter," and he added that he was "not in a position to judge" the legitimacy of the lunch-counter protests. Acting separately, however, representatives of the Justice Department gave limited assistance to the direct-action movement. In response to black protests, the department filed suit in May against officials of Harrison County and the city of Biloxi, Mississippi for denying blacks access to beach facilities. Government lawyers claimed federal jurisdiction in the case because of the use of federal funding in the beach's antierosion project and seawall.

In early June, the Justice Department also extended its good offices in an effort to resolve the drugstore segregation controversy. Attorney General Rogers invited representatives of the F.W. Woolworth's S.H. Kress, and W.T. Grant chains to an informal meeting to discuss the possible desegregation of their lunch-counter facilities. Two months later, the variety-chain executives informed the attorney general of their willingness to desegregate lunch counters in sixty-nine Southern communities. Their action represented an important breakthrough, for 70 percent of the outlets affected had not yet witnessed sit-in protests. A delighted Rogers proclaimed that the outcome demonstrated the superiority of solutions obtained "when responsible local citizens take the first steps." Elsewhere, however, voluntary acceptance of integration by local entrepreneurs was not so easily achieved. In Jacksonville, Florida, sit-ins led to violence, and a petition by 1,400 blacks in late August for administration assistance went unheeded. Nevertheless, by the end of 1960, 50,000 blacks were engaged in direct-action campaigns in the South, including sit-ins, walk-ins, stand-ins, and pray-ins. Although approximately 3,600 protestors were arrested for violations of public order or segregation statutes, the demonstrations forced the integration of public facilities in 126 Southern cities, primarily in the Upper South.

Despite the increase of direct action and the new law-enforcement challenges it produced, White House attention to civil rights in 1960 was diverted by the political concerns of the upcoming November presidential election. With Eisenhower not eligible to succeed himself, the job of carrying the administration's record to the public fell to the vice president. On the surface, it appeared that a Nixon candidacy signaled a greater Republican commitment to federal civil rights activism in the future. As a congressman, Nixon had voted against the poll tax and for a fair employment practices commission. In his vice-presidential duties as Senate presiding officer

and as chairman of the President's Committee on Government Con-
tracts, Nixon had gained additional notoriety within the administration as a civil rights advocate.

The vice-president's support for black rights, however, rarely
had advanced beyond the level of symbolic gestures, and his public
utterances on civil rights usually had been shaped according to partisan needs. Nixon's actual philosophy of the role of the federal
government in civil rights differed but marginally from Eisenhower's. He wrote in his campaign biography, *The Challenges We
Face:* "In the world-wide struggle in which we are engaged, racial
and religious prejudice is a gun we point at ourselves." But he also
affirmed that administration policy "is not now, and should not be,
immediate and total integration." Asked for a written interview by
the Pittsburgh *Courier,* Nixon's answers (drafted primarily by campaign staffers) revealed the candidate's limited commitment to civil
rights. Declaring "I am against *forced* segregation," the vice-president endorsed the administration's civil rights program and emphasized the importance of voting rights: "There is nothing more
basic to progress in a democracy than for citizens to exercise their
right to vote." Nixon's primary aim in the field of civil rights was
the purification of the moral image of the United States abroad. "I
believe that the civil rights issue is vitally important to our nation
because it is basically a moral issue. Stated briefly, it is this: When
we say we stand for equality under law, do we mean it or not?"

Nixon did not seek to soften his public image as a civil rights
supporter before the party's nominating convention, for his main
challenge for the nomination came from Governor Nelson A. Rockefeller of New York. Entering the convention with an unshakable
grip on the presidential nomination, the vice president still sought
assurances of Rockefeller's active support in the general election. In
addition, Nixon wished to avoid being outflanked on civil rights by
a stronger Democratic platform plank. As a result, he engaged in
three-way negotiations with Rockefeller and platform committee
representative John Tower of Texas and lobbied platform committee delegates for a strong civil rights plank. The eventual Republican platform statement pledged the "full use of the power, resources, and leadership of the federal government" in combatting
discrimination, recited the Eisenhower record of accomplishment,

and even "affirmed" the right of "peaceable assembly" to protest private discrimination—a clear reference to the sit-in movement.

Once the Nixon general election campaign began, however, the candidate immediately backtracked from his preconvention posture of civil rights advocacy. Warned of the displeasure of Southern Republicans with the party platform, Nixon aides issued letters to supporters in the region denying any Nixon connection or affiliation with the NAACP. In a speech on August 17 at Greensboro, North Carolina, the birthplace of the direct-action movement, Nixon issued a personal disclaimer from vigorous federal action in civil rights, asserting that "law alone . . . is not the answer" and "is only as good as the will of the people to obey it." The Nixon campaign, following the Eisenhower lead, also solicited and received the help of South Carolina's former governor and segregationist leader James F. Byrnes, who assiduously avoided Joseph P. Kennedy's courtings in behalf of his son. Dismaying Morrow and Val Washington by using only Jackie Robinson as a black campaign spokesman and by ignoring the black press, Nixon persisted in avoiding any unqualified declarations of support for civil rights. Asked for his position during a Southern swing in Jackson, Mississippi, on September 24, the vice-president replied only, "I know that you are aware of my deep convictions on this issue."

Given his predecessor's success in employing a "Southern strategy" in winning the presidency, Nixon could be excused for attempting to duplicate it in 1960. But popular awareness of civil rights as a moral question was much greater in 1960 than in 1952 or even 1956. Eisenhower himself, despite his consistent sympathies for the white South, had demonstrated in 1956 his recognition of the political need to provide additional gestures of support for civil rights beyond those offered four years earlier. By 1960, rhetorical retreat on civil rights did not suit a Northern voting public growing more aware of Southern discrimination and measuring the moral fitness of presidential candidates in part on the basis of their public allegiance to the principle of equal opportunity. In its political task of providing a successful blend of rhetorical moral urgency and moderate policies, the Nixon campaign failed miserably. Breaking with the Eisenhower pattern, Nixon in 1960 did not even make a campaign appearance in Harlem. Running mate Henry Cabot Lodge, assuming the role of civil rights spokesman Nixon had once played, did promise the appointment of a black to the cabinet, only to have his "trial balloon" punctured by Nixon campaign aides. With the vice president's advisers insisting that all appointments would be made strictly on "merit," an embarrassed Lodge was forced to repudiate his statement during a Winston-Salem, North Carolina, appearance.

The Nixon campaign's biggest civil rights blunder, however, stemmed from the October 19 arrest of Martin Luther King by local police in Atlanta, Georgia, for participation in a department store sit-in. Having been given a suspended sentence six months earlier for a traffic violation, the civil rights leader was sentenced by a DeKalb County judge to four months at hard labor for violating probation. Fearful for King's physical safety, his associates pleaded with the administration to intervene with the judge to reduce the sentence. Although the vice president, who had conferred with King on several previous occasions, agreed that the civil rights leader had received a "bum rap," he refused to act in his capacity as a lawyer to telephone his protests to the judge. Such an action would be "improper," Nixon felt, and he notified reporters through Press Secretary Herbert Klein that he would have "no comment" on the matter. The candidate believed that any obligation to take action on King's behalf lay with the President, for in his politically safe position as a "lame duck," Eisenhower could respond freely without fear of the electoral consequences.

Upon the urgings of Attorney General William Rogers, a Nixon ally, Deputy Attorney General Walsh drafted a statement for delivery by James Hagerty, the presidential press secretary, protesting King's "fundamentally unjust arrest" and claiming that the President had directed the Justice Department "to take all proper steps to join with Dr. Martin Luther King in an appropriate application for his release." Eisenhower, however, never gave the necessary final approval for release of the statement. John F. Kennedy's campaign staff seized the opportunity to capitalize on the incident and secure the support of black voters and sympathetic whites. Following the advice of former CRC staffer and campaign aide Harris Wofford, Kennedy, not known as a forceful advocate of civil rights, transmitted a message of sympathy to Coretta Scott King. Campaign manager Robert Kennedy, although initially skeptical of the political benefits of intercession, had his own legal objections to the sentence relayed to the judge. The following day, in an action that apparently underlined the effectiveness of the Kennedy communications, King was released from jail.

It was the supreme irony of the campaign that the Nixon candidacy stumbled because of the vice president's failure to capitalize upon the King arrest through a symbolic gesture of help. Nixon had been one of the most willing and able practitioners of racial symbolism in the Eisenhower administration. But his failure, in Eisenhower's words, to "make a couple of phone calls" led to a spurt in black Democratic support that boosted Kennedy's national lead in the campaign's final two weeks. Kennedy supporters encouraged the trend by distributing literature on the King incident to black churches the Sunday before the election. On Election Day, Kennedy won the White House by a slim national margin of only 120,000 popular votes and 84 electoral votes, despite a white voter majority of 52 percent for Nixon. Postelection polls of black voters showed that they had preferred the Democrat by better than a 2–1 margin, and perhaps as high as 3 to 1. The Kennedy advantage among blacks roughly held irrespective of differences in age, sex, region, or community size. Without his margin of black support, Kennedy could not have carried the key states of Illinois, Michigan, New Jersey, Texas, and South Carolina. In contrast, Nixon's level of black support represented a disappointing slippage of between 5 and 10 percent from the Republican figures of 1956.

By electing John F. Kennedy, the American public had narrowly endorsed a change in party leadership in the White House. With twinges of regret mixed with a considerable sense of relief, officials of the Eisenhower administration prepared for the transition of power and for their departure from positions of official responsibility. Although their control over racial issues was less complete than they had hoped, Eisenhower and his advisers had nevertheless helped shape a legacy of philosophical assumptions and national policies that would continue to affect the national political consideration of racial issues for years to come. Initially the Republican administration had been content to issue executive orders continuing military desegregation, removing discriminatory sanctions from the nation's capital, appointing blacks to visible but unimportant executive positions, and creating fact-finding committees on minority employment. Dedicated to slowing the onward march of centralized government power, they had turned aside suggestions for a greater federal enforcement role in guaranteeing fair employment and housing. The times had been kind to them in their effort to minimize federal intervention in the private economy, for the general prosperity of the 1950s had defused much of the political interest in additional government economic activism, whether in the civil rights field or elsewhere.

If left to their own desires, Eisenhower and his subordinates likely would not have ventured beyond the initial boundaries of their policy of racial symbolism. But they had not been able to seize sufficient control over the march of events to prevent additional entanglement in the legal and moral confrontations over Jim Crow discrimination in the South. Forced by the Truman administration into taking a stance on public school segregation, the Eisenhower Justice Department reluctantly had filed briefs upholding the right of the Supreme Court to employ the Fourteenth Amendment as a tool to strike down Jim Crow. Challenged in the aftermath of the *Brown* decision by Southern "massive resistance," the administration had taken the first halting steps toward the enforcement of court-ordered desegregation decrees. In their desperate search for ways to free themselves from further involvement, administration officials had turned to the advocacy of voting rights as a means of providing blacks with a tool for self-protection, and the results were manifested in the civil rights acts of 1957 and 1960. In addition, the creation of the U.S. Commission on Civil Rights had provided the administration a bipartisan forum from which to shame the South, and the rest of the nation, into compliance with democratic ideals without itself becoming directly involved.

In explaining its approach to racial issues, the Eisenhower administration had given both voice and official sanction to a new and more respectable kind of civil rights conservatism, although the President himself had preferred the label "moderation." The Eisenhower doctrine of civil rights, which had supported the removal of official sanctions mandating discrimination but had preferred to leave additional progress to the private sector, represented a repudiation of the older white-supremacist tradition of conservative racial thought. At the same time, however, it was a rejection of the newer tradition of government fiscal and regulatory intervention in the private sector symbolized by the New Deal and

the Fair Deal. The President's philosophy of civil rights did succeed in jettisoning the unpalatable overt racism of Jim Crow,
allowed actions aimed at removing federal segregation and project-
ing an official image of racial democracy, and fused these elements
within a general domestic program aimed at limiting governmental
intrusions upon private freedom. By the 1970s, Eisenhower's anti-
statist doctrine, which declared support both for general civil
rights principles and for limitations on federal enforcement powers, had become so popular among conservatives of both parties
that even such former champions of white supremacy as Alabama's
George Wallace and South Carolina's Strom Thurmond had incor-
porated it into their political rhetoric.

In spite of the Eisenhower administration's uneasiness with
the exercise of federal power, the heightened focus upon black
constitutional rights that was a byproduct of its confrontations
with Jim Crow had meant that by the end of the decade Americans
did possess a rudimentary "progress chart" of legal equality. By the
time of the inauguration of John F. Kennedy, executive orders and
regulatory judgments formally barred discrimination in the military services and in federal hiring. Federal rulings prohibited segregation in interstate transportation and public services in the District of Columbia. National legislation promised equal black access
to the voting booth and set down limited criminal and civil sanctions for the protection of other minority citizenship rights. The
federal courts banned officially mandated segregation in public
schools, invalidated restrictive covenant enforcement and zoning
for discriminatory purposes, and barred racial exclusion from jury
service. Because of Eisenhower's decision, however uncharacteristic, to intervene at Little Rock, precedents existed even for the
application of federal troops to enforce court-ordered school
desegregation.

Nevertheless, given their philosophical and partisan objections
to federal "coercion," Eisenhower and his subordinates had displayed a consistent pattern of hesitancy and extreme political caution in defending black legal rights. As black aide E. Frederic Morrow later observed, "Civil rights in the Eisenhower administration
was handled like a bad dream, or like something that's not very nice,
and you shield yourself from it as long as you possibly can, because
it just shouldn't be." Much of the blame for the administration's
excessive caution lay squarely with the President himself. In 1954,

criticizing a group of senators for lacking backbone on another matter, Eisenhower had written: "They do not seem to realize when there arrives that moment at which soft speaking should be abandoned and a fight to the end undertaken. Any man who hopes to exercise leadership must be ready to meet the requirement face to face when it arises; unless he is ready to fight when necessary, people will finally begin to ignore him." Measured by his own standards, the President's leadership in the civil rights struggle had fallen short. His failure to commit himself unequivocally to racial justice, his willingness to settle for the political containment of racial problems rather than their solution, and his reluctance to intervene in matters of divided federal-state jurisdiction meant that white Southern resistance to black legal equality persisted as an immediate civil rights challenge to the Kennedy administration.

In time Eisenhower's immediate successors demonstrated a greater willingness to use the enforcement machinery of the federal government to uphold black legal and political rights. But other aspects of the Eisenhower administration civil rights legacy helped frustrate black attempts to initiate an extended governmental response to the problems of material disadvantage that underlay continuing racial inequality. The optimistic rhetoric of symbolic equality employed by the Eisenhower administration in the 1950s had encouraged white Americans to believe that the attainment of racial democracy would require only the removal of the official buttresses of discrimination. The achievement of racial equality, official spokesmen had claimed, would be not only painless but actually therapeutic to white consciences and white pocketbooks alike. Immersed in what historian Robert Wiebe had described as a "myth of middleclassness," the Eisenhower administration had never confronted the possibility that the realization of genuine racial equality might require white material sacrifices or the adoption of redistributionary fiscal policies.

When the enactment of legal prescriptions for equality alone did not produce universal black social advances, many whites assumed that the blame lay with the disadvantaged themselves, rather than in the basic assumptions supporting federal racial policy. By 1963, although a vast majority of white Americans professed no longer to believe in black inferiority, fully two-thirds concluded that blacks were "less ambitious." At the same time, black leaders who had based their previous strategies upon nonviolent moral protest and governmental legal response began to question the depth of the white commitment to racial equality. Writing from the Birmingham city jail, Martin Luther King observed, "Over the past few years I have been gravely disappointed with the white moderate. I have almost reached the regrettable conclusion that the Negro's great stumbling block in his stride toward freedom is not the White Citizen's Counciller or the Ku Klux Klanner, but the white moderate, who is more devoted to "order" than to justice; who prefers a negative peace which is the absence of tension to a positive peace which is the presence of justice."

The major civil rights accomplishments of the Kennedy and Johnson administrations—the 1964 Civil Rights Act and the 1965 Voting Rights Act—were logical and essential extensions of federal power in the pursuit of black citizenship equality, a search that had been revived in the 1950s. . . .

To many black observers in the late 1960s and the 1970s, the stillborn reforms of the Great Society, the murder of Martin Luther King, the diversion of national resources to the Vietnam War, and the continuing white resistance to redistributionary policies, when taken together, represented nothing other than a triumph of tokenism. Describing at an early stage the depth of black frustration with the American political system, in 1966 Le Roi Jones issued a personal condemnation of the self-imposed limitations even of liberal politicians:

> Liberals are people with extremely heavy consciences and almost nonexistent courage. Too little is always enough. And it is always the *symbol* that appeals to them most. The single futile housing project in the jungle of slums and disease eases the liberals' consciences, so they are loudest in praising it—even though it might not solve any problems at all. The single black student in the Southern university, the promoted porter in Marietta, Georgia—all ease the liberal's conscience like a benevolent but highly addictive drug. And, for them, "moderation" is a kind of religious catch phrase.*

If the liberals of the 1960s were guilty of being satisfied with symbolic victories over racism, however, their limitations of vision and political courage were but a logical outgrowth of the racial politics

---

*Le Roi Jones, "tokenism: 300 years for five cents," *Home* (New York, 1966).

of the Eisenhower years. It would remain for subsequent generations of black Americans to provide the definitive judgment as to
whether the symbolic promise of equality contained in the rhetoric
of official America—the dominant civil rights legacy of the Eisenhower administration—had ultimately borne the fruits of genuine
racial progress or the bitter harvest of hypocritical national self-
deception.

Michael S. Mayer

EISENHOWER AND RACIAL MODERATION

While conceding that Eisenhower was moderate in his views and cautious in his actions, Michael S. Mayer maintains that Eisenhower and his
administration deserve more credit for their contributions to civil rights
than most historians have given them. The Eisenhower administration
undertook to end segregation in Washington, D.C.; made substantial
strides toward desegregating the armed forces; hired a larger number
of African Americans, and to unprecedented positions, in the executive
branch; obtained passage of the first civil rights legislation since Reconstruction; and appointed liberal and moderate judges to the federal judiciary in the South. Mayer contends that these constituted real and
significant, if limited, gains for civil rights. Yet as Mayer points out,
Eisenhower's vision of racial progress was a gradual one. Eisenhower's
reaction to the Supreme Court's decision in *Brown v. Board of Education* exemplified the president's approach toward civil rights.

[Dwight] Eisenhower's response to the issue of civil rights demonstrates the dominance that he exercised over policy within his administration and the political maneuvering with which he sought to
implement his policies. A careful examination of his handling of
civil rights also destroys forever the neat lines of traditional histori-
ography, which glorifies the contributions of Harry S. Truman and

Portions of this text first appeared in Michael S. Mayer, "With Much Deliberation
and Some Speed: Eisenhower and the *Brown* Decision," *Journal of Southern History*,
vol. LII (February 1986), 43-76. Footnotes omitted. Reprinted by permission.

John F. Kennedy and portrays Eisenhower's two terms as an intervening period of quiescence. Neither, however, do the facts indicate that Eisenhower was an unequivocal advocate of racial equality.

Complex and at times ambiguous, Eisenhower's personal attitudes towards desegregation were refracted through his perception of his duty as president of the United States. Personally, he believed it wrong to deny the rights of citizenship or equality of opportunity to anyone because of race, and, as president, he considered it his duty to ensure that all citizens received equal treatment at the hands of the government. Thus, he determined that the activities of the federal government should do nothing to support and should in no way be tarnished by segregation. He sympathized, however, with southerners whose social system would be disrupted, and he shared some of their misgivings towards blacks. He believed that rapid desegregation would affront southerners and that forced contact between whites and unassimilated blacks would result in conflict, thus setting back the cause of desegregation. His course of action reflected these concerns and resulted in a policy aimed at gradual, noncoercive desegregation, which at times seemed to be working at cross purposes.

The first year of Eisenhower's presidency witnessed landmark gains such as the end of segregation in the nation's capital, the unprecedented appointment of blacks to clerical and administrative positions in the executive branch, significant steps towards the actual desegregation of the armed forces, and a commitment to end segregation and discrimination in federal employment. All of this was accomplished with as little fanfare as possible. For the most part, subordinates implemented policies and announced those that required public articulation. Eisenhower's hand remained invisible, and he associated himself publicly with the policies only to a limited extent. Moreover, all of these reforms affected areas in which the federal government exercised sole jurisdiction and the executive branch possessed unilateral authority. Eisenhower wanted no part of a noisy, partisan battle with Congress. Nor did he desire any confrontation with the states over principles of federalism. Indeed, in such a conflict, he tended to side with the states, a concern that constituted the primary distinction between Eisenhower and the liberal Democrats of his era with respect to civil rights.

In the spring of 1954 the focus of civil rights changed dramatically. On May 17 the U.S. Supreme Court declared unanimously that segregated public schools violated the Constitution of the United States. The decision culminated a decades-long struggle waged in the courts by the National Association for the Advancement of Colored People. The Court postponed granting relief, however, until after it could hear arguments on that issue in the fall. . . . Despite the significant advances of Eisenhower's first year or so in office, no one could predict just what his response would be. While he had committed his administration to desegregating the armed forces and the nation's capital city and to ending discrimination in federal employment, the president had also maintained his opposition to a federal Fair Employment Practices Committee. Moreover, Eisenhower had made clear "his displeasure with 'punitive or compulsory federal law' " in this area and opposed as "extraneous" (as did many liberals) the attempts of Congressman Adam Clayton Powell, Jr., to forbid the allocation of federal funds to any recipient who practiced or sanctioned segregation.

From the preinaugural period the school segregation cases had presented a dilemma to the newly elected president and his administration. In the last of days of Truman's presidency the Justice Department filed a brief as an *amicus curiae* on behalf of black children seeking admission to previously all-white schools. . . .

When Eisenhower took the oath of office, the Supreme Court had already heard arguments on school segregation in cases from South Carolina, Kansas, Virginia, the District of Columbia, and Delaware. On June 8, 1953, the Supreme Court announced that it wished to hear reargument on October 12 and set out a series of five questions to which counsel were to address themselves. The questions posed by the Court concerned the intention of the framers of the Fourteenth Amendment, the power of Congress and the courts to abolish segregation, and whether or not the Court had power to grant gradual relief. At the same time the Court invited the attorney general to file a brief and participate in the oral arguments.

The [top officials in the new administration's Justice Department], Herbert R. Brownell, Jr., attorney general; William P. Rogers, deputy attorney general; and J. Lee Rankin, assistant attorney general, met [outgoing members of Truman's Justice Department]. According to Philip Elman, Rogers expressed the prevailing view of the Republicans when he said, in effect, "Jesus, do we really *have* to file a brief?" Whether or not he was as reluctant as Elman has suggested, Brownell did remove the case from the solicitor general's office and bring it into his own, under the supervision of his fellow Nebraskan, Rankin.

The Court's request that the government submit a memorandum of fact and an opinion concerning the intention of the Fourteenth Amendment made Eisenhower uncomfortable. He considered the rendering of an "opinion" by the attorney general on this kind of question to constitute an invasion of the authority of the Supreme Court. On August 19 he telephoned the attorney general to present this view. Brownell, whose political judgment and legal abilities Eisenhower admired greatly, persuaded him that answering such a question posed by the Court in no way violated its integrity or authority, and the brief submitted by the government contained an opinion on the intent of the Fourteenth Amendment.

The president's reluctance to have his Justice Department submit a brief revealed an important aspect of the assumptions that he brought to the problem of civil rights in general. While he strove to make sure that the federal government in no way supported segregation, he rejected federal legislative leadership on two grounds: it would usurp powers that belonged properly to the states, and it would be ineffective. He rejected other coercive steps towards desegregation on similar grounds.

On July 20, 1953, Eisenhower had lunch with his friend James F. Byrnes, the governor of South Carolina and former secretary of state in the Truman administration, who had come to discuss the possibility of a ruling by the Supreme Court that would abolish segregation in public schools. In his diary Eisenhower noted that Byrnes was "very fearful of [the] consequences in the South" that such a decision would bring about. The governor brought up the possibility of riots, ill feeling, and defiance, but only briefly. He stressed instead that a number of southern states would immediately cease support for public schools. Several times he told the president that the South had no great problem in dealing with adult blacks, but they were "frightened at putting the children together," a position with which Eisenhower was not completely out of sympathy. Eisenhower also observed that "the

Governor was obviously afraid that I would be carried away by the hope of capturing the Negro vote in this country, and as a consequence take a stand on the question that would forever defeat any possibility of developing a real Republican or 'Opposition' Party in the South." The president declined to give Byrnes an opinion on a Supreme Court decision that had not yet been handed down, but assured him that his "convictions would not be formed by political expediency." He also took great pains to make Byrnes "well aware" of his own convictions that "improvement in race relations is one of those things that will be healthy and sound only if it starts locally. I do not believe that prejudices, even palpably unjustified prejudices, will succumb to compulsion." He then predicted that any attempt to impose federal law on the states would result in a conflict of police powers between state and federal government that "would set back the cause of progress in race relations for a long time."

Several weeks later he wrote a letter to Byrnes contending that the best way to avoid such a conflict would be for state officials to cooperate with desegregation. . . .

As the date of the oral arguments approached, Eisenhower received letters from three southern governors, Allan Shivers of Texas, Robert F. Kennon of Louisiana, and Byrnes, all of whom had supported him in 1952. They stressed the local nature of school systems, the limited authority of the Supreme Court, and the threat to the federal system if the Supreme Court extended federal control into the area of public schools. Eisenhower answered Shivers and Kennon politely and sent a more revealing letter to Byrnes. His note to Byrnes stated that he was "primarily interested in progress," but that he hoped for a solution that would "progressively work toward the goals established by abstract principle, but which would not, at the same time cause such disruption and mental anguish among great portions of our population that progress would actually be reversed." He challenged, however, the "equal but separate" alternative that would have brought black schools up to parity with white schools, but allowed them to remain separate. On practical grounds alone, Eisenhower argued that it would involve "extraordinary expenditures," and he "wonder[ed] just what officials of government would be charged with the responsibility for determining when facilities [were] exactly equal." Once again, the president at-tempted to convince Byrnes that "no political consideration of any kind [would] be given any weight whatsoever."

During the preparation of the brief a split developed within the administration. Brownell, Rankin (who would argue the case), and others within the Justice Department favored a strong stand against segregation. Some members of the administration, includ-ing Wilton B. Persons, head of the congressional liaison staff, and Secretary of the Treasury George M. Humphrey, hoped to draw disaffected southern Democrats into the Republican camp and were loath to alienate potential political allies. The disagreement delayed preparations, and in July the Justice Department asked the Court for a postponement, which the justices gladly granted. The Court rescheduled the oral arguments for December 7.

As the Supreme Court prepared for the fall term of 1953 and one of the most significant cases in its history, a major shock rocked the institution—the death of Chief Justice Fred M. Vinson. . . . Eisenhower now faced the task of appointing a successor. When Tru-man had appointed his old friend from the Senate to the nation's highest judicial office, Vinson took over the helm of an extremely di-vided Court. He proved to be a weak chief justice, and the rift had deepened by the time of his death. Personal as well as philosophical issues divided factions led by Justices Hugo L. Black and Robert H. Jackson. In addition, the prestige of the Court had come to one of its periodic low ebbs. This decline resulted in large part from Tru-man's four appointments, whom political scientist Clinton Rossiter described as "about the least distinguished in history."

Bent on restoring prestige as well as some degree of unity to the Court, Eisenhower wanted a man of national stature, proven administrative ability, and statesmanship. . . . [In a letter to his] older brother Edgar, a successful lawyer, president of the American Bar Association, and a right-wing Republican, . . . Eisenhower also revealed something of what he wanted in a chief justice. "Almost without exception," he wrote, "if a lawyer recommends someone, that individual is now a practicing judge, or at the very least a suc-cessful practicing lawyer. Almost everybody else seems to favor some man who has been experienced in more phases of our gov-ernmental life than merely the legal." He concluded that, "for myself, the only thing I am determined to do is to make certain that I shall do my part in attempting to restore some of the prestige that the Court has lost.". . .

In yet another letter to Edgar the president ruminated on what made a great chief justice. "So far as I can find out," he related, "there seems to be universal respect for Hughes, Taft, and Stone as Chief Justices. None of them had any great experience as a judge—indeed, they were principally known for efforts in work other than the law. This did not apply to Stone, who was Dean of Columbia's Law School. But the point is that he was *not* a practicing lawyer, nor a judge. As I recall the life of John Marshall, the same applied to him." Demonstrating a far better understanding of the internal workings of the Supreme Court than many so-called experts, Eisenhower proposed that "a Governor with a *good* legal background just might be about the best type we could find—provided, of course, that he had a successful record of administration and experience and was nationally known as a man of integrity and fairness." Finally, he once again expressed the hope of avoiding a man who reached "the voluntary retirement age of seventy in two years."

It is difficult to determine whether Eisenhower had [Earl] Warren in mind all along, or if the Californian simply met the requirements that the president had worked out on his own. Various accounts of the relationship between the two men suggest different answers. Warren remembered that Eisenhower telephoned him not long after the election to say that there would be no place for him in the cabinet. Warren had received consideration for the position of attorney general, but Brownell had been a trusted political adviser during the campaign, and the president-elect wanted to retain his political advice as well as his legal counsel. Eisenhower then remarked that he intended to offer Warren the first vacancy on the Supreme Court. But they both understood that the commitment was not concrete, and when Vinson died, Eisenhower shopped around. Brownell's recollection coincides with Warren's on this point. Eisenhower himself recalled speaking with Warren before Vinson's death and coming away impressed with him as a man of "high ideals and a great deal of common sense." He also remembered telling Warren that he had him in mind for the Supreme Court should a vacancy arise. Eisenhower was not, however, thinking of him as a prospective chief justice, but to everyone's surprise, the first vacancy occurred in that position. . . .

. . . Eisenhower commented on his reasons for choosing Warren. He told the newsmen that he "certainly wanted a man whose reputation for integrity, honesty, middle-of-the-road philosophy, experience in Government, experience in the law, were all such as to convince the United States that here was a man who had no ends to serve except the United States, and nothing else." He also sought a man in good health who was relatively young—"if you can call a man of approximately my age relatively young. . . ."

The appointment generated widespread favorable reaction. . . .

With Hugo Black administering the oath of office, Warren took his place on the bench as an interim appointment on October 5, 1953. . . .

In November the Justice Department entered the final stages of drafting [its] brief [in the school segregation cases]. On Monday, November 16, Brownell called the president to express his opinion that a decision by the Supreme Court on the constitutionality of segregation would be necessary. Eisenhower remarked that Byrnes was coming to dinner, and he might have a chance to speak with him. In any case, Byrnes had an appointment to see the attorney general on Wednesday morning. Eisenhower asked Brownell what would happen if the southern states abandoned public education. Brownell responded that he would try to convince Byrnes that "under our doctrine it would take a period of years, and he wouldn't have to 'declare war,' so to speak."

Eisenhower's Justice Department did not enter the case with a blank slate. The brief the government had filed in 1952, written by Elman and submitted over his own signature and that of [Attorney General James P.] McGranary, conceded that the Court could decide the cases without overturning *Plessy* v. *Ferguson,* the Supreme Court's decision of 1896 that provided the basis for the separate but equal rule. The brief stated that the *Plessy* decision said nothing about limiting considerations of equality to physical plants; so if segregation produced damaging effects on students, the justices could invoke *Plessy* to end segregated public schools. If, however, the Court wished to come to terms with its earlier decision, it should overturn it; experience had shown separate and equal to be a contradiction in terms. Moreover, the *Plessy* decision constituted "an unwarranted departure, based on dubious assumptions of fact combined with a basic disregard of the basic purpose of the Fourteenth Amendment," and the age of the precedent did not "give it immunity from re-examination and rejection."

Apparently pleased with Elman's work on the *Thompson* case, which ended segregation in Washington's restaurants, Brownell assigned him to write the government's brief answering the questions posed by the Court for reargument in *Brown*. Aided by a staff of eight, Elman produced a massive six-hundred-page document, which his superiors approved and the government filed in late November. Submitted as a supplement to the brief filed the year before, it did not call explicitly for a decision overturning *Plessy*. It concluded that the evidence regarding the legislative history of the Fourteenth Amendment provided no definite answer as to the intention of its framers. The amendment did, however, establish "the broad constitutional principle of full and complete equality of all persons under the law, and that it forbade all legal distinctions based on race or color." Moreover, the framers clearly intended the amendment to "prohibit all state action based upon race or color," and therefore "all segregation in public education." Elman, Brownell, and Rankin wanted to write a direct statement requesting that the Court strike down segregation. Some observers have suggested that Elman did not include it because he believed that it would receive little sympathy from within the White House and that the president himself would not favor it. Brownell has stated that the brief was filed in direct response to the questions submitted by the Court, and addressed itself to those questions only. At the same time, Brownell did advise the president that if the question arose during oral argument, the Justice Department would take a position in favor of striking down segregation.

Oral arguments began on December 8, 1953, and lasted for an unprecedented ten hours over three days. The arguments presented covered everything from the historical background and intent of the Fourteenth Amendment to the psychological and social impact of segregation on black school children. . . .

Rankin . . . stood to present the government's views. He had not spoken very long when Justice William O. Douglas broke in with a question. Commenting on the equivocal nature of the brief,

Douglas asked Rankin if the government took a position on the constitutional controversy. Rankin answered affirmatively and went on to say that the government believed that "segregation in public schools cannot be maintained under the Fourteenth Amendment. . . ." Douglas then asked Rankin if the Court could properly decide the case either way. Rankin replied that the Court "properly could find only one answer." This position must have pleased the NAACP greatly; the government had taken their side. Rankin's responses to questions on the possible implementation of an antisegregation decision gave them less cause for elation. He argued that the Court had power to issue gradual decrees and that the situation would best be handled by local solutions, not a national timetable.

On January 12, 1954, a month after the oral arguments ended, Eisenhower sent the Warren nomination to the Senate. Most observers expected a swift termination of Warren's uncomfortable interim status, especially with the obviously important segregation cases awaiting a decision. . . . Warren received approval from the Senate on March 1, 1954.

During the period between the arguments and the Court's decision, Eisenhower maintained a close watch over the case through his attorney general. On January 26, 1954, Brownell informed him that the Court might decide the constitutionality of segregation that spring, but postpone the problem of a remedy until fall. Obviously struggling with the issue, Eisenhower replied vaguely, "I don't know where I stand, but I think that the best interests of the U.S. demand an answer in keep [*sic*] with past decisions." When the attorney general suggested that the Court wanted to defer the matter as long as possible, the president laughingly responded that perhaps they would defer the matter until the next administration.

If Eisenhower entertained any serious hopes along those lines, the Court shattered them on May 17. As Brownell predicted, the Court found segregation unconstitutional but held off on the question of relief. Chief Justice Earl Warren, speaking for a unanimous Court, ruled that "in the field of public education the doctrine of 'separate but equal' has no place. Separate educational facilities are inherently unequal." Segregation, he continued, deprived the plaintiffs and all others similarly situated of the equal protection of the laws guaranteed by the Fourteenth Amendment.

Noting that these cases had wide applicability and that there existed a variety of local conditions, the Court found the formulation of decrees in these cases to "present problems of considerable complexity." In order to deal with these problems, the Court ordered the cases restored to the docket and requested counsel for both sides to provide further argument for implementing the decision that fall. The Court invited the attorney general of the United States to participate again and also invited arguments from the attorneys general of all states that required or permitted segregation in their public schools. On the same day, Warren read another unanimous decision, striking down segregated public schools in the District of Columbia on the ground that separate schools in the nation's capital violated the due process clause of the Fifth Amendment.

In spite of the assertion in his memoirs that "I definitely agreed with the unanimous decision," Eisenhower harbored serious misgivings about the Court's ruling in *Brown*. Arthur Larson, Eisenhower's under secretary of labor, later wrote that the president unequivocally disagreed with the Court's decision. Similarly, Emmet John Hughes, a speechwriter, related a conversation in which the president said to him, "I am convinced that the Supreme Court decision *set back* progress in the South *at least fifteen years.* . . . We can't demand *perfection* in these moral questions. All we can do is keep working toward a goal and keep it high. And the fellow who tries to tell me that you can do these things by *force* is just plain *nuts.*" Sherman Adams, on the other hand, claimed that Eisenhower believed "that progress toward school integration had to be made "with considerable deliberation." Adams further described Eisenhower as thinking that "in general principle . . . the Supreme Court decision was correct and personally he had no quarrel with it."

These contrasting opinions need not be mutually exclusive. Eisenhower believed in the morality, necessity, and inevitability of desegregation, but he thought it best accomplished through a slow process, beginning at the graduate and professional level and working down slowly, perhaps at the rate of one grade per year. Graduate and professional schools could integrate immediately on the basis of merit because they concerned "mature and relatively purposeful students." He might also have added, very few blacks. Eisenhower recognized that his scheme was "probably too slow to fit the aspirations of many Negroes. But it would, [he] was convinced, effect real progress and would insure an orderly integration process." To his way of thinking, a process of education and public acceptance had to precede other gains, and he rejected the idea that segregation should end by a summary court order or federal statute. To Larson and Hughes, it may well have seemed that he opposed the Court's decision.

The day after the *Brown* decision, the president met with James Hagerty, his press secretary, to discuss a news conference scheduled for the following day, May 19. Eisenhower indicated that he would simply say that the Supreme Court was the law of the land, that he was sworn to uphold the Constitution, and that he would do so. He told the press precisely that and repeated the position years later in his memoirs, concluding, "this determination was one of principle." Having once expressed an opinion of a decision, he argued, he "would be obliged to do so in many, if not all, cases." Eventually he would be drawn into a statement disagreeing with the Court, that would, if nothing else, create doubt as to the vigor with which he would enforce the decision.

In his briefing with Hagerty, Eisenhower expressed considerable concern over the effect of the ruling. He worried primarily about the possibility that southern states would abolish public education altogether and institute "private" schools supported by state aid. Such a system, he continued, would handicap blacks and "poor white" children. Eisenhower especially feared the reaction of Georgia and its governor, Herman E. Talmadge. His fears proved to be well-founded. The initial reaction to the decision in the South was generally muted, but one of the few rebel yells emitted came from the governor of Georgia.

Although Eisenhower made it a point not to announce his discomfort with the Court's decision, hints of his displeasure emerged nonetheless. During the press conference of May 19, Harry C. Dent, a reporter for the Columbia, South Carolina, *State and Record,* noted that the *Brown* decision had been made under a Republican administration. Eisenhower retorted: "The Supreme Court, as I understand it, is not under any administration." Moreover, at every chance, he reiterated that he did not believe "you can change the hearts of men with laws or decisions." Not once throughout the summer between the *Brown* decision and the arguments on implementation did the president make a statement supporting the Court's decision or directly calling for compliance with it. His tremendous personal popularity would have provided an invaluable ally to the beleaguered Court. Nor did he answer the segregationists who on the floor of Congress and on television advised their constituents to defy the federal courts. Such silence also gave encouragement to southern states preparing to argue for the slowest possible implementation when the Supreme Court convened that fall.

Not all of the signals emanating from the White House during this period were hostile, however. Immediately after the Court struck down segregated schools in the District of Columbia, Eisenhower declared that there was no need for a judicial order to make the federal government recognize its responsibilities and that the District of Columbia would serve as a model for the nation by desegregating voluntarily and immediately. His actions extended beyond rhetoric; he summoned the District of Columbia commissioners to the White House and told them he expected the district to take the lead in desegregating its schools. Under pressure from the White House, the district government had no choice but to comply. Hobart M. Corning, the district's superintendent of schools, drew up a plan to reorganize the capital's school system along nonsegregated lines. The Board of Education adopted the Corning plan on June 2, after rejecting complete desegregation beginning in September 1954. On September 20, Samuel Spencer, president of the board of commissioners of the District of Columbia, wrote to Eisenhower to inform him of the completion of the first week of the fall semester under a nonsegregated system. He reported further that the transition had proceeded smoothly and without disturbances. Of the district's 158 schools, 116 had "biracial attendance," and the teaching staffs of 37 schools included members of both races. Moreover, the enrollment figures showed that it would be possible to accelerate the original plan.

As the fall of 1954 approached, the president made another important concession to the Court's determination to end segregation. When Justice Robert H. Jackson died in October, Eisenhower selected John Marshall Harlan III, the grandson of the lone dissenter in *Plessy* v. *Ferguson*, to replace him. The appointment was significant for its symbolism. Southern senators, fearing he would share his grandfather's belief that the "Constitution is color-blind," voiced their displeasure with the appointment and questioned the nominee extensively about his views on the United Nations, "one worldism" (he was a Rhodes scholar), and, of course, segregation. Despite Harlan's exceptional qualifications, southerners delayed his confirmation for four months. The Senate finally approved the nomination on March 16, 1955. Though Harlan had a reputation as a moderate conservative, his conservatism clearly did not extend to civil rights.

Eisenhower's most direct impact on the outcome of *Brown II* (as the decision dealing with implementation came to be known) came through his participation in the *amicus curiae* brief that the Justice Department prepared. Interest in the department's position extended beyond the president to others within the White House. Electoral politics influenced the way in which some of Eisenhower's aides assessed what position the Justice Department and the administration should adopt regarding desegregation. While recognizing the potential of black voters, particularly in the urban North, they also saw a chance to make inroads into another bloc of Democratic voters, the disaffected southern Democrats who had walked out of the 1948 convention. A compromise therefore interested the administration not only because it might insure peace and unity, but also because it could benefit the Republican party.

Opinion within the Justice Department differed from that within the White House. The [lawyers] responsible for the preparation of the *Brown* case in the department were unanimous in their commitment to end segregation. Philip Elman had written or assisted in the writing of every major brief filed by the government in a civil rights case since the *Sweatt* and *McLaurin* cases. A vocal and effective advocate of civil rights, he could claim a large share of the responsibility for involving the government in *Brown*. Herbert Brownell was a major architect not only of the Eisenhower administration's entry into *Brown*, but also of the Civil Rights Act of 1957 and the federal intervention at Little Rock. He believed that segregation was wrong and that the time to end it had arrived. J. Lee Rankin shared the beliefs of his boss in this matter. He had less to do with preparing the briefs and arguments on implementation, however, because by the fall of 1954 the Eisenhower administration had appointed its own solicitor general.

Simon E. Sobeloff, who as solicitor general presented the government's plan for implementing the *Brown* decision to the Court, came to the job as an outspoken and active opponent of racial inequality. During the 1930s he had opposed segregation and the exclusion of blacks from public housing. In 1933 he went before the Senate Judiciary Committee to plead for the passage of a federal antilynching bill. He continued his unvarnished opposition to segregation in his native Baltimore throughout the 1940s. Addressing a meeting of the city's Advertising Club, Sobeloff lashed out at segregation, chiding theater owners for allowing blacks into their establishments to appear onstage but not as patrons, and telling his audience that the prejudiced man injures not only his target but himself, for his bigotry "degrades his humanity." His fellow Baltimorian, Thurgood Marshall, the man who more than any other individual was responsible for the desegregation of graduate, professional, and public schools, recalls that "when I started my hard battle in Baltimore, he was one of only three white lawyers who were at all interested. He stuck with me from the beginning to the end." Sobeloff's beliefs on civil rights were such that when Eisenhower appointed him to the United States Fourth Circuit Court of Appeals in 1955, southern senators, led by Samuel J. Ervin, Jr., of North Carolina, Olin D. Johnston of South Carolina, and James O. Eastland of Mississippi, held up his confirmation for a year. As a judge, and later chief judge of the Fourth Circuit, he led that court to a reputation as a highly progressive court and wrote several landmark desegregation opinions.

While Eisenhower cautiously isolated himself from the *Brown* decision, the Justice Department prepared itself for the coming arguments on implementation. Sobeloff, with the aid of Elman, arrived at a position for the government in a preliminary draft of the government's brief. In it, they argued that the Court did not need to order immediate relief and that the issuance of a decree ordering a gradual adjustment would fall within the proper exercise of the Court's equity powers. If, however, the Court were to order a gradual adjustment, the vindication of the constitutional rights involved in the cases should be "as prompt as possible," for relief short of immediate admission to nonsegregated schools necessarily implied the continuing deprivation of these rights. Further, they urged prompt action because the "personal and present right of a Black child to not be segregated while attending a public school [was] one which, if not enforced when the child [was] of school age, lost its value."

At the same time, they recognized that the public interest required an "intelligent, orderly, and effective solution" to various problems that might be encountered in complying with the decision. When the Court overruled segregation, it struck down an institution whose "origins and development [were] woven in the fabric of American history." In ordering the cases for reargument the Court had recognized that these difficulties could not "be resolved by a single stroke of the judicial pen." The problems they considered relevant involved administrative and financial adjustments the states would face in changing to nonsegregated schools. (At the same time, they pointed out that equalizing all-black schools would have cost far more than desegregation and that ending the maintenance of separate school systems would further reduce costs.) Because of the compelling nature of the children's right to an equal education, however, they stated that "there should be no delay in the full vindication of the constitutional rights involved in these cases, and if delay is required, it should be kept at a minimum."

The brief then turned to the problem of popular hostility with which school authorities would have to cope and the threats of various states to withdraw funds from public education. Such hostility, contended the government lawyers, should not be allowed to interfere with the implementation of the Court's decision and the vindication of the rights of black children. . . . As to the threat that violence would follow integration, they argued that scattered disturbances provided no basis for supposing that local officials would tolerate such action.

Finally, because of the "wide variance in local conditions," the brief submitted that no single formula or blueprint readily applied to all localities. The formulation of any practicable program for ending segregation required a knowledge of the special problems and needs of that community. Therefore, rather than frame a blanket decree, the Court should remand the individual cases to the courts of first instance, which would consider plans for ending segregation submitted by the defendants in light of guidelines established by the Supreme Court. It would be essential for the

Justices to lay down clear guidelines for the lower courts, specifying what the Supreme Court would or would not consider acceptable. The Justice Department suggested that "a remand for further proceedings without more, would add to the uncertainty and doubt which already exist and would serve only to make the process of adjustment more difficult." In addition, the Court should be sure to enter no order that "might have the practical effect of slowing down desegregation."

Soboloff then presented suggestions for the decrees he and Elman believed the Court should frame. First, they suggested that the Court reiterate its declaration that segregation in public schools violated the Constitution and emphasize that all provisions of law requiring or permitting such segregation were unconstitutional. Second, the lower courts should receive instructions to require that the school boards admit the plaintiffs, and others similarly situated, "forthwith to public schools on a non-segregated basis or to propose promptly, for the court's consideration and approval, an effective program for accomplishing the transition as soon as possible." If the school authorities wished any postponement, they would bear the burden of proof to establish the need for extra time. Where no "solid obstacles to desegregation" existed, any delay was "not justified and should not be permitted." Third, to insure a prompt start towards implementing the decision, the justices should direct the lower courts to enter orders requiring school boards to submit plans for ending school segregation within ninety days. If the local boards failed to submit a satisfactory plan within the ninety-day period, the lower courts should be instructed to issue appropriate orders directing the admission of the plaintiffs and others similarly situated to nonsegregated schools at the beginning of the next school term. Upon submission of a plan by the school board, the appropriate lower court would hold a hearing to determine if the plan provided for a transition to nonsegregated schools "as expeditiously as the circumstances" permitted; the lower court should sanction no program that did not call for immediate commencement of the procedures necessary to accomplish the transition. During the transitional period, the lower courts would require the defendants to submit detailed periodic reports on the progress of desegregation. Moreover, the Supreme

Court should retain jurisdiction for the purpose of making further orders, if such were necessary, to carry out its mandate.

In a Saturday morning conference, held on November 20, 1954, Sobeloff met with Eisenhower and other members of the administration at the White House to discuss the brief he had prepared. The meeting produced several changes in the wording of the brief that altered the tone of the document. . . .

The first change concerned the speed with which desegregation was to proceed. Sobeloff had written that "the vindication of the constitutional rights should be as prompt as possible." The phrase "as prompt as possible" was very similar to the phrase "at as early a date as possible" that Robert Carter, who represented the black children in *Brown,* would use several months later in the oral arguments before the Supreme Court. The conference that Saturday morning produced the following change in wording: "the vindication of the constitutional rights should be as prompt as feasible." The word "feasible" replaced the word "possible" at every instance in which Sobeloff had used it. In a later interview Philip Elman discounted the importance of the change, maintaining that if one were not aware of it, the substitution of the words would not affect the import of the brief. He admitted, however, that the word "possible" could be taken to mean that only administrative and physical problems would properly be considered as causes for delay and that "feasible" could be read to include nontangible problems, perhaps even community hostility. *Webster's Dictionary* defines "possible" as "within the powers of performance, attainment" and "feasible" as "capable of being . . . dealt with successfully." That distinction may well have been the nuance Eisenhower desired; he believed that immediate desegregation would not succeed.

. . . Even a cursory review of Eisenhower's personal correspondence, the comments and changes he made in drafts of his speeches, and the several handwritten drafts of the famous Guildhall speech delivered at the end of World War II (which he wrote without assistance) reveals him to be a careful wordsmith. It seems highly unlikely that he would have insisted on such a change unless he intended it to have some significance. Moreover, the substitution of the word coincides with other alterations made during the course of the meeting.

Other, more obvious changes made that Saturday morning had a similar effect. Soboloff had included a passage citing the positive results produced by rapid desegregation of the armed forces. He asserted that "experience has shown that normal contacts between people, in groups or as individuals, serve to diminish prejudice while enforced separation intensifies it. Race relations are improved when individuals, without distinction as to race or color, serve in the armed forces together, work together, and go to school together." The implication was that desegregation should commence immediately. Essentially, this answered the argument that community hostility necessitated a delay in beginning desegregation. As a result of the conference, however, this passage was removed altogether from the brief.

Finally, Eisenhower himself inserted an additional passage. The president's suggestions formed the basis for the following excerpt from the brief.

> The Court's decision in these cases has outlawed a social institution which has existed for a long time in many areas throughout the country—an institution, it may be noted, which during its existence not only has had the sanction of decisions by this Court but has been fervently supported by great numbers of people as justifiable on legal and moral grounds. The Court's holding in the present cases that segregation is a denial of Constitution rights involved an express recognition of the importance of psychological and emotional factors; the impact of segregation upon children, the Court has found, can so affect their entire lives as to preclude their full enjoyment of constitutional rights. In similar fashion, psychological and emotional factors are involved—and must be met with understanding and good will—in the alterations that must now take place in order to bring about compliance with the Court's decision.

This passage left no doubt as to its meaning. It implied that the time allowed for the period of adjustment should not be merely time enough to allow administrative adjustments to take place, but time for the shock to wear off and for southern attitudes at least to begin to change. While it is probable that Eisenhower did not mean to suggest the interminable period of time that actually elapsed, it is clear that he did not support the position taken by Soboloff and other members of the Justice Department that desegregation could and must begin immediately.

The changes Eisenhower effected in the brief reflected a position he maintained throughout the period between the decision of May 1954 and the Court's ruling on implementation. A month before he met with Sobeloff and Brownell to rework the government's brief, the president discussed the issue of implementation in a letter to his friend and confidant, Swede Hazlett. He believed that the segregation issue would "become acute or tend to die out according to the character of the procedure orders that the Court will probably issue this winter. My guess is that they will be very moderate and accord a maximum of initiative to local courts." At a news conference held on November 23, after the president's meeting with Sobeloff and Brownell but before the government filed its brief, Harry Dent asked Eisenhower to comment on his personal views on implementation. The president took the opportunity to lobby for the views he had injected into the brief. Expressing certainty that the country wanted to obey the Constitution, he pointed out that desegregation presented "a very great practical problem" and involved "deep-seated emotions." "What I understand the Supreme Court has undertaken as its task," he continued, "is to write its orders or procedure in such fashion as to take into consideration these great emotional strains and the practical problems, and try to devise a way where under some form of decentralized process we can bring this about. I don't believe they intend to be arbitrary, at least that is my understanding."

Submitted on the last day of November, the government's brief was the last of a seemingly endless procession of briefs to reach the Court. At the time of the Court's decision on May 17, 1954, twenty-one states had mandatory or permissive segregation laws. Since the ruling affected them all, the Court invited each of them to file briefs and participate in the oral arguments on implementation. The invitation constituted not only a conciliatory gesture on the part of the Court, but an astute political move as well. Participation by the southern states in the process of determining implementation amounted to a tacit acceptance of the original decision. Significantly, Georgia, Louisiana, Alabama, and Mississippi ignored the invitation; and several of these states indicated that they would not permit integrated schools within their borders, regardless of what decrees the Court might formulate. Maryland,

Florida, Arkansas, Oklahoma, North Carolina, and Texas accepted the Court's offer to participate.

Predictably, the attorneys for the southern states sought a drawn-out period of adjustment. . . . While not formulated in precisely the same terms, the basic positions of all of the briefs submitted by the southern states, including those that accepted the Court's invitation to participate as an *amicus curiae,* were virtually the same. Their positions can be summed up along the following lines: any attempt to desegregate school facilities would encounter grave obstacles, stemming primarily from community hostility to mixing the races in the classroom; overcoming these obstacles would take a long and indefinite period of time; in the process of desegregation, school children should not be "martyred" in the institution of new social policy; and due to these factors, the Court should not formulate detailed decrees, but rather should leave it to the courts below to determine when and how integration could be accomplished without disrupting the school systems or endangering the welfare of the children.

The attorneys for the NAACP conceded that desegregation was probably not possible overnight everywhere, or even advisable, but warned against undue delay. They charged that many advocates of a gradual transition intended, in actuality, to stall the process indefinitely. Therefore, their brief called on the Court to effectuate the *Brown* decision by "decrees forthwith enjoining the continuation" of segregation. Such a decree, as envisioned by the NAACP's lawyers, would have required the immediate initiation of administrative procedures to end segregation and to admit the plaintiffs and others similarly situated to white schools by the beginning of the following academic term. In granting any postponement of relief beyond that date, the lower courts were to understand that school authorities bore the "affirmative burden" of proof to establish that there existed "judicially cognizable advantages greater than those inherent in the prompt vindication of the appellants' adjudicated constitutional rights." Judges should remain aware of the especially heavy burden in these cases, since the rights were "personal and present," and since each day of delayed relief produced a "day of serious and irreparable injury."

Because of the protracted debate over John M. Harlan's nomination, the Court postponed the oral arguments originally scheduled for December 6, 1954, until Monday, April 11, 1955. The oral presentations largely followed the lines of argument established in the briefs. . . .

On the third day of the arguments Soboloff rose to speak for the government. Once again he rejected both specific decrees and the "other extreme," which asked the Court to set no criteria for guidance to the lower courts. Delay for its own sake was inexcusable. Arguing beyond the bounds established in the government's brief, Soboloff contended that the Court should leave no doubt that the cases were being remanded "for the purpose of effecting the decision as soon as feasible . . . ," and "feasible" did not mean that the courts should wait for a change of attitude.

Ideological commitments to judicial restraint, shared to a surprising extent by even the most activist justices, militated against a decision to formulate detailed decrees ordering immediate desegregation. Although such ideological considerations went into the formulation of the Court's decree, practical reasons influenced the Court as well. It was apparent to the Court and to those who heard or read the arguments of lawyers representing the southern states and the public statements of southern political leaders that the Deep South would not cooperate with any decree and would overtly defy one calling for immediate desegregation. Moreover, it was also clear that no help was forthcoming from Congress. The Court, particularly the chief justice, believed that it could expect little more from the president. Warren's memoirs indicate that he believed Eisenhower to be an unalterable opponent of desegregation. No significant legislation on civil rights had a chance of passing the southern-dominated House and Senate, and, after his order to desegregate the District of Columbia's public schools, Eisenhower's words and deeds seemed to give as much comfort to the Court's southern opponents as it did to the justices. In any enforcement crisis the Court had to depend on the executive to lend weight to its pronouncements, and the president's public coolness towards the *Brown* decision was not lost on the Court.

On May 31, 1955, a unanimous Court, again speaking through the chief justice, announced its ruling on implementation.

Desegregation, declared Warren, should begin immediately and proceed "with all deliberate speed." The Court's decision followed closely the plan submitted by the Justice Department. It differed, however, in one respect. The justices chose not to include the Justice Department's ninety-day time limit for school boards to submit a satisfactory plan for desegregation or be faced with court-ordered integration the following school term. Nevertheless, the decision won the support of the most staunchly liberal magazines, such as the *Progressive* and *New Republic*. Thurgood Marshall and Robert Carter [an attorney for the NAACP Legal Defense Fund] lent their public assent to the decision in an article published not long after the Court's ruling. In it they evaluated the decision not to set a deadline by which time the process of desegregation would have to be completed and concluded that "the decision was a good one." They even judged that desegregation might proceed more smoothly than if "a more stringent order had been issued."

The *Brown* decision constituted an important milestone for the Eisenhower administration as well as for the rest of the nation. Prior to the Supreme Court's decisions of May 1954 and 1955, the administration had proceeded rapidly and effectively with its program of quiet, limited gains in areas over which it had unquestioned jurisdiction. After *Brown* that policy became an instant anachronism. Eisenhower dug in his heels and attempted to put a brake on the accelerated rate and scope of change. He supported the Court's ruling when necessary, but only to the minimum extent he believed the law required, and while the programs begun earlier continued, no major new ones were undertaken until the introduction of civil rights legislation in 1956. Now traveling uncertain and uncharted waters, Eisenhower and his men cast about for a way to avoid what they considered the extremes of too-rapid desegregation that would result in southern defiance and the alternative of no progress at all.

Eisenhower's hesitancy expressed itself during the furor which arose following the Court's decision when he repeatedly declined to give the decision his personal endorsement. Maintaining what he considered to be a "neutral" posture, he refused to comment publicly on his views regarding desegregation. Instead, he adopted the position that it was his job to carry out decisions of the Supreme Court, not to pass judgment on them. Nor did he use the power of the chief executive to uphold the substantive rights of blacks when they faced threats from recalcitrant southerners. When he reluctantly sent troops to Little Rock in 1957, he made it clear that he did so to enforce the orders of a federal court, not for the purpose of integrating Central High School.

Although Eisenhower never used the presidency as a pulpit from which to speak out for acceptance of the Court's decision, he and his administration began slowly to take concrete steps to advance the cause of desegregation. In the field of legislation the Eisenhower administration sponsored two civil rights acts and pushed them through Congress, the first such legislation since . . . Reconstruction. These accomplishments, achieved in the face of the heated, partisan battle with Congress that the president had earlier hoped to avoid, should not be underestimated.

Eisenhower's appointments to federal judgeships, especially to the fourth and fifth circuits, constituted his greatest contribution to the cause of civil rights. The liberals and moderates whom he appointed to the areas most affected by the *Brown* decision quietly insured a continuing process of desegregation. When compared to the appointments made by his predecessor and successor, his achievement stands out in dramatic relief. Although engineered by Brownell, Eisenhower knew of and cleared these appointments, which fit with his vision of desegregation. The [judges] he appointed would enforce the Supreme Court's ruling, but by the very nature of the American legal system, the process would be a gradual one.

The *Brown* decision played a crucial role in determining the administration's policy. Initially, it functioned to inhibit Eisenhower's attempts to advance the cause of civil rights. While Eisenhower could agree in principle with the decision's intent, he had doubts about the federal government or the courts taking such an active role. Moreover, he believed that a court ruling (or compulsory, immediatist legislation for that matter) would fail to bring about equality for blacks. He worried that a backlash would wipe out advances that had already been made.

Because they have devoted so much of their attention to the *Brown* decision, many historians have misinterpreted Eisenhower's purpose and his role in the struggle for civil rights. Clearly, the Court's decision in the segregation cases deserves the continuing attention of scholars, and the president's response to such a significant event reveals much about his policies towards blacks. However, focusing on *Brown* without placing it in the context of Eisenhower's attitudes and activities on the broader question of race obscures the nature and intent of his policies. While he was not the obstructionist that some historians have portrayed, Eisenhower did have his doubts about *Brown*. His quarrel was with the Court's methods, not its intent. He had qualms about the exercise of judicial power represented in the school segregation decision and even more serious doubts about the extension of federal power. These doubts did not, however, extend to the *principle* of desegregation.

IV

Eisenhower and Foreign Policy

Eisenhower met with Soviet Premier Nikita Khrushchev (as well as the leaders of Great Britain and France) at the Geneva Summit in 1955. While the conference failed to resolve any of the significant issues dividing the U.S. and USSR, it did produce some cultural exchanges and the first thaw in the Cold War. Eisenhower proclaimed that the conference achieved "a new spirit of conciliation and cooperation." In this photo, Eisenhower and Khrushchev display "the Spirit of Geneva." (UPI/Corbis-Bettman)

Robert A. Divine

EISENHOWER AND THE COLD WAR

Many of the earliest reappraisals of Eisenhower's presidency focused on his foreign policy. These accounts stressed his extensive knowledge of and experience in foreign affairs. They also gave Eisenhower credit for avoiding potential disasters; although he confronted as many dangerous situations as any president of the cold war era, Eisenhower's record contained no catastrophes like the Bay of Pigs or Vietnam. Robert A. Divine, a professor of history at the University of Texas at Austin and author of numerous books on foreign policy, finds much to admire in Eisenhower's restraint. While acknowledging that Eisenhower failed to achieve a permanent lessening of cold-war tensions and control of the arms race, Divine concludes that Eisenhower "used his sound judgment . . . to guide the nation safely through the first decade of the thermonuclear age."

World War II would serve ever after as Eisenhower's point of reference on world affairs. In common with others of his generation, he viewed appeasement and the Munich conference as the epitome of diplomatic folly. Isolationism was just as bad; "no intelligent man can be an isolationist," he commented to the people of Abilene, Kansas, in June 1945. The United States must remain active in the world, assuming its rightful role of leadership. Despite his service in the Philippines, he was European-centered in his thinking. He shared the Eastern establishment's foreign policy view that American security rested on a stable and friendly Europe, and he had little patience for those Republicans who were oriented toward Asia. Above all, he saw himself as a champion of peace, the soldier who would cap his service to the nation by working for international harmony. Yet even here he had little patience for those who spoke of an ideal world without conflict. Peace, to Eisenhower, was a practical matter. Nations would always have competing interests; the real task was to avoid the resort to armed force. "We must learn in this world," he told John Gunther [a journalist] in 1951, "to accommodate ourselves so that we may live at peace with others whose basic philosophy may be very different."

Eisenhower's outlook on the world grew directly from his personality. Just as he believed that common sense and good will could resolve almost any problem between individuals, he felt that nations could exist in harmony despite their differences. Throughout his career, he had displayed, as Gunther noted, an "instinctive ability to understand the other person's point of view." This empathy, combined with a buoyant optimism, set him at odds with Cold Warriors who believed that the United States was locked in a struggle for survival with the Soviet Union. The clash with the Russians, which he inherited from Truman, was a problem to be managed, not an all-consuming crusade against the forces of evil. . . . He had the ability to stand aloof from the passions of the moment and to assess the broader implications of each situation. . . . What some perceived as excessive caution and even indecision would prove in time to be admirable qualities of patience and prudence that enabled Eisenhower to deal effectively with many of the international crises of the 1950s.

* * *

The Cold War was at its height in the spring of 1952 when Dwight Eisenhower decided to seek the Republican nomination. The Marshall Plan had helped to put Europe back on its feet economically, but the process of creating an effective NATO defense force had barely gotten started under Eisenhower. There were only a dozen NATO divisions to counter the more than one hundred Soviet formations, and the problem of German rearmament still divided the Western allies. In Asia, the Korean War had settled into a stalemate after the Chinese intervention in late 1950; truce talks that had begun in mid-1951 were stalled over the delicate issue of repatriating unwilling prisoners-of-war. The most ominous development came in the nuclear field, where the Soviets had broken the American atomic monopoly by detonating their first bomb in August 1949. The United States had responded with a crash program to perfect the far more awesome hydrogen bomb, and after a crucial theoretical breakthrough in the spring of 1951, the American H-bomb program was in high gear, with the first test explosion set for the fall of 1952. And the Soviets were only a few months behind in their secret quest for the H-bomb.

Foreign policy posed a difficult political problem for the Republican party. In both the 1944 and 1948 elections, the GOP had chosen not to challenge the Democrats on international affairs, opting instead for a bipartisan position. John Foster Dulles, an experienced international lawyer and diplomat, had advised defeated candidate Thomas Dewey to pursue such a policy, but by the spring of 1952 Dulles had changed his mind. He felt it was vital for the Republicans to challenge the Democratic policy of containment and to promise the American people a new and bolder stance in world affairs.

In early May, Dulles flew to Paris to confer with Dwight Eisenhower at his NATO headquarters. He brought with him an essay he had written on American foreign policy which would be published three weeks later in *Life* magazine. Warning that containment would lead ultimately to both excessive reliance on military power and to a heavy drain on the American economy, Dulles outlined two new approaches. The first he called retaliation. Instead of investing so heavily in conventional military power to contain the threat of Communist aggression, Dulles suggested a reliance on America's air and nuclear superiority. Without ever mentioning the atomic bomb, he hinted at a willingness to use it as a threat against the Soviet Union. ". . . the free world," he argued, should "develop the will and organize the means to retaliate instantly against open aggression by Red armies, so that, if it occurred anywhere, we could and would strike back where it hurts, by means of our own choosing."

The use of nuclear weapons to neutralize Soviet conventional superiority would enable the United States to implement a new political strategy of liberation. Bemoaning the postwar Russian domination of Eastern Europe, Dulles advocated a moral and spiritual offensive to free these captive nations. The United States should abandon the static policy of containment and instead make it "publicly known that it wants and expects liberation to occur." He did not, however, advocate the use of force. He spoke vaguely about using Radio Free Europe to encourage people to escape from behind the Iron Curtain, and the organization of "task forces" to develop "freedom programs" for each of the captive nations. It might take a decade or more for liberation to occur, but he was confident that in the long run the forces of freedom and democracy would triumph over those of oppression and tyranny.

Eisenhower, who had read earlier drafts of Dulles's essay, was impressed by the concepts of retaliation and liberation. They fitted in with his belief that containment could lead to eventual American bankruptcy. He made no comment about liberation, but he challenged the simplistic notion that all Communist moves could be met with the threat of nuclear war. He wondered how retaliation could be used to counter "Soviet political aggression, as in Czechoslovakia," which "successively chips away exposed portions of the free world." From his experience with NATO, Eisenhower realized the importance of conventional forces "to convey a feeling of confidence to exposed populations, a confidence which will make them sturdier, politically, in their opposition to Communist inroads."

After their meeting in France, Dulles agreed to support Eisenhower's candidacy, but he withheld any public announcement while he strove to hammer out a Republican foreign-policy plank acceptable to both the general and to his main opponent, Senator Robert Taft. The document that finally emerged, after considerable amendment by Taft's supporters, was highly partisan in tone. The Republicans accused the Democrats of abandoning the peoples of Eastern Europe to Communist rule in the "tragic blunders" made at Teheran, Yalta, and Potsdam. A specific repudiation of the Yalta agreement was coupled with a ringing call for the liberation of "captive peoples." Instead of continuing "the negative, futile and immoral policy of 'containment,' " the GOP platform promised to "revive the contagious, liberating influences which are inherent in freedom." Eisenhower accepted this partisan rhetoric, presumably as the price he had to pay for party unity, but he drew the line at the inclusion of the phrase "relatiatory striking power" in the platform. The general felt this meant exclusive reliance on air power and the abandonment of all that he had done to build up NATO. . . .

After winning the Republican nomination, Eisenhower seemed willing to embrace the second Dulles slogan, "liberation," in the fall campaign. The promise to take the offensive in the Cold

War had great domestic political appeal, especially to ethnic groups such as Polish-Americans who normally voted Democratic. Thus in his first major foreign-policy speech, given at the American Legion convention in late August, Eisenhower declared his opposition to the Soviet tyranny, "a tyranny that has brought thousands, millions of people into slave camps and is attempting to make all humankind its chattel." Without specifying how it would be done, he called upon the American people to join with him in a great moral crusade to liberate the captive peoples. . . . The next day, after a long conference with the candidate, Dulles reaffirmed the liberation concept, telling reporters that what the United States needed to do was to "try to split the satellite states away" from Russia. "The only way to stop a head-on collision with the Soviet Union is to break it up from within," Dulles concluded.

The Republican liberation rhetoric sent a shudder through Western Europe. Frightened by the prospect of a nuclear war to free the captive nations, Europeans wondered what had happened to the prudent Eisenhower they had known and trusted. At home, the Democrats made the most of their opportunity. Candidate Adlai Stevenson spoke sadly about the risk of a war which would "liberate only broken, silent and empty lands.". . .

Eisenhower himself was disturbed by the implications of liberation. Upset that Dulles had failed to stress the vital qualification that liberation should be achieved only by peaceful means, the candidate berated him for this omission after a speech in Buffalo in which Dulles talked about air-drops of supplies to anti-Communist freedom fighters. In his next major foreign policy address, the general restated the liberation concept in carefully qualified terms, saying that he intended "to aid by every peaceful means, but only by peaceful means, the right to live in freedom." Then he stressed his devotion to peace by concluding, "The one—the only—way to win World War III is to prevent it."

This speech in Philadelphia on September 4 marks the end of Eisenhower's reliance on liberation in the campaign. He dropped all further references to captive peoples, save for one brief Pulaski Day statement, and he no longer relied on Dulles for drafts of foreign policy speeches. For Eisenhower, the political advantages in liberation were more than outweighed by the implication that he favored a policy that could lead to war with the Soviet Union. His own devotion to peace prevailed.

* * *

Eisenhower's handling of the Korean War issue showed that he was still willing to exploit foreign policy for political gain. When the war first broke out in June 1950, he staunchly backed Truman's decision to fight, and he stood behind the President when he removed General MacArthur. The stalemate in Korea had made the war increasingly unpopular by 1952, and even though other Republicans sniped at Truman's policy, Eisenhower remained loyal. In his first press conference after declaring his candidacy in June, the general expressed his doubts about launching a major offensive in Korea to achieve victory and then added, "I do not believe that in the present situation there is any clean-cut answer to bringing the Korean War to a successful conclusion."

By the fall, Eisenhower felt differently. Surveys of public opinion and voter sentiment revealed a growing national concern with the stalemated conflict and a belief that Eisenhower could furnish the new leadership needed to end the fighting. The candidate began making references to the war in Korea, defending Truman's decision to fight but questioning his conduct of the war. In early October, he took a new line by suggesting that the administration was wrong in making American youth bear the brunt of battle. "That is a job for Koreans," he said in Illinois. "If there must be a war there, let it be Asians against Asians, with our support on the side of freedom." A few days later in San Francisco, Ike stressed the heavy casualties the United States had suffered in Korea and then for the first time stated that if elected he would give "full dedication to the job of finding an intelligent and honorable way to end the tragic toll. . . ."

Even as Eisenhower was speaking, the dormant war sprang to life. The Communists broke the lull with a major offensive on October 6; a week later, General Mark Clark ordered a counter-strike. For two weeks, American troops, engaged in bitter, hand-to-hand fighting in the "Iron Triangle" area, suffered heavy casualties. The Democrats, on the defensive, accused the Republican candidate of trying to wring votes out of "our ugly, miserable, bloody ordeal" in Korea. President Truman, angry at Eisenhower's intimation that he knew how to end the conflict, dared Ike to come forward with his remedy.

Truman's challenge played directly into the hands of the Republican strategists. Several of Eisenhower's advisers, including speechwriter Emmet Hughes, thought that Korea was a perfect issue on which to apply the general's reputation as a military expert. Hughes wrote a speech in which the candidate would promise to go to Korea if he were elected. He gave it to campaign manager Sherman Adams, who immediately approved, but they were afraid that Ike would reject it as too theatrical. When they showed the text to the general, however, his eyes lit up, he reached for a pencil, and quickly made a few changes to sharpen the impact of the key sentence.

Eisenhower made his famous pledge at the height of the campaign, in a speech in Detroit on October 24. He singled out Korea as the tragedy that "challenges all men dedicated to the work of peace." After accusing the Democrats of mishandling the war, he came to his climax. The first task of a new administration, he declared, would be "to bring the Korean war to an early and honorable end." "That job requires a personal trip to Korea," he continued. "I shall make that trip. . . . I shall go to Korea."

"That does it—Ike is in," reporters told Sherman Adams. Nearly all the political commentators agreed that the pledge to go to Korea clinched the election for Eisenhower. He repeated the promise in subsequent speeches, driving home the belief in the minds of voters that the architect of victory in World War II would surely find a way to conclude the limited war in Asia. The beauty of the pledge, however, lay in its very vagueness. All that Eisenhower promised was to make the trip. He left himself complete freedom of action in dealing with the Korean conflict as President. He had thus been able to take political advantage of the Korean War without committing himself in advance to any specific course of action.

After Eisenhower's decisive victory at the polls over Adlai Stevenson, most observers assumed that one of his first acts as President-elect would be to appoint John Foster Dulles as secretary of state. Instead, Ike delayed the appointment for several weeks while he canvassed the field. For a time he considered offering the position to John J. McCloy, a leading member of the foreign policy establishment and former American High Commissioner to Germany. Eisenhower finally settled on Dulles, partly out of his respect for his knowledge and experience in foreign policy and partly because Ike knew that the appointment would please the Taft wing of the GOP.

In the course of time, the legend grew that Eisenhower turned over foreign policy completely to his secretary of state, intervening only occasionally to soften the unyielding line that Dulles pursued toward the Soviet Union. . . .

There is much in the relationship of the two men, however, which does not fit this simple picture. From the outset, Dulles was insecure in his relations with Eisenhower. The President kept him dangling before he appointed him secretary of state, and throughout his presidency, Eisenhower kept a set of independent foreign-policy advisers on hand at the White House. Dulles constantly struggled to prevent men like C. D. Jackson, Nelson Rockefeller, and Harold Stassen from using their White House posts to influence the course of American foreign policy. Adams tells of the frequency of Dulles's visits to the President's office and of the constant telephone calls from the secretary of state, a fact confirmed by the logs kept by the White House staff. In his own memoirs, Ike refers casually to the fact that while traveling abroad, "Secretary Dulles made a constant practice . . . of cabling me a summary of the day's events." After six years, Ike recalled, the cables and other memoranda from Dulles made a stack more than four feet high—hardly an indication of a secretary of state making policy on his own.

In essence, Eisenhower used Dulles. Confident of his own grasp of world affairs, he needed someone who had the knowledge and skill to conduct diplomacy yet would defer to the President. Ike also realized the importance of having a secretary of state who could keep ardent Cold Warriors, especially right-wing Republican senators, happy with administration policy. He knew how helpless Dean Acheson had become, called constantly to testify before congressional committees to justify Truman's policies, which were in fact tough and unyielding toward the Soviet Union. Dulles could serve as the lightning rod, absorbing domestic criticism and warding off attacks from the right with his moralistic rhetoric. On occasion, Ike would complain that "Foster is just too worried about being accused of sounding like Truman and Acheson," but he understood the advantage of having the secretary of state as the target of criticism. ". . . the Democrats love to hit him rather than me," Ike commented to Emmet Hughes. And Ike never had any doubts about who called the shots. ". . . there's only one man I know who has seen *more* of the world and talked with more people and *knows* more than he does," Eisenhower told Hughes, "—and that's me."

The two men formed an effective team. Eisenhower enjoyed the confidence of the American people, and he had a personal relationship with many of the world's leaders. Pragmatic by nature, he was committed to an effort to keep the Cold War manageable, to reduce tensions, and to avoid the dread possibility of a nuclear war. Dulles had a more theoretical cast of mind. Convinced of America's moral superiority, he sought to put the Communists on the defensive. His moralistic and often ponderous public statements gave him the reputation, which he cherished, of being a dedicated crusader against the Soviets; behind the scenes, he proved to have a lucid understanding of the realities of world politics and a surprising gift for the give-and-take of diplomacy. Dulles, the civilian lawyer, had a fondness for the threat of force, while Eisenhower, the military man, preferred the language of peaceful persuasion. The secretary tended to become uneasy in moments of crisis; the President was at his best when the situation became the most tense. One close associate commented about Eisenhower's air of calm relaxation during a critical period: "I realized as never before why a President is so important—to be able to give others, at such a time, an impression of unruffled assurance and confidence.". . .

Above all, the two men complemented each other. Ike lacked the stamina and enthusiasm for the daily grind of diplomacy that Dulles took in stride. Though the President was knowledgeable about European issues, he was much weaker on Asia, Latin America, and the Middle East. Dulles helped fill in many of the gaps in Eisenhower's understanding of world affairs. Eisenhower's serene self-confidence helped offset Dulles's personal insecurity. When the secretary fretted about public opinion and the reactions of others, the President could offer him the necessary reassurance, telling him to ignore his critics. And there was no doubt in either man's mind who made the decisions that counted. "The truth is that Dulles did Eisenhower's bidding in matters of high policy," comments presidential biographer Peter Lyon, "and also served as the convenient butt for any criticism of that policy. . . ." Ann Whitman, Eisenhower's private secretary, wrote to a friend after Dulles's death to play down reports of a "new" Eisenhower finally taking command of American foreign policy. "He isn't any different—he has always taken the lead," she wrote. "Perhaps now it is more obvious, but Dulles and the President consulted on every decision and then Dulles went back to the State Department and carried them out."

* * *

From the outset of his administration, Eisenhower moved to revitalize the National Security Council and thereby ensure his continuing control over all major foreign policy decisions. The NSC, created in 1947 to coordinate diplomatic and military policy, had never achieved its full potential under President Truman. He had met with the statutory members, who included the secretaries of state and defense, the chairman of the Joint Chiefs, the director of civil defense, and the head of the CIA, infrequently, preferring to arrive at his major decisions independently. Eisenhower asked aide Robert Cutler, a Boston banker, to design a more orderly and systematic procedure, and then in March directed Cutler to put his recommendations into effect under the title, Special Assistant for National Security Affairs. Under the new system, the NSC was broadened to include the secretary of the treasury and the budget director, as well as other officials on an *ad hoc* basis when their expertise was needed. Cutler headed up a Planning Board which prepared a paper on some aspect of national security each week. Cutler circulated the document in advance, briefing the President the day before the NSC met to consider it.

The weekly meetings of the NSC revealed Eisenhower's intense interest and concern for foreign policy. CIA Director Allen Dulles normally opened the sessions with an intelligence briefing, and then Cutler summarized the issue to be discussed. For the next two hours, the members debated the various aspects of the problem before them. Eisenhower followed the discussion closely, trying to stay quiet at first so that others would speak their minds freely, but gradually joining in and expressing his views. The President waited until after the meeting to inform Cutler of the decisions he had reached, and sometimes he called a select few into his office to carry on a further discussion of particularly sensitive topics. Cutler then drew up a Record of Action and supervised its implementation.

Eisenhower liked the new process. He much preferred oral briefings to the reading of long memoranda; in the give-and-take of NSC debate he could weigh the various alternatives and reach carefully reasoned conclusions. He could balance the ideas and suggestions of John Foster Dulles against the views of other advisers. By April, he was telling members of Congress that the NSC had become "the central body in making policy." "Its sessions are long, bitter, and tough," he commented. "Out of that sort of discussion we're trying to hammer policy." Ike attended nearly all the NSC meetings, missing only twenty-nine in eight years, and he was the focal point of the group's discussion. "All remarks were addressed to him," Cutler noted. "When he spoke, everyone listened." Those who attended NSC meetings regularly soon realized that the President, not the secretary of state, was in charge of the administration's foreign policy. "The mythical Eisenhower," commented one NSC member, "who left decision-making to subordinates . . . cannot be found in these records of the most important business he conducted for the nation."

* * *

In their early months in office, Eisenhower and Dulles had to deal with two issues they had raised in the campaign—liberation and the Korean War. The Republican platform's denunciation of the Yalta agreements and the call for liberation rather than containment led to expectations of a new departure in the administration's policy toward Eastern Europe. In his first State of the Union message to Congress in early February 1953, the President sought to reassure the Republican right. He promised a "new, positive foreign policy" and declared that the United States would not "acquiesce in the enslavement of any people." He would soon ask Congress, he pledged, "to join in an appropriate resolution making clear that this government recognizes no kind of commitment contained in secret understandings of the past with foreign governments which permit this kind of enslavement."

Those who expected an early renunciation of the Yalta agreements were in for a disappointment, however. The President soon realized that repudiation would endanger existing American rights in West Berlin and Vienna as well as run into stiff opposition from the Democrats in Congress. In a press conference in mid-February, Eisenhower commented that he did not feel that it was "feasible or desirable" to deny the entire substance of the Yalta and Potsdam agreements, admitted that he had not found any additional secret agreements, and even defended the secrecy of the wartime accords on military grounds. Concerned about several sweeping "captive nations" resolutions introduced into Congress, Eisenhower and Dulles moved to preempt extreme action by sponsoring a joint resolution that accused the Soviet Union of violating the Yalta agreements "to bring about the subjugation of free peoples."

Democrats, who had maintained all along that it was Soviet violations, not the agreements that Roosevelt and Truman had negotiated, that had led to Communist domination of Eastern Europe, quickly threw their support behind the administration's proposal. The House Foreign Affairs Committee gave its unanimous approval, but in the Senate conservative Republicans, led by Robert Taft, objected. At first they sought an amendment which made it clear that the resolution did not signify a congressional validation of the disputed agreements. When the Democrats refused to accept this reservation, Senator Taft finally permitted the resolution to die in committee after the death of Joseph Stalin in early March. Eisenhower and Dulles, who argued that the change in Russian leadership made it inappropriate to proceed with the captive nations resolution, were relieved to have such a potentially embarrassing and politically divisive issue shelved.

The emptiness of liberation was even more graphically demonstrated in June when rioting broke out in East Berlin and spread to several other cities within the Soviet-occupied zone of Germany. Workers, angered at the imposition of heavier production goals, burned Communist banners on the Unter den Linden and broke open East German jails to free political prisoners. The Soviet Union moved swiftly to restore order; within twenty-four hours the Russian army had brutally crushed the spontaneous uprising. The United States carefully avoided taking any positive action beyond opening food kitchens in West Berlin to feed refugees from East Germany. Eisenhower, who had been aware of the danger of liberation from the outset, kept silent about the Soviet action and refused to let Dulles take any steps that would lead to a confrontation.

* * *

The President played a much more active and successful role in redeeming his own personal campaign pledge to end the fighting in Korea. Three weeks after the election, he quietly slipped out of the country for a three-day tour of the fighting front. He conferred briefly with Syngman Rhee, the President of the Republic of Korea, but he spent most of his time visiting American units and talking with the UN commander, General Mark Clark. Clark had prepared a detailed estimate of the forces required for a major offensive to win the war; to his surprise, Eisenhower never asked him what it would take to achieve victory. Instead, the President-elect made it clear that he was more interested in negotiating an honorable peace. In his memoirs, Ike recalled that he quickly concluded that "we could not stand forever on a static front and continue to accept casualties without any visible results. Small attacks on small hills," he decided, "would not end this war."

Over the next few months, Eisenhower considered the alternatives in Korea. Determined not to have the stalemate continue, he examined the possibility of widening the war and launching a general offensive which would include aerial strikes against Manchuria and a blockade of the Chinese coastline. Dulles tended to favor such a course, believing that it was necessary to win in Korea in order to prevent further Chinese advances in Asia. . . . But Eisenhower felt differently. He realized that England and other American allies would oppose an all-out effort in Korea, with the inevitable risk of touching off a world war. "If you go it alone in one place," he told Sherman Adams, "you have to go it alone everywhere. No single nation can live alone in the world."

Another possibility would be to resort to nuclear weapons. General Douglas MacArthur had made this suggestion to Eisenhower shortly after his return from the Korean trip. A solemn warning to the Soviet Union of American intentions to use the atomic bomb would be enough to end the war, MacArthur argued, but he went on to suggest both the "atomic bombing of enemy military concentrations and installations in North Korea and the sowing of fields of suitable radio-active materials . . . to close the major lines of enemy supply. . . ." Eisenhower saw no insurmountable moral problem in the use of atomic weapons, but he shared the doubts of the Joint Chiefs of Staff about the effectiveness of tactical bombs on the deeply entrenched Communist forces in Korea. He also realized the rift this would open up with our allies, and he worried about a possible Soviet response against the defenseless cities of Japan.

The President finally chose a variant of MacArthur's proposal. Instead of publicly warning the Soviet Union that we planned to use nuclear weapons to end the Korean conflict, Eisenhower decided to let the Chinese, Russians, and North Koreans know that the United States was prepared to "move decisively without inhibition in our use of weapons" unless there was satisfactory progress in the peace talks. "In India and in the Formosa Straits area, and at the truce negotiations at Panmunjom," Eisenhower recalled, "we dropped the word, discreetly, of our intention. We felt quite sure it would reach Soviet and Chinese Communist ears."

Stalin's death may have been as influential as the veiled threat of nuclear force. In late March, the Chinese suddenly responded favorably to an earlier American request for an exchange of sick and wounded prisoners-of-war. More significantly, the Communists also indicated a willingness to renew negotiations, suspended since the fall of 1952, on the key issue—American refusal to permit forced repatriation of prisoners-of-war. A large proportion of the more than 100,000 North Korean and Chinese captives did not want to return to their homelands. China had rejected an earlier Indian proposal for a neutral repatriation commission to decide the fate of those unwilling to go home, but in the talks that resumed in Panmunjom on April 6, the Communist representatives accepted voluntary repatriation in principle. Presumably either direct pressure from the Soviet Union or Chinese uncertainty of Russian support for a hard line after the death of Stalin had led to this sudden change in Communist policy.

When the truce talks reached an impasse in mid-May, Eisenhower decided it was time to step up the pressure. In the course of a two-day visit to India, Secretary Dulles informed Prime Minister Nehru that the United States might feel compelled "to use atomic weapons if a truce could not be arranged." Eisenhower and Dulles were sure that Nehru would pass along this warning to Peking. At the same time, the President sent new orders to General Mark Clark in Korea authorizing him to break off the truce talks if the Chinese rejected the final American offer. If the fighting resumed, Clark commented in his memoirs, "then I was to prosecute the war along lines we had not yet taken to make the Communists wish they had accepted our terms." Finally, the administration transferred atomic warheads to American bases in Okinawa.

The Chinese responded in early June by accepting the American formula for the repatriation of prisoners-of-war. A last-minute attempt by Syngman Rhee to sabotage the truce negotiations by releasing 25,000 Communist prisoners held in South Korea delayed the final negotiations, but on July 27, 1953, UN and Communist representatives signed eighteen copies of the armistice agreement at Panmunjom. Syngman Rhee expressed his displeasure by boycotting the ceremony, and several Republican senators criticized the Eisenhower administration for failing to achieve a unified Korea. The American people, however, were relieved that a long and unpopular war had finally come to an end. The President struck the appropriate note of caution in his message to the nation on the truce: "we have won an armistice on a single battleground, not peace in the world."

It was still an impressive achievement. Six months after taking office, Eisenhower had fulfilled his implicit campaign promise and ended the divisive Asian conflict. He quite properly had given it priority in the early months of his administration, and he clearly was the architect of the successful strategy. Stalin's death helped by adding a new element of uncertainty in the Communist ranks and thus inclining China toward a peaceful solution. The President had steered a careful course between Dulles's urging of a military victory and MacArthur's call for a public nuclear challenge. Several years later, Dulles would try to claim the credit by telling a reporter that he had gone to the brink of war to achieve the Korean settlement and thus stirred up a controversy over "brinksmanship." But it was Eisenhower, in his own characteristically quiet and effective way, who had used the threat of American nuclear power to compel China to end its intervention in the Korean conflict. Perhaps the best testimony to the shrewdness of the President's policy is the impossibility of telling even now whether or not he was bluffing. . . .

* * *

. . . During his last few months in office [Eisenhower] was unable to regain the momentum he had been trying to create toward easing Cold War tensions. Instead, he found himself the prisoner of events. In Cuba, the emergence of Fidel Castro led to a growing antagonism and finally a break in diplomatic relations; the sudden grant of independence to the Congo by Belgium caused grave instability in Africa; growing Communist insurgency in South Vietnam and an abortive right-wing coup in Laos created a sense of danger in Southeast Asia that foreshadowed the tragic Vietnam War of the 1960s. In the fall, the President watched helplessly as Nikita Khrushchev came to the United Nations in New York and attracted worldwide attention by pounding his shoe on the table. His greatest disappointment came in November, when Richard Nixon spurned his help until the climax of the presidential campaign and then lost narrowly to John F. Kennedy, a man Eisenhower felt lacked the experience and maturity to conduct American foreign policy.

The sense of a heightened Cold War troubled Eisenhower as he left office. His fondest wish had been to use his skills to reduce tension and lessen the possibility of a nuclear holocaust. His record, however, was far better than the crises of 1960 would suggest. He had halted the Korean War six months after taking office. In the ensuing seven-and-a-half years he had kept the United States at peace. In the Middle East he had managed to contain the Suez crisis and restore temporary stability to that troubled region; in Asia, he had balanced the somewhat flamboyant rhetoric of his secretary of state with his own restraint and achieved a delicate stand-off between the Nationalists and the Chinese Communists in the Formosa Straits; in Europe, he had stood fast before Khrushchev's threats over Berlin, maintaining the American commitment to that city while avoiding a resort to force. And if he had failed in his most ambitious undertaking, the control of the arms race, at least he had achieved a cessation of nuclear testing, with its potentially deadly fallout, during the last two years of his term.

The very nature of Eisenhower's presidential style obscured his successes and led to the contemporary belief that he was a lazy and ineffective leader. His fondness for indirection robbed him of the credit, as well as the blame, for the actions of the men he let take the limelight, such as John Foster Dulles and Harold Stassen. Yet those close to Eisenhower realized that he alone was making the important decisions and was in full control of his more visible subordinates. . . . Eisenhower believed that his job was to make the decisions; he left the role of advocacy and debate to others.

The essence of Eisenhower's strength, and the basis for any claim to presidential greatness, lies in his admirable self-restraint. Emmet Hughes had this quality in mind when he wrote: "The man—and the President—was never more decisive than when he held to a steely resolve *not* to do something that he sincerely believed wrong in itself or alien to his office." Nearly all of Eisenhower's foreign policy achievements were negative in nature. He ended the Korean War, he refused to intervene militarily in Indochina, he refrained from involving the United States in the Suez crisis, he avoided war with China over Quemoy and Matsu, he resisted the temptation to force a showdown over Berlin, he stopped exploding nuclear weapons in the atmosphere. A generation of historians and political scientists, bred in the progressive tradition, have applied an activist standard to Ike's negative record and have found it wanting. Yet in the aftermath of Vietnam, it can be argued that a President who avoids hasty military action and refrains from extensive involvement in the internal affairs of other nations deserves praise rather than scorn.

Eisenhower left behind a mixed legacy. His efforts to liquidate the Cold War and ease the burdens of the arms race failed; he bequeathed to John F. Kennedy situations in Cuba and Vietnam that led to grave crises in the 1960s. But at the same time, his moderation and prudence served as an enduring model of presidential restraint—one that his successors ignored to their eventual regret. Tested by a world as dangerous as any that an American leader has ever faced, Eisenhower used his sound judgment and instinctive common sense to guide the nation safely through the first decade of the thermonuclear age.

Robert J. McMahon

EISENHOWER AND THE THIRD WORLD

Robert A. Divine's was one of a number of revisionist studies in the early 1980s that established Eisenhower's central role in foreign policy and praised his restraint in the management of foreign affairs. The portrayal of Eisenhower as the prime mover in his administration's foreign policy has emerged as an established paradigm. However, some historians of Eisenhower's foreign policy have subsequently questioned his restraint. This group is sometimes referred to as "postrevisionist." Many of those historians have focused on Eisenhower's policies toward the Third World. Robert J. McMahon, a historian at the University of Florida, summarized the arguments of the postrevisionists in 1986. At the end of his article, McMahon raises some of the most substantial problems with the postrevisionist analysis. These authors stress continuity in American foreign policy, particularly with respect toward the Third World. Is it fair, then, to single out the Eisenhower administration for criticism?

Within the past decade, revisionism about Dwight D. Eisenhower's presidency has become a veritable cottage industry. . . . Certainly the new scholarship on Eisenhower is not uncritical, nor is it unanimous in its judgments on the various facets of the administration's record. Nonetheless, there does appear to be a consensus developing on the part of the majority of the new Eisenhower scholars that, at least within the realm of foreign affairs, Eisenhower must rank as one of the most skilled and probably the most successful of all the postwar presidents.

Fueled by a combination of new sources and fresh perspectives, revisionist accounts of the Eisenhower presidency have chal-

From Robert J. McMahon, "Eisenhower and Third World Nationalism: A Critique of the Revisionists," from *Political Science Quarterly*, vol. 101, no. 3 (1986), 453–473, footnotes omitted. Reprinted with permission.

lenged earlier studies on two broad grounds: first, the Eisenhower revisionists have portrayed the general, in the words of one scholar, as a "skilled tactician and a master of his administration"; and, second, they have argued that his foreign policy was astute, restrained, and largely successful. The two contentions, of course, deal with separate issues and are often advanced by scholars with different sets of interests.

Given the weight of evidence presented by the Eisenhower revisionists, the first contention now appears virtually unassailable. . . . As Richard H. Immerman has persuasively argued, contrary to the conventional wisdom, Eisenhower exercised strong executive control in foreign affairs, often reining in his bombastic secretary of state. Even Arthur M. Schlesinger, Jr., hardly a sympathetic observer, concedes that "the Eisenhower papers . . . unquestionably alter the old picture. . . . Eisenhower showed much more energy, interest, self-confidence, purpose, cunning, and command than many of us supposed in the 1950s."

These new revelations about Eisenhower's leadership capabilities and uses of presidential power have added an important dimension to our understanding of the man and his presidency. Despite the intrinsic value of such work, however, it has serious limitations for the student of American foreign relations. For those interested in examining the goals and results of American diplomacy during the 1950s, the preoccupation with the decision-making process appears at best peripheral. This debate focuses on the means of presidential leadership, not the ends. . . .

The second contention, involving longer-term perspectives and more intricate standards of evaluation, has inevitably sparked more controversy. Do Eisenhower's accomplishments in foreign affairs place him in the first rank among the postwar presidents? Despite inevitable differences on particulars, the revisionists are virtually unanimous in applauding Ike's consistent exercise of mature judgment, prudence, and restraint and in celebrating his signal accomplishment of maintaining peace during an unusually perilous period in international relations.

Robert Divine has ably summarized the revisionist perspective in his recent book, *Eisenhower and the Cold War.* . . . Despite the general consensus among Eisenhower revisionists on the success of his diplomacy, these scholars have been curiously ambivalent on one major topic: the efficacy of Eisenhower's approach to the emerging nations of the Third World. As Robert Divine's examples—Korea, Indochina, Suez, the Taiwan Straits—would suggest, the wisdom of the President's policies toward the Third World constitutes an important element in the favorable assessment of at least some historians. To the litany of achievements cited by Divine, moreover, other scholars have added the limited but effective use of force to help overthrow unfriendly governments in Iran and Guatemala and to help prop up a friendly one in Lebanon. Other Eisenhower scholars, however, including Peter Lyon, Charles C. Alexander, and Stephen E. Ambrose, have criticized the President's handling of certain Third World problems. They have nonetheless concluded their evaluations by praising the President's overall diplomatic legacy. Thus Lyon, whose critique of the administration's record in the Third World is both sustained and sharp, closes his largely sympathetic "portrait of the hero" with the observation that Eisenhower must be praised for the pacific nature of his two terms in office.

This seeming contradiction is actually quite easily explained. Regardless of whether they see success, failure, or a mixed record in the Third World, the Eisenhower revisionists do not consider that aspect of Ike's diplomacy crucial to their overall evaluation. It is such issues as maintaining the peace, managing relations with the Soviet Union, gaining control over the nuclear arms race, and understanding the limits of American power that these scholars typically emphasize when calculating the balance sheet on the Eisenhower years. Given that perspective, Third World issues fade in importance; only the President's refusal to commit American troops to any open-ended Third World conflict appears critical to the new consensus on Eisenhower.

That perspective, however, is certainly open to question. Undoubtedly the concerns mentioned above were critical ones during the Eisenhower years. With the ever-present threat of nuclear confrontation—a threat compounded by the advent of the H-Bomb and intercontinental ballistic missiles—U.S.–Soviet relations certainly had to top Ike's diplomatic agenda. Still, the single most dynamic new element in international affairs during the 1950s was the emergence of a vigorous, broad-based, and assertive nationalism throughout the developing world. Those nationalist stirrings, moreover, constituted not only a major challenge to the world order that Eisenhower and his advisers sought to preserve, but promised as well to exacerbate tensions between Washington and Moscow as the two superpowers competed for the loyalty and resources of the newly emerging areas. The nature of the administration's response to Third World nationalism, in its varying manifestations, must therefore rank as a fundamental consideration in any overall assessment of Eisenhower's diplomatic record. This article will argue that the failure of the Eisenhower revisionists to appreciate the centrality of Third World nationalism has led them to present a distorted and oversimplified view of American foreign relations during a critical eight-year period.

The publication in recent years of a series of detailed studies on U.S. relations with different parts of the developing world, either focusing specifically on the Eisenhower years or spanning a broader time frame, has considerably enhanced our understanding of this important subject. Considered as a whole, this work offers an assessment of Eisenhower's foreign policy sharply at odds with that drawn by the revisionists. Indeed, a brief review of some of the more important recent work on U.S. relations with Asia, the Middle East, Latin America, and Africa reveals that Eisenhower scholarship actually is moving in two very different directions. Instead of applauding restraint, the authors of these studies often criticize intervention; instead of seeing a prudent administration aware of the limitations of American power, they often see an administration self-consciously expanding American involvement in all corners of the globe and trying to manage the internal affairs of other nations to an unprecedented degree.

Although recent literature on U.S.–Third World relations during the Eisenhower years varies considerably in scope, quality, depth of research, and interpretive thrust, it does suggest the plausibility of an alternative interpretation of Eisenhower's foreign policy. That view might be summarized as follows. The Eisenhower administration grievously misunderstood and underestimated the most significant historical development of the mid–twentieth century—the force of Third World nationalism. This failure of perception, furthermore, constituted a major setback for American diplomacy. The Eisenhower administration insisted on viewing the Third World through the invariably distorting lens of a Cold War geopolitical strategy that saw the Kremlin as the principal instigator of global unrest. As a result, it often wound up simplifying complicated local and regional developments, confusing nationalism with communism, aligning the United States with inherently unstable and unrepresentative regimes, and wedding American interests to the status quo in areas undergoing fundamental social, political, and economic upheaval. Rather than promoting long-term stability in the Third World, the foreign policy of the Eisenhower administration contributed to its instability, thus undermining a basic American policy goal. In this critical area, then, the Eisenhower record appears one of persistent failure. The new Eisenhower revisionism, which largely overlooks, downplays, or misinterprets this record, may consequently be a castle built upon sand.

Asia

Eisenhower's response to Asian developments well illustrates this larger theme. Nearly all of the new revisionist writers applaud the President's decisions to extricate the United States from the Korean quagmire and to avoid the considerable pressures for American intervention at Dienbienphu in Indochina. In addition, most of these scholars similarly praise Ike's astute avoidance of conflict with China over the Quemoy and Matsu imbroglio. The President, Herbert Parmet contends, was "cautious and fully cognizant of the hazards involved in military commitment, held the controls during the Indochinese crisis of 1954 and, together with John Foster Dulles, maneuvered with care and skillfully avoided enticements to involvement during two crises over the islands of Quemoy and Matsu."

The revisionist reasoning in this regard is as logical as it is compelling: the former general, who well understood the limits of military force, carefully steered the nation clear of open-ended military commitments, a policy of restraint that stands in sharp relief when compared to that pursued by both his predecessor and successors in the Oval Office. At least in the case of Indochina, this judgment appears sound. John Prados's *"The Sky Would Fall,"* a book based on newly declassified records, concludes that the pressures for intervention were even stronger than previously suspected. Accordingly, Ike's firm stand against U.S. military involvement in the face of strong contrary advice from many of his leading military and civilian advisers appears both bold and far-sighted. Despite the considerable evidence that Prados amasses to demonstrate how close the United States did come to intervention, the salient fact remains that the President ultimately exercised sound judgment. In a new study of "the day we didn't go to war," George C. Herring and Richard H. Immerman conclude that "there seems little reason to quarrel with the view that the administration acted wisely in staying out of war in 1954."

The Korean case is somewhat more problematic. . . . Critics of his policy . . . suggest that [the President] may have relied far too heavily on the threat of nuclear weapons to break the negotiating logjam, thus initiating a "brinksmanship" policy that gravely endangered world peace.

Scholars have advanced similar arguments with regard to the Taiwan Straits crises of 1955 and 1958. Divine approves of the President's brinksmanship in those twin showdowns with China, arguing that "the beauty of Eisenhower's policy is that to this day no one can be sure whether or not . . . he would have used nuclear weapons." That brandishing nuclear weapons could be a thing of beauty under any circumstances is a value judgment that some historians have been unwilling to make. Lyon faults the President for placing the United States in "an untenable position" during the 1958 crisis, "which, by maladroit diplomacy, was transformed into an intolerable dilemma, one that could apparently be resolved only by nuclear catastrophe or Chinese restraint." Likewise, John Gaddis's brief account of these episodes in his suggestive book, *Strategies of Containment,* also raises serious doubts about the efficacy of Ike's brinksmanship. "Far from validating the administration's strategy," he writes, "these incidents—particularly the one of 1958—in fact thoroughly discredited it in the eyes of the American public and allies overseas by revealing how little it would take to push the administration into a war with China involving the probable use of nuclear weapons." Decrying the riskiness of brinksmanship in the Taiwan Straits and elsewhere, Gaddis argues that "in retrospect the most startling deficiency of the administration's strategy was its bland self-confidence that it could use nuclear weapons without setting off an all-out nuclear war."

The real problem with the interpretation of the President's Asian policy advanced by the Eisenhower revisionists is not just that their assessments of his remarkable restraint in the incidents noted above are open to question. Rather, it is that they build a case based on a narrow, highly selective, and episodic approach that largely ignores the crucial question of nationalism. How well did the President accommodate American foreign policy to the transforming dynamic of Asian nationalism? Given the framework sketched above, that question should be critical to any rigorous analysis of Eisenhower's diplomatic record in Asia. Yet it is missing from most of the revisionist accounts. Most important, posing that question necessitates a very different evaluation of the administration's policy toward Asia since, according to much of the recent literature, its response to Asian nationalism was often inadequate and at times even disastrous.

Indochina is a case in point. While the revisionists routinely cite Ike's nonintervention at Dienbienphu to bolster their overall interpretive thrust, they rarely evaluate the more general issue of American policy toward Indochina during the post-Geneva period. Those revisionists who do discuss this aspect of the administration's record invariably temper their judgments. Lyon, for example, praises the President for his staunch refusal to aid the French in 1954, but adds that "the decisions to make massive commitments of military and financial aid to the puppet government in Saigon were Eisenhower's, as were the decisions to authorize hostile acts, 'dirty tricks,' acts of war against the Viet Minh undertaken by Americans under the direction of Americans." George C. Herring's important study of U.S. involvement in Vietnam, *America's Longest War,* renders a harsh verdict on Eisenhower's Vietnam policy. "Certain that the fall of Vietnam to Communism would lead to the loss of all of Southeast Asia," he writes, "the Eisenhower administration after Geneva firmly committed itself to creating in the southern part of the country a nation that would stand as a bulwark against Communist expansion and serve as a proving ground for democracy in Asia." But this experiment in nation building, Herring argues, was a "high-risk gamble" that by the close of Eisenhower's second term was on the verge of collapse. Despite massive military and economic assistance—aid that by 1961 had catapulted South Vietnam to fifth place among recipients of U.S.

support worldwide—the Americans never succeeded in laying the foundation for a genuinely independent nation; on the contrary, the American financial stake tended to foster dependence. As renewed guerrilla warfare erupted in the south in 1957, the inefficacy of the U.S. effort became painfully apparent. Only "the quirks of the electoral calendar," Herring contends, "spared Eisenhower from the ultimate failure of his policies in Vietnam."

The administration's record in Laos, conveniently ignored by most of the Eisenhower revisionists, constituted another effort at nation building whose outcome was less than a triumph for U.S. policy objectives. Charles Stevenson, whose book *The End of Nowhere* remains the most detailed and informed account of American relations with that struggling young country, offers a scathing indictment of the Eisenhower policy. He charges that the administration was animated exclusively by that nation's supposed significance to the Free World in its struggle against international communism. But by reducing complex Lao developments to broad Cold War categories, the United States almost completely misread and distorted the internal dynamics of Lao society. Stevenson demonstrates the futility of the U.S. effort to create an anticommunist bastion in Laos by pumping enormous sums of money into the Lao army. As Ike's second term came to a close, the deepening U.S. involvement in Laos had elevated a limited, local struggle against a communist-led guerrilla movement to global significance. Yet, as in Vietnam, U.S. objectives were further from realization than ever before.

U.S.–Indonesian relations, another subject largely ignored by the Eisenhower revisionists, provide even more dramatic evidence of the administration's failure to understand the depth and appeal of Asian nationalism. Specialists in this area have argued that the Eisenhower administration's virtual obsession with the prospects for a communist takeover of Southeast Asia's largest and most important nation blinded it to the complex internal developments that were shaking Indonesian society to its very core. The result was a policy that proved almost entirely counterproductive in terms of long-range U.S. objectives in that country. By providing clandestine support to Indonesian dissidents, whose long-simmering regional rebellion erupted into full-scale civil war in 1958, Eisenhower apparently hoped that he could help topple President

Sukarno's left-leaning regime and replace it with a more pliant, moderate, and pro-American government. But the administration's bold gamble backfired when Sukarno quickly suppressed the rebels; not only did the United States support the losing side, but its covert support for that side was embarrassingly exposed when Sukarno's troops shot down a CIA pilot flying bomber missions for the rebels. The heavy-handed U.S. intervention wound up strengthening Sukarno's hand while simultaneously offending nationalists of nearly all political hues with what was universally denounced as imperialist intervention. As a former Indonesian Foreign Minister later recalled, "the general opinion in Indonesia was unanimous that the CIA had a hand in the rebellion" and this suspicion "was to linger on for a long time and was the main cause of further deterioration in Indonesia–U.S. relations. . . ."

In comparison to the continuing crises in Indochina and Indonesia, U.S.–Philippine relations during the Eisenhower years appear remarkably placid. Indeed, as a recent study by Stephen Shalom makes clear, by the mid-1950s U.S. policy makers looked upon the Philippines as a real American success story: the Huk rebellion had been suppressed; economic collapse had been averted; a staunch U.S. ally, Ramon Magsaysay—with timely help from the CIA—had been installed in the presidency; U.S. economic and strategic interests had been secured; and nationalist sentiment appeared largely neutralized. Beneath this surface tranquility, however, lay festering problems, and Shalom shows how pent-up Filipino frustrations with their nation's neocolonial status—symbolized by the mammoth U.S. military bases and the unequal trade relationship between the two nations—led to an explosion of nationalist sentiment in the mid-1950s. As a result, the negotiations over a revised military bases agreement became harshly acrimonious and were broken off in 1956 as the United States could not satisfy Filipino demands for even limited sovereignty. It was U.S. recalcitrance in the face of enhanced Filipino nationalism, Shalom argues, that led both to the collapse of the talks and to a searching reexamination by Manila of its relationship with Washington. The significance of the Philippine case is that it demonstrates how, even in the most moderate, American-oriented Asian nation, nationalism posed a formidable threat to American objectives; the American response to that nationalist challenge proved at best halting and inadequate.

Another important topic rarely examined by the Eisenhower revisionists, U.S. policy toward South Asia, can best be understood as part of this general pattern. Recent work in this area by scholars such as Selig S. Harrison, M. S. Venkataramani, and Stanley Wolpert has suggested that the Eisenhower administration proved incapable of appreciating the deeply felt neutralist stance of the region's most important power, India. Instead of cultivating India's friendship as the key to regional stability, the Eisenhower administration made a major strategic blunder by aligning itself with Pakistan, first through a military assistance agreement in 1954, and subsequently through Pakistani membership in the Southeast Asia Treaty Organization (SEATO) and the Baghdad Pact. This decision, based on a global geopolitical approach that viewed Pakistan as a valuable strategic asset and thus an important anchor in America's worldwide containment network, proved counterproductive, however; it helped foster an arms race between India and Pakistan, rendered an amicable resolution of the tangled Kashmir dispute increasingly unlikely, alienated Afghanistan, and opened the door for greater Russian involvement in both India and Afghanistan. In short, the Eisenhower administration's decision to provide Pakistan with arms and to align it with the West increased regional instability and, as Indian Prime Minister Jawaharlal Nehru charged at the time, brought the Cold War to South Asia.

Latin America

As in other regions, so too in Latin America an explosive nationalism posed the principal challenge to American interests during the Eisenhower years. Recent literature on inter-American relations during this period, much of which draws heavily on documentation from the Eisenhower Library, suggests that the administration adapted poorly to the problems—and opportunities—presented by this renewed nationalism. Only the threat of communist penetration could arouse high-level interest in Latin American issues during Ike's presidency; otherwise, the administration pursued a policy of benign neglect, calculating that in comparison to more pressing international hot spots Latin America could safely be placed on the proverbial back burner. The result of this policy, according to most recent accounts, was nothing short of disastrous. Throughout the 1950s inter-American relations steadily deteriorated, a fact dramatically illustrated by the angry mobs that greeted Vice President Richard Nixon in Venezuela and elsewhere during his goodwill tour in 1958, the establishment of a revolutionary regime in Cuba in 1959, and Eisenhower's belated efforts to repair relations within the hemisphere during the waning months of his presidency. In his new study of U.S. relations with Central America, *Inevitable Revolutions,* Walter LaFeber states flatly that the Eisenhower administration simply could not "come to terms with history." Even the episode that some Eisenhower revisionists point to as a successful and limited defense of American interests—the CIA-led overthrow of the leftist Jacobo Arbenz regime in Guatemala in 1954—has been severely criticized in recent works.

The studies of Blanche Weisen Cook, Stephen Schlesinger and Stephen Kinzer, and Richard Immerman offer the fullest account yet of the Guatemalan coup, an operation still shrouded in secrecy. They agree that the intervention in Guatemala was not only unjustified by nearly any standard, but set a dangerous precedent for the expanded use of covert operations as an instrument of American policy. Cook insists that the Guatemalan model has been used time and again, with only minor modifications. There are important differences in emphasis in these works. In *Bitter Fruit,* Schlesinger and Kinzer argue that the American intervention was motivated by concern with the confiscation of the properties of the powerful United Fruit Company. In *The CIA in Guatemala,* Immerman takes a broader and more convincing view, suggesting that an all-embracing Cold War ethos led the United States to fear radical social experimentation in Guatemala and equate it, despite the lack of hard evidence, with communism. They do agree wholeheartedly, however, on the baleful impact of the operation. Of course, it was a resounding short-term success; Arbenz was ousted and replaced by a leader beholden to the United States. In the long run, though, Immerman and Schlesinger and Kinzer see the intervention as detrimental not only to the evolution of democratic institutions in Guatemala, but also to the achievement of long-term U.S. interests in the country and in the region. Arbenz sought to end centuries of social and economic injustice, Immerman asserts, but "the CIA's 1954 coup made moderation impossible." He sees the guerrilla struggle currently raging in Guatemala as "the final irony—and legacy" of the Eisenhower administration's intervention in that tragic land. Schlesinger and Kinzer are equally biting in their indictment of the CIA's meddling in Guatemala. "Over the longer term" they contend, "the coup gravely damaged American interests in Latin America. The gusto with which the United States had ended the Guatemalan revolution embittered many Latins, and strengthened deep-seated anti-Americanism throughout the continent." Partly as a result of the coup, they conclude, "movements toward peaceful reform in the region were set back, dictators were strengthened and encouraged, and activists of today look to guerrilla warfare rather than elections as the only way to produce change."

U.S. insensitivity toward the rising tide of Latin American nationalism took a less dramatic form in Brazil, but the results were just as detrimental to the accomplishment of long-term American objectives in the hemisphere. In his essay, "The United States, Brazil, and the Cold War, 1945–1960," Stanley E. Hilton contends that the Eisenhower administration's neglect of the region's largest and most important nation brought about an eclipse in the special relationship between the two countries that had long served U.S. and Brazilian interests. As a result, by the late-1950s the Brazilian leadership began to replace dependence on and cooperation with the United States with a more independent policy, one that would eventually lead Brazil to proclaim solidarity with the neutralist nations of the Third World and to seek common cause with fellow Latin states. The Truman and Eisenhower administrations "bear responsibility for that shift," according to Hilton. By foolishly ignoring its leaders' incessant pleas for the maintenance of a privileged relationship, he writes, "Washington alienated Brazil, formerly an eager ally in hemisphere matters. It also contributed powerfully to the long-range decline of American influence in the region by propelling Brazil along the path of solidarity with its historical antagonists, the Spanish Americans."

Stephen G. Rabe's important new book on U.S.–Venezuelan relations presents another chronicle of insensitivity and missed opportunities during the Eisenhower era. "Perhaps what distinguished its policies from the previous administration," Rabe notes, "was the Eisenhower administration's unabashed embrace of military dictatorships and its failure to criticize, however mutely, the rampant political and civil repression in Latin America." This failure was particularly evident in Venezuela, where the U.S. heaped medals and accolades on the brutal dictator, Marcos Pérez Jiménez, for his staunch anticommunism and his favorable treatment of U.S. oil companies. When Pérez Jiménez was toppled in January 1958, the unqualified support for a leader who had managed to alienate nearly all segments of Venezuelan society produced a vicious backlash against the United States. The angry mob that nearly killed Nixon in Caracas in May 1958, "shocked the United States," Rabe writes; "relations with the model Latin American country were in a shambles." In the aftermath of the assault on the Vice President, the Eisenhower administration scrambled to repair relations with some limited success. Support for the liberal democrat Romulo Betancourt certainly represented a welcome reversal of previous policy. Nonetheless, Rabe contends that the Eisenhower administration's failure to adapt to the stirrings of economic nationalism in Venezuela laid the seeds of future problems. The Eisenhower administration continually blocked any Venezuelan efforts to gain more control over their only important resource: oil. And when the President announced price cuts and import quotas on Venezuelan petroleum in 1959, Venezuelan leaders responded by founding the Organization of Petroleum Exporting Countries (OPEC), a cartel that would raise fundamental problems for the United States in succeeding years.

Without doubt, Fidel Castro's revolution in Cuba presented the most serious immediate threat to the accomplishment of the administration's objectives in the region. It is the verdict of much recent scholarship on Cuban–American relations that the Eisenhower administration's response to that challenge was rash, poorly planned, and ultimately counterproductive. As former Ambassador Philip W. Bonsal recalled in a 1972 memoir: "The Russian presence in Cuba is largely the consequence of the American reaction to Castro's provocations. . . . Russia came to Castro's rescue only after the United States had taken steps designed to overthrow him." Richard E. Welch's *Response to Revolution,* the most recent and balanced account of these events, concludes that "the Cuban policy of the Eisenhower years can only be judged a failure. Its legacy was one of defeat and animosity." Eisenhower, moreover, must be charged with the primary responsibility for the Bay of Pigs fiasco. "It was Eisenhower," writes Peter Lyon, "who had ordered that the attack be prepared, just as the operation was carried out under the purview of officials . . . who were completing what they had begun at Eisenhower's instigation." Peter Wyden, whose *Bay of Pigs: The Untold Story* is the fullest account to date of that failed operation, offers a savage indictment of an ill-conceived and poorly planned "wild gamble" that he calls "Eisenhower's baby." Even Cole Blasier, who accepts the still hotly debated theory that Eisenhower was correct in believing that Castro, from the very inception of his rule, sought to radicalize Cuban society and establish close relations with the Soviet Union, insists that the President's decisions "to arm a counterrevolutionary force and cut the sugar quota were counterproductive. . . . U.S. policies seem to have removed whatever slight chances may have existed for Castro's demise and facilitated his alignment with the USSR."

Conclusion

The foregoing review raises some troubling questions about the new Eisenhower revisionism. Certainly the revisionists are to be congratulated for combining new evidence with fresh perspectives to give us a challenging reinterpretation of the Eisenhower presidency. Many of their findings, moreover, appear basically sound; that the general was a strong leader who often exercised prudence and restraint in the conduct of international relations seems veritably unassailable now. In their zeal to revise, however, some revisionists have badly overstated their case. This paper has tried to demonstrate that they often ignore, downplay, or misinterpret major elements of the President's policies toward the Third World, and thus seriously distort the Eisenhower record. It is particularly revealing that the revisionists offer judgments about American diplomacy that are widely at variance from those drawn by scholars who have focused more narrowly on U.S. relations with particular developing nations or regions. If one accepts the premise that Eisenhower's response to the Third World, and especially its nationalist stirrings, must be at least one critical ingredient in any overall evaluation of his foreign policy, then the revisionist case for Ike appears far weaker than many recent accounts would have us believe.

There are several possible explanations for the contrasting perspectives offered in the two sets of literature. Since the nature and availability of documentary evidence inevitably shapes the judgments rendered by scholars, it is tempting to see interpretive differences as a function of the reliance on different sources. Such an explanation, however, would risk gross oversimplification. To be sure, many of the studies of U.S.–Third World relations discussed above are painstakingly researched, while some of the revisionist works—Robert Divine's *Eisenhower and the Cold War* is a prime example—are general accounts based solely on secondary literature. Yet other revisionist works certainly do mine important primary sources. Herbert Parmet, Peter Lyon, Fred I. Greenstein, and Stephen E. Ambrose all rely heavily on newly released documentation from the Eisenhower Library. Ambrose's magisterial biography, *Eisenhower, The President,* reflects its author's exceptional grasp of the available primary sources.

Depth and breadth of research alone simply cannot explain such sharp differences in interpretation. . . .Varying perspectives and conflicting methods of evaluation more accurately explain these contradictory trends in Eisenhower scholarship. What criteria does one use to evaluate the relative success or failure of any administration in international affairs? On this crucial question the revisionists and their critics differ profoundly. As noted above, the revisionists emphasize several key considerations in analyzing Eisenhower's foreign policy: maintaining the peace, managing relations with the Soviet Union, and understanding the limits of American power. On every point they award Ike high marks, contrasting his accomplishments, either implicitly or explicitly, with those of other postwar occupants of the White House.

Rather than reject these sweeping claims directly, many specialists in the field of U.S. relations with the developing nations simply investigate areas and topics outside the standard purview of the revisionists. Thus many of the nations discussed above—Laos, Indonesia, India, Pakistan, Egypt, Iraq, Brazil, Venezuela—are virtually ignored in revisionist accounts of Eisenhower's presidency. Yet the issues raised by these case studies speak directly to the conclusions reached by revisionist scholars. Using different standards of measurement—such as the *impact* of American actions on developing nations and the gap between goals and results—they reach strikingly different conclusions. If these authors are correct about the meager results of American initiatives, the detrimental long-term effects of many U.S. actions, and the chasm between expectations and accomplishments in so many parts of the world, then it becomes nearly impossible to view Ike's foreign policy in such a favorable light. Nor do the occasionally rash and often counterproductive actions detailed in these studies bolster the image of Ike's administration as consistently wise, prudent, and restrained.

Most important, this work on U.S.–Third World relations provides the basis for a fuller and more sophisticated understanding of Eisenhower's foreign policy. It promises to move the traditionalist/revisionist debate to a new plane. If any one theme emerges clearly from the recent literature on postwar American diplomacy it is the global nature of American interests. To understand a global foreign policy requires a systematic examination of *all* the areas of the world in which the United States tried to exert influence or affect developments. The studies discussed above certainly move us closer to that ultimate goal.

As the authors of those studies typically emphasize the continuity in American policy toward the developing nations, another question must be addressed: Is it fair to single out the Eisenhower administration for criticism in this area? Or, to rephrase the question: Is the Eisenhower administration any more to blame for American policy failures in the Third World than those of Harry S. Truman, John F. Kennedy, Lyndon B. Johnson, or other recent presidents? Although that question cannot be answered with precision until far more detailed work on U.S.–Third World relations during those administrations has been published, it is certainly germane to this discussion. If Eisenhower's policies toward the Third World are in fact just part of a continuum in postwar American foreign relations, as some of the studies discussed above suggest, then this article's emphasis on the failures of one particular administration may be misplaced. At the same time, the revisionists' emphasis on discontinuity—the heart of their argument for Ike's diplomatic success—might be equally misplaced. . . .

American Culture
in the 1950s

Levittown. William J. Levitt pioneered the construction of standardized, low-cost housing. The first Levittown was built on Long Island, N.Y. The virtually identical houses provided homes for homogenous suburban populations. Critics of conformity, such as Willliam Whyte, regarded Levittown as yet another threat to individualism. (AP/Wide World Photos)

Richard H. Pells

THE LIBERAL MIND IN A CONSERVATIVE AGE

In the 1960s and 1970s, many intellectuals and historians dismissed the 1950s as an intellectually stagnant era. Beginning in the 1980s, however, historians and critics demolished that notion with careful studies of the powerful, often dissenting, perspectives put forward by intellectuals in the 1950s. One such study is Richard H. Pells's *The Liberal Mind in a Conservative Age.* Pells, a professor of history at the University of Texas at Austin, maintains that American intellectuals of the 1950s developed profound critiques of their own society. Moreover, in doing so, they "created the vocabulary and the mental framework with which the next generation of Americans assaulted the nation's political institutions and social values." Pells finds the origins of both the New Left and the New Right in social critiques developed in the 1950s.

This is a book about intellectuals. More specifically, it is a book about the way certain American writers in the 1940s and 1950s interpreted and tried to cope with the major events of their time. I have chosen to call these writers "liberal" but I intend to use that word in its loosest possible sense. During these years, the terms liberal and conservative had already begun to shed whatever precise political meanings they may have once possessed. Moreover, several of the intellectuals I discuss continued to describe themselves as socialists or social democrats, while others had grown weary of politics of every sort. A few were even well embarked on a journey to the right, although they did not arrive at their final destination until the 1970s. Nevertheless, given the American political landscape between 1941 and 1960, most of them still occupied the territory from the center to the left—this at a moment when their countrymen and the leaders of their government were becoming increasingly conservative in foreign policy and domestic affairs.

Yet their liberalism, however broad or vague, was not the principal characteristic of their books and articles. Nor did I select these men and women for study because of their particular philosophies, specialties, career patterns, or proximity to people in power. Rather, I decided to write about them because they seemed to me to be fulfilling the essential function of the intellectual in a modern society. Whether they were known officially as sociologists, political theorists, historians, economists, literary critics, or magazine editors, they succeeded in translating their fields of expertise into a form of general communication; they used the language of their disciplines to address the most important issues of the war years and the postwar era.

My book, therefore, is not meant to be a comprehensive survey of American culture in the 1940s and 1950s. I make no effort to treat literature, the arts, music, religion, methodological schisms within university departments, mass circulation magazines and newspapers, or the fluctuations in public taste and opinion. Still, because I think the intellectuals in this book did focus on the central problems of modern American life, the strengths and deficiencies of their analyses may serve as a measure of how effectively or how poorly the nation adapted to a new age. So though I chose to write only about intellectuals, I found myself inevitably writing about larger cultural and social developments as well.

Like their fellow citizens, American intellectuals confronted a series of crises for which their prior experiences furnished few guidelines. In the space of twenty years, they had to deal with the military and technological impact of a second global war that in its ferocity and destructiveness far outdistanced World War I, with a tenuous peace that rapidly disintegrated into an interminable political and ideological conflict between the United States and the Soviet Union, with a cascade of investigations into "subversive" influences in every area of domestic life, and with the complex and contradictory effects of an unprecedented and apparently permanent prosperity.

But the intellectuals brought to this turbulence a special set of memories and assumptions. Although they did not constitute a single or unified generation, some having risen to prominence in the midst of the Depression while the rest launched their careers during or after the war, they all shared a disenchantment with the political and cultural radicalism of the 1930s together with the felt need to ask new questions about and explore the new tensions of a "postindustrial" society. Thus their work was suffused with the conviction that the troubles of the postwar years were very different from those of the past. Whether they concentrated on the specter of totalitarianism abroad or the centralization of power at home, whether they sought to redefine or move beyond the perceptions and programs traditionally associated with liberalism, whether they scrutinized the role of the mass media or the monotony of modern work or the emptiness of life in suburbia or the failures of education or the pressures of conformity, they insisted on the uniqueness of their concerns if not the originality of their arguments.

Because of these suppositions, they neither proposed nor trusted any sweeping solutions to the difficulties of their time. At most, they urged their contemporaries to resist wherever possible the seductive blandishments of the state, the bureaucracies, the media, and the organizations for which almost everyone now labored. In this way, they hoped the citizen might assert his individuality and protect his freedom within the constraints of the existing social order.

Such precepts hardly amounted to a grand or utopian vision of the future. Yet they unexpectedly created the vocabulary and the mental framework with which the next generation of Americans assaulted the nation's political institutions and social values in the 1960s. Inadvertently and often unhappily, the postwar intellectuals became the parents and teachers—literally and spiritually—of the New Left, the partisans of the counterculture, the civil rights activists, and the movement to end the conflagration in Vietnam. And just as inadvertently, though less unhappily, they introduced in the 1950s the attitudes that informed the rhetoric of neoconservatism in the 1970s and 1980s. Their significance, then, lies as much in their legacy to their successors as in the issues they raised in their own era.

In the course of these pages, I am frequently skeptical about their ideas and positions. I believe that many of them were too eager to embrace established political and economic practices, too reluctant to reevaluate the diplomacy of the Cold War, too enamored with the role of leaders and experts, too cooperative with McCarthyism, and too obsessed with the psychological and moral agonies of the middle class—a preoccupation that led them to neglect the systemic diseases of urban decay, racism, and poverty.

But I also admire enormously much of what they said. I consider them neither complacent nor mean-spirited defenders of the status quo. On the contrary, because of their hostility to and liberation from the ideological dogmas of the prewar Left, their preference for asking questions instead of inventing answers, and their desire to act as free-floating intellectuals rather than as spokesmen for a mass movement, I think they offered more provocative and imaginative criticisms of their society than one can find in the manifestos of either the 1930s or the 1960s. Indeed, I regard Hannah Arendt's *The Origins of Totalitarianism,* David Riesman's *The Lonely Crowd,* William Whyte's *The Organization Man,* John Kenneth Galbraith's *The Affluent Society,* Paul Goodman's *Growing Up Absurd,* Daniel Bell's "Work and Its Discontents," Dwight Macdonald's *Against the American Grain,* Louis Hartz's *The Liberal Tradition in America,* Daniel Boorstin's *The Image,* and C. Wright Mills's *The Power Elite* as superior in quality to any comparable collection of works produced in America during other periods of the twentieth century. Consequently, those of us who came afterward remain in their debt even as we try to transcend their perspective. . . .

One of the major consequences of America's postwar prosperity was that writers turned their attention to the social predicaments of the middle class. Their interest in the subject was not unprecedented. During the Progressive era, journalists, social critics, academics, and city planners had sought to reform the urban-industrial environment on behalf of the native bourgeoisie. The crusade against political machines, the exposés of graft and corruption, the desire to "Americanize" the immigrants as swiftly as possible were all motivated by the assumption that middle-class values ought to guide national policy. After World War I, the enlightened burgher cherished by the Progressives became in the minds of the expatriates a Philistine and a Babbitt from whom they could only flee in disgust. Still, the novelists and intellectuals of the 1920s retained their fascination with the middle class; for all their scorn, they sometimes seemed unable to write about anything else. The Depression encouraged the Left to hope that the middle class might join with the workers and the poor—if not for a revolution, then at least for a New Deal. Indeed, the history of radicalism in the 1930s, particularly during the height of the Popular Front, might be viewed as a case study of how socialist ideas in the United States were gradually diluted to fit the tastes and aspirations of the bourgeoisie. In each of these episodes, the middle class served as a symbol for whatever the intellectuals at any moment admired, courted, or despised.

By the 1950s, however, the middle class was less a repository for political or artistic fantasies than an inescapable presence in American life. The signs of its dominance were everywhere. . . .

For intellectuals in the postwar years, there were no longer any shelters from the middle class. One could hardly sustain the illusion that the man in the gray flannel suit was a reformer or an incipient revolutionary. Nor could writers depart for bohemia; the price of a picturesque cottage in Provincetown or on Martha's Vineyard was now exorbitant, the reigning spirit of Greenwich Village seemed ever more commercial, and the United States was successfully exporting both its products and its culture to Europe. Under these conditions, the intellectual had no choice but to confront the problems of the American middle class as harbingers of the fate toward which the entire world was apparently hurtling.

The compulsion to scrutinize the attitudes and life-styles of the bourgeoisie led intellectuals in the 1950s to markedly different conclusions from those of their predecessors in the 1920s. Nearly every observer in each decade grumbled about the political passivity of the middle class, its avoidance of social causes, its fear of public controversy, and its preoccupation with personal gain. Yet where these complaints gave writers in the 1920s a justification for satire and flight, some commentators in the 1950s suspected that political apathy was a mask for private discontent. In a wealthy society, overt ideological and social quarrels rarely erupted; class antagonisms remained muted; the real difficulties of life were minimized or ignored in the electoral campaigns. But this did not mean that America was a land without strain, unresolved conflicts, or nagging frustrations.

In fact, several writers besides Dwight Macdonald recognized that the central issues of the 1950s had to be addressed in novel ways, that one could not expect political parties or mass movements to express much dissatisfaction in a time of breathtaking prosperity. "Almost all the problems that were once called 'political,' " a contributor to *Commentary* remarked, "now belong to a different context, psychological, sociological, and cultural." At the end of *Political Man,* Seymour Lipset acknowledged that his title might well be inappropriate: "Since domestic politics, even liberal and socialist politics, can no longer serve as the arena for serious criticism from the left, many intellectuals have turned from a basic concern with the political and economic systems to criticism of other sections of the basic culture of American society, particularly of elements which cannot be dealt with politically." Thus some of the most characteristic essays and books of the postwar years— Dwight Macdonald's *Against the American Grain,* Mary McCarthy's *On the Contrary,* Daniel Bell's "Work and Its Discontents," Norman Mailer's "The White Negro," Paul Goodman's *Growing Up Absurd,* Clement Greenberg's *Art and Culture,* Robert Warshow's *The Immediate Experience,* Daniel Boorstin's *The Image,* William Whyte's *The Organization Man,* David Riesman's *The Lonely Crowd* and *Individualism Reconsidered,* C. Wright Mills's *White Collar* and *The Power Elite*—concentrated less on the plight of the disadvantaged or the programs of various administrations than on the psychological, moral, and cultural tensions plaguing the middle class.

From one point of view, these writers' disinterest in the details of political and economic policy seemed another example of the intellectual community's unwillingness to engage in a systematic critique of postwar America. Yet seen from another perspective, their lack of curiosity about legislative proposals and their relative indifference to presidential campaigns freed them to examine for the first time the dilemmas of a postindustrial society. Since they believed (like the rest of their contemporaries) that the tasks of capital accumulation, economic development, and modernization had all been completed, since they supposed that the historic afflictions of hunger and poverty were being eradicated, they could contemplate those problems that had no obvious institutional solutions.

Liberated from the assumptions of the 1930s, many intellectuals in the 1950s attacked the social order not because it was politically unjust or economically oppressive, but because it seemed impersonal, bureaucratic, and inhumane. No longer awaiting the inevitable collapse of capitalism or the revolutionary fury of the working class, they began to assess the moral impact of mass consumption and material success. Less haunted than the prewar generation by the specters of unemployment and economic disintegration, they evaluated the uses of leisure time, the manipulative effects of advertising and popular culture, the quality of human relationships in an age of affluence. Frightened by the totalitarian implications of state ownership and centralized planning boards, they explored the sense of powerlessness and alienation felt by the ordinary citizen whose voice was never heard at the highest levels of government.

Given their trust in the permanence of prosperity, they considered it more urgent at present to study the plight of the privileged than to catalogue the hardships of the poor. Accordingly, they analyzed the monotony of factory labor and white-collar office work, the middle-class yearning for comfort and security rather than adventure and risk, the emptiness of life in modern suburbia, the traumas of adolescence, the absorption of the individual into a mass society.

Above all, having rejected the notion that political ideologies and organized social movements would provide some form of salvation for themselves and their society, the postwar intellectuals reemphasized the virtues of privacy and personal fulfillment. Where the search for community had captured the imagination of the Left in the 1930s, the search for identity inspired the writers and artists of the 1950s. Where social critics had once insisted on the need for collective action, they now urged the individual to resist the pressures of conformity.

Such concerns indicated how far writers had journeyed from the ideas of Marx to those of Tocqueville, Sartre, and Freud. In their eyes, the contemporary obsession with status and prestige had replaced the traditional issues of class and property. Opinion molders and tastemakers seemed more powerful than the men who owned the means of production. The possession of great wealth appeared less significant than the ability to make the crucial decisions about war and peace. The primary danger was no longer social inequality but standardization and uniformity, not economic exploitation but the moral consequences of abundance.

These were not the sorts of problems that liberal reformers or socialist theoreticians could readily address. Yet as a result of having jettisoned the ideals and commitments of the 1930s, some intellectuals in the 1950s were able to offer a profound and far-reaching indictment of modern American life, often more challenging and provocative than anything found in the social thought of the Depression years. Writers like Dwight Macdonald, Paul Goodman, Normal Mailer, Mary McCarthy, Daniel Bell, Clement Greenberg, Daniel Boorstin, William Whyte, David Riesman, and C. Wright Mills continued to function as critics, persisting in the quest for alternative values if not for alternative institutions. Although they had ceased (apart from Mills) to be "radical" about political or economic affairs, they remained subversive on questions of culture and society.

And they left a legacy for the future. In their works, one discovered a country filled with paradox and potential discord. Here was a population choking on material goods but vaguely uneasy about its addiction to consumerism, a thoroughly urban civilization whose most respectable inhabitants scampered to the suburbs to evade the deterioration and eventual collapse of their most spectacular cities, an opulent and highly mobile nation with large segments of its citizenry still imprisoned in poverty and ghettos, a middle-class society whose children resigned themselves without enthusiasm to their prospects inside the giant corporations and bureaucracies that dominated the economy, an apolitical and inward-looking people whose government harbored global ambitions beyond the influence or control of the average voter.

This was a portrait of America that could have radical implications in another time and under other circumstances. Indeed, most of the moral and cultural quandaries depicted in the articles and books of the postwar intellectuals were transmitted intact to the 1960s. But in the following decade these no longer seemed the subtle contradictions of an economically stable if emotionally insecure nation. Rather, they were at the heart of the political and social crises ripping the country apart. And they shaped the perspective of people too young to have experienced the strains and ambivalences of the postwar years. So, far from being part of a silent generation of complacent apologists, the writers of the 1950s became (whether they wished to or not) the prophets of rebellion and the sires of the New Left. . . .

Eventually, most intellectuals who tried to maintain their critical perspective faced a frustrating dilemma. Since they assumed that prosperity was a permanent feature of American life, and that pragmatic reforms were preferable to ideological strife, they doubted the likelihood of and necessity for a radical transformation of the nation's political and economic institutions. But they could not ignore the psychological and cultural costs of middle-class affluence, or the moral compromises involved in the individual's readiness to embrace the attitudes and expectations of his peers. So while they accepted the basic structure of society, they believed that the private citizen must somehow resist the enticements of material comfort and the pressures to conform.

Two writers, William Whyte and David Riesman, were especially alert to the tension between the American's desire to fit in and his occasional impulse to rebel. Hoping to resolve this conflict, they sought to revive neither the individualism of the nineteenth century nor the collectivism of the 1930s. Instead, they explored the possibilities of personal freedom *within* the existing social order. Because of the questions they raised, the answers they offered, and the phrases they introduced into the national lexicon, Whyte's *The Organization Man* (1956) and Riesman's *The Lonely Crowd* (1950) emerged as the decade's classic critiques of American society.

William Whyte was not a typical member of the postwar intellectual community. Although he grew up during the Depression, he graduated from Princeton—a few miles away yet a world apart from the doctrinal clashes that kept the young revolutionaries at CCNY in tumult. After the war, Whyte found a home not with the little magazines or in the universities, but at *Fortune* magazine. While a number of other writers labored at various times for Henry Luce (Dwight Macdonald, James Agee, John Hersey, John Kenneth Galbraith, Daniel Bell), they looked upon their journalistic interludes as incidental to their main pursuits. Whyte remained a correspondent and an editor for most of his career. *The Organization Man* began as a series of articles for *Fortune,* and its success derived as much from its reportorial style and wit as from its sociological insights. Whyte skillfully blended interviews, anecdotes, autobiographical vignettes, generalizations about American history and culture, and personal commentary. In these respects, *The Organization Man* was a precursor of the next decade's "new journalism."

Whyte also differed from his contemporaries in forswearing any radical or satiric intent. Where many intellectuals represented themselves as critics of American life, even when they sprinkled their works with plaudits for the political and economic system, Whyte denied that his book was a "plea for nonconformity" or a "censure of the fact of organization society." The reader would be spared the usual "strictures against ranch wagons, or television sets, or gray flannel suits." Nor did Whyte have in mind a "paradise lost," an "idyllic eighteenth century" in contrast with a "dehumanized twentieth." Actually, he thought there was much to be said in favor of social cooperation, shared responsibilities and the benevolence of modern institutions—particularly when compared to the exploitation and poverty of the past.

Despite these disclaimers, Whyte's discussion of the large corporations, the governmental bureaucracies, the multiversities, and suburbia was about as nonjudgmental as Thorstein Veblen's insistence that "conspicuous consumption" should be taken as a neutral term with no invidious connotations. Whyte did refrain from denouncing the political and economic implications of concentrated power, but this freed him to focus on what he regarded as an equally important issue: "the personal impact that organization life has had on the individuals within it." It was exactly this preoccupation with the psychological effects of organizational values on the middle class that made Whyte's portrait so unflattering—and therefore so central to the critical outlook of the 1950s.

Perhaps the element in Whyte's book that seemed most characteristic of the postwar mood was his barely concealed antagonism to the collectivist sentiments of the 1930s. From the opening pages, he complained about America's recent conversion from the Protestant ethic to a "social ethic": the "belief in the group as the source of creativity"; the notion that "belongingness" was the "ultimate need of the individual"; the conviction that each person

could feel worthwhile only when he restrained his ego and collabo-
rated with his peers in some common enterprise. According to this
credo, public agreement, psychological adjustment, and a sense of
"total integration" with others were the goals toward which everyone thought they must strive; disorganization, conflict, tension,
fluidity, "solitary and selfish contemplation," were the "evils from
which man should be insulated." Ideally, no fundamental disputes
between the citizen and society ought ever arise, merely "misun-
derstandings" or "breakdowns in communication." In the end, as
Whyte described it, the group was supposed to bring out the best
in the individual; when people worked together, they could produce a "combustion of ideas" and a consensus on the proper "lines
of action" beyond the capabilities of anyone thinking or struggling
alone. This philosophy first sprouted in the Depression years as a
radical alternative to the capitalist emphasis on competition and
personal gain. But to its postwar proponents—bureaucrats, business executives, personnel experts, senior partners of law firms,
university administrators, consultants to foundations—the social
ethic had become in Whyte's opinion a rationale for conformity
and conservatism.

The social ethic also furnished the ideological impetus for the
emergence of organization men as the "dominant members of our
society." These were not ordinary white-collar employees who toiled
sullenly in offices and department stores, Whyte cautioned, but middle-class professionals who identified completely with the purposes
of the government agency, the corporation, the bank, the hospital or
private clinic, the Wall Street law factory, the aerospace contractor,
the military, the trade union, the church hierarchy. In short, they
were the bulwarks of "our great self-perpetuating institutions"; it
was their values that now shaped the "American temper."

Whyte's depiction of the organization man's mentality,
though couched in dispassionate prose, could hardly have been
more biting. The new functionaries, he charged, cared less about
their own creativity than about supervising the work of their subordinates. Concentrating almost exclusively on the "personality relationships within the group," they preferred cooperation to open
rivalry, managerial efficiency to disruptive debate, the "practical
team-player" to the eccentric genius, getting along with others to
getting ahead. On all occasions, company loyalty mattered more

than displays of imagination, curiosity, or independence. In Whyte's view, the supreme objective of the well-rounded organization man was not to rise to the top but to remain in the middle—to be "obtrusive in no particular, excessive in no zeal." And at the end of the day, unwinding on the commuter train or navigating the freeway to suburbia, the organization man dreamed not about wealth but about job security and the "good life." Nevertheless, it was the firm, rather than the suburb, that gave him a stable home and a feeling of having "roots" in a nation where everyone seemed on the move.

At times, Whyte abandoned his impartial pose and attacked both the premises and the consequences of the social ethic. Deriding the "wishful vision of total harmony now being touted," he argued that a "conflict of allegiances" between one's private aspirations and the "demands of the system" was natural and essential. In fact, the current hostility within the organization to strong, assertive personalities, the suspicion of "anyone who has ideas of his own or who differs with others on basic policy," the reliance on staffs and committees to cobble together compromise proposals, all appeared "more repressive" to creative thinking and personal freedom than the decrees of an authoritarian chairman of the board. The individual soon discovered that it was his "moral duty" to participate in joint activities, however much he might feel "imprisoned in brotherhood." On balance, Whyte began to appreciate the old-fashioned boss: "What he wanted primarily from you was your sweat" whereas the organization asked for "your soul."

These compulsions were enormously difficult to combat. The organization, after all, was not malign or nakedly coercive. On the contrary, Whyte pointed out, its "very beneficence," the "democratic atmosphere" it cultivated, the comfort it offered in moments of personal distress, made the individual less able to "justify *to himself* a departure from its norm." The average citizen submitted voluntarily to the group; he internalized its attitudes; his tyranny was "self-imposed." Still, this form of intimidation seemed to Whyte and his contemporaries the most ominous result of the postwar affluence, and a forerunner of the totalitarian state of mind. As George Orwell had warned, when people deferred gratefully to their leaders, when they longed to be relieved of the burdens of choice, when they finally learned to love Big Brother, there was no hope for rebellion.

Whyte did not believe that the organization had yet evolved into an animal farm. But like most writers in the 1950s, he could imagine no movements or programs to challenge the established social arrangements. The modern organization, with all its pressures and constraints, was a necessary component of every advanced technological society, and was obviously here to stay. So for Whyte the crucial problem lay not in America's institutions but in people's blind "worship" of organizational values—particularly the elevation of the social ethic into a religion of human behavior. Since the fault rested with attitudes rather than structures, Whyte concluded that the individual would have to reassess his own commitments to the organization before any other changes could occur.

Given his pessimism about the chances of altering the procedures or spirit of the organization, Whyte limited himself to analyzing the ways in which the individual might broaden his freedom within the perimeters of collective work. One need not be entirely subservient to the group. The key to personal liberation, Whyte declared, was to *understand* rather than to deify the organization. The individual must recognize the existence of options, and demonstrate his independence whenever feasible. He also had to grasp the differences between altruism and conformity, agreement and capitulation. Once he attained this higher consciousness, he could fight his peers without sounding stupid or self-destructive. In extreme situations, Whyte noted, the individual's capacity to "champion the unpopular view" depended psychologically on his willingness to move from one firm to another. But absolute freedom was an illusion. Most of the time, others would determine the contours of one's life. In Whyte's estimation, each person could control his destiny only to the extent that he realized when to cooperate with and when to resist whatever organization he presently served.

This was hardly an expansive conception of human liberty, much less a call to arms. Whyte pictured the successful American (typically a chief executive rather than a middle-level manager) as resourceful, moderately ambitious, sensitive to the disparity between his inner drives and the requirements of the organization, aloof from his peers and indifferent to their code of good-fellowship yet adept at office politics, inclined to take only those risks whose consequences he had calculated in advance, fully capable of manipulating the system to his own advantage but always careful to play by the rules of the game. Rarely faced with a genuine crisis of integrity, Whyte's hero knew how to survive and prosper inside the narrow boundaries of his bureaucratic world.

Whyte clearly implied that it was all right for the individual to deceive his colleagues so long as he remained true to himself. Assuming that the essential framework of the modern organization remained intact, the conduct Whyte urged might seem morally ambiguous but it was certainly realistic. The more troubling dilemma was whether Whyte's recommendations really aided the individual at all, or only the institutions for which he worked.

Sometimes Whyte suggested that, the issue of personal freedom aside, organizations themselves would improve if they adopted his advice. The primary defect of the social ethic, he observed, was its refusal to see that the individual's isolation from and disagreements with the group might "eventually discharge the greater service" to society. The nonconformist actually helped the community remember its nobler ideals; he was the devil's advocate, infuriating his fellow citizens for their own good. Similarly, the executive's readiness to resign from his current post not only increased his leverage over his peers, but also ensured that corporate policy would never become too "static" or complacent. Whyte's disparagement of business schools followed the same logic. The interests of the organization could be more effectively promoted if universities did not give their students a specialty or practical instruction in how to handle other people, but instead provided better training in the "fundamental disciplines." This in turn would guarantee a steady flow of graduates who valued basic research, original ideas, and unorthodox opinions, rather than companionship, conferences, and teamwork. In the long run, Whyte hinted, everyone would benefit: The individual could fulfill his potential while the organization grew more productive.

Still, despite the ambivalence of his arguments, Whyte wanted to strengthen the individual's ability to question the organizational mystique. If people were aware of and utilized their opportunities for dissent, they might at times transcend both the organization and the social ethic. Beyond this, Whyte would not go. For him, and for other intellectuals in the 1950s, outright rebellion was pointless. The best one could do was bend (though not surrender) to the demands of a managerial society, hoping to preserve some small areas of privacy and self-respect in the bargain. . . .

The most unsatisfying feature of *The Lonely Crowd* and *The Organization Man* was how sketchily each author resolved the problems his book raised. Aside from a phrase here, a metaphor there, an afterthought somewhere else, neither Riesman nor Whyte devoted much space to outlining in any detail the strategies by which conformity could be overcome. But they were not alone in this respect; the same haste in suggesting alternatives to the present social arrangements was evident in the work of Richard Hofstadter, Louis Hartz, Dwight Macdonald, Daniel Bell, Daniel Boorstin, and Paul Goodman. Having discarded the "smelly orthodoxies" of the 1930s, suspicious even of the search for certitude, many intellectuals in the 1950s were more interested in posing questions, pursuing new fields of inquiry, and offering tentative hypotheses than in describing with ideological assurance or theoretical clarity what a different America might look like in the future.

These predilections underscored the dramatic reversal of those ideas associated with the Depression years. Reading Whyte or Riesman, one sensed a profound shift in language, or in the connotations assigned to the same words. What the writers of the 1930s called "community," the postwar intelligentsia labeled "conformity." Cooperation now became "other-direction"; social consciousness had turned into "groupism"; solidarity with others implied an invasion of privacy; "collectivism" ushered in a "mass society"; ideology translated into imagery; economic exploitation yielded to bureaucratic manipulation; the radical activist was just another organization man.

The change in vocabulary indicated a change in orientation as well. The intellectuals of the 1950s had transferred their attention from the substance of politics to styles of behavior, from the sharecropper to the suburbanite, from labor to leisure, from "conditions" to consciousness, from revolution to resistance.

Behind this new rhetoric and outlook lay a new set of values. The planned, orderly, equitable nation envisioned by the Old Left gave way to an admiration for any signs of marginality, eccentricity, self-expression, and private indifference to public life. Alienation was no longer a problem to be surmounted, but a virtue to be nourished. The individual had to free himself, not from the chains of capitalism, but from the smothering embrace of "other people."

It is easy to see the limitations of this perspective. By minimizing the need for alterations in America's political and economic institutions, by insisting that the country's most serious predicaments were cultural and psychological, by focusing almost exclusively on the possibilities of inner rejuvenation in an otherwise stable society, the majority of postwar intellectuals had obscured the links between the social order and personal discontent. One seldom encountered in their books and essays the suggestion that the psyche of the organization man could not be remodeled without restructuring the organization itself, that the number of "autonomous" individuals might multiply only when they could affect the policies of those in power, that true freedom consisted not merely in making choices but also in the choices made.

Yet whatever the weaknesses in their analyses, writers like Whyte and Riesman were neither conservative nor complacent. Their attack on conformity contained radical implications from which they drew back because the one alternative theory they could imagine—socialism—seemed responsible for the very collectivist attitudes they condemned. But in their willingness to raise questions without supplying answers, in their critique of the quality of middle-class life, in their efforts to encourage self-awareness and higher forms of consciousness, and in their appreciation for individual resistance and dissent, Whyte and Riesman (as well as Macdonald and Goodman, Bell and Boorstin, Hartz and Galbraith) were challenging the official tenets of the 1950s and articulating many of the issues that would galvanize the young in the following decade.

Peter Biskind

PODS AND BLOBS

Movies inevitably reflect the concerns of a society. Peter Biskind, a film critic, contends that real insight into the America of the 1950s comes not from overtly ideological films, which failed to please either the public or critics, or from the major movies of the decade. His book *Seeing Is Believing* focuses on what he describes as "everyday" films. Biskind argues that genre films, such as westerns and science fiction movies, reflected concerns about the cold war, the red scare, conformity, minorities, gender roles, delinquency, and sex. Like many other observers, Biskind posits a fundamental change from the 1930s, when an alliance of the left faced off against an alliance of the right. In the fifties, liberals and conservatives made common cause against extremes of the left and the right. This corporate liberal alliance dominated politics, intellectual discourse, and films of the fifties. In the excerpt below, Biskind deals with two well-known science fiction films from the first half of the decade.

When Ben Peterson (James Whitmore), a New Mexico state trooper, comes across a little girl wandering around in the desert, clutching a doll to her chest in Gordon Douglas's *Them!* (1954), he knows there's something amiss. "Look, she's in shock," he says, and sure enough, she is. Her dad has just been killed and their trailer squashed like a beer can. The sides are caved in, the interior is a mess, and curiouser and curiouser, there are sugar cubes strewn about the ground, not to mention strange tracks in the sand. Pretty soon the scene of the crime is crawling with fingerprinters and police photographers, but no one can make head or tail of the sugar cubes, tracks, and above all, the peculiar high-pitched ringing sound that fills the air with a maddening throb. No money has been taken, and the whole thing "doesn't make sense," as one cop says to another. Indeed, the police procedure seems completely inappropriate. As in *12 Angry Men* and *Panic in the Streets*, reality

The advertising poster for the movie *Them!* (1954).

defies common sense; this is clearly a job for experts, not professionals; docs, not cops.

Later, we find out that the culprits were oversized ants who have a correspondingly lusty appetite for sweets, and that the destruction of the trailer was incidental; it happened while they were rummaging around for sugar, which they love more than life itself. But what may not have been so incidental is the identity of the little girl's dad, the ants' first victim: he was an FBI agent on vacation. The ants, in other words, spawned in the desert of the Southwest, have struck at J. Edgar Hoover's G-men, agents of the federal authority from the East.

Them! goes on to build this whisper of regional rivalry into a structural contrast by cutting between shots of desert locales, with the ants wreaking havoc and spilling sugar every which way, and shots of Washington, D.C. When the dry, dusty landscape of the Southwest fades away and the U.S. Capitol Building, lit up like a Christmas tree on a dark Washington night, fades in, we breathe a sigh of relief. We know that once the authorities in Washington are alerted to the danger, everything will be under control. In other words, if the threat arises in New Mexico, strikes at Washington through the death of the FBI agent, and then against Los Angeles, a major urban center, the solution moves from the national to local. When the time comes to declare martial law, and the words we have been waiting for boom out over the loudspeakers—"Your personal safety and the safety of the entire city depend on your full cooperation with the military authorities"—we know it's true. People in the street after the curfew are subject to arrest by the MPs, but we don't care. After all, it's a national emergency. *Them!* has effectively established the legitimacy of state power.

The federal government in Washington responds to the crisis by dispatching Dr. and Pat Medford (Edmund Gwenn and Joan Weldon), a father/daughter team of "myrmecologists" from the U.S. Department of Agriculture, . . . a general, and an FBI agent named Robert Graham (James Arness) bringing up the rear. Although the national elite, the coalition of the center, runs the show, it does not sweep aside local authority, but works through it, forming an alliance with Ben Peterson, the state trooper. He becomes the agent of the federal government within the local community. Federal interests are administered, mediated by local officials.

It is the scientists who have pride of place. Dr. Medford is a benign, avuncular fellow, a far cry from the demented Thorkels of yesteryear. Although he wonders what God hath wrought ("We may be witnessing a biblical prophecy come true. . . . The beasts will reign over the earth"), he also knows that the test tube is mightier than the cross, and that once again, if it was science (in this case nuclear testing) that had caused the problem, science would solve it too.

Them! reflects the new prestige of science by placing scientists at the center of world-shaking events. Dr. Medford meets with the president, lectures top public officials, and is able to command the full resources of the state. In the same way that the mayor in *Panic* had to take orders from Dr. Reed, so here the general has to take orders from Dr. Medford. In fact, he flies Medford around in his Air Force plane like a chauffeur, and Pat Medford observes, "It's like a scientist's dream." Poor agent Graham complains that the scientists are keeping him in the dark and won't tell him their theory. "We're on this case, too," he says plaintively. The cachet of science is so great that it even seems to upset the traditional hierarchy of sex roles. When the men get ready to climb down into the ants' nest, Pat Medford wants to go along. "It's no place for you or any other woman," says agent Graham manfully, but she puts up a fight. "Somebody with scientific knowledge, a trained observer, has to go," she says, and not only does she have her way, she takes over, ordering the men to torch the queen's chamber. Far from resisting her power, agent Graham falls in love with her, raising the prospect that the alliance between science and the military, or, in this case, the law, will be ratified by marriage.

Often, in films like *Them!*, the military was not able to use its big guns because it was fighting on its own turf. Even the army, eager to bomb the ants in the desert, hesitated to nuke Los Angeles, so that the search for the appropriate weapon, more discriminating and selective than the H-bomb, became a major theme in corporate-liberal sci-fi, a distant echo of the fight within the defense establishment over big bombs or tactical nuclear weapons. The search for a flexible, limited response to the alien threat reflected corporate liberals' uneasiness with the all-or-nothing strategy of massive retaliation championed by conservatives like Dulles. In *Them!*, the appropriate weapon is gas, not guns; in *The Beginning of the End,* it is sound, not bombs, a sonar imitation of the grasshoppers' mating call, that lures them to a watery death in Lake Michigan.

While the scientists and soldiers were quarreling among themselves over the appropriate weapon, another group of scientists and soldiers was having its own troubles up north, in Howard Hawks's *The Thing* (1951). This film was based on a 1938 novella called *Who Goes There?* by John W. Campbell. Like *Them!*, *The Thing* is not only preoccupied with hierarchies of authority, the authority of groups, and groups in conflict, but also with the struggle between science and the military, and the nature of aliens. *The Thing,* however, is a conservative film, and so the outcome of these conflicts is somewhat different.

When Air Force Capt. Pat Hendry (Kenneth Tobey) arrives in a remote Arctic outpost of scientists to help them investigate a strange item buried in the ice, he finds an enormous object apparently shaped like a frying pan. His men fan out around it and quickly find that they have made a circle. "We found a flying saucer," someone shouts, and indeed they have. "This isn't any metal I know," says another, examining a fin protruding from the ice.

But Hendry's problems are just beginning, because it seems that the passenger aboard the saucer has survived; it is the Thing-from-Another-World, as the ads put it, and it lives on blood. As if this weren't bad enough, Hendry discovers that the head scientist at the base, Nobel Prize-winner Dr. Carrington (Robert Cornthwaite), is almost as dangerous as the Thing. . . . We're tipped off right away by his goatee (facial hair in the fifties was about as popular as bad breath) and his Russian-style fur hat. When he's not wearing that, he's attired in a dressing gown and ascot, a thinking man's David Niven, out of place among the rough-and-tumble soldiers.

Carrington is no Medford. He's a borderline mad scientist, and in *The Thing* the tension between science and the military that was latent in *Them!* not only becomes much more pronounced, it is resolved in favor of the military. FBI agent Bob Graham complained in *Them!* that he couldn't understand the Medfords because they used too many big words ("Why don't we all talk English?" he says testily), but Graham was something of a clod anyway, and if he couldn't make out their technical lingo, it was probably his own fault. But when Captain Hendry asks a question and gets only mumbo jumbo in return, it's another matter. "You lost me," he says, and this time it's the scientists' fault, a symptom of technocratic arrogance. In *Them!*, Medford's admiration for the "wonderful and intricate engineering" of the ants' nest is reasonable, not unseemly or unpatriotic. But in *The Thing,* Dr. Carrington's scientific curiosity is given a sinister twist. He develops an altogether unhealthy interest in the Thing. "It's wiser than we are," he says. "If only we could communicate with it, we could learn secrets hidden from mankind." Whereas Medford merely restrains the military because he wants to find out if the queen is dead, Carrington betrays it, defecting to the Other side. He helps the Thing reproduce itself, finds a nice warm spot in the greenhouse for it to lay its spores, and even sabotages Hendry's attempts to kill it.

Carrington's scientific disinterest, which reflects the value-free pragmatism of the corporate liberals, is regarded as appeasement. "There are no enemies in science, only phenomena to be studied," he says, but he's wrong. There are no neutrals. When he rushes up to the Thing, alien groupie that he is, crying "I'm your friend," it swats him aside like a fly. The enemy is remorseless and cruel; negotiations with it are useless, and those who try are self-deceiving at best. Carrington is an unreliable element—private, moody, reclusive. He's soft on aliens, a Thing-symp, the J. Robert Oppenheimer of the Arctic base. The genial scientist and expert of *Them!* is transformed into an extremist "egghead," a head-over-heart zealot, a man who can't be trusted because "he doesn't think like we do," a man who has contempt for the average and is therefore dangerous. Unlike Dr. Medford, Carrington is derided as a genius or superman. "These geniuses," says Hendry with contempt. "They're just like nine-year-olds playing with a new fire engine." Carrington's behavior justifies the soldiers' mistrust of science, even turns them against the Bomb itself. "Knowledge is more important than life. We split the atom," Carrington shouts in a transport of enthusiasm. "That sure made everybody happy," comes the sour reply from one of Hendry's men.

But even here, science is by no means rejected wholesale. There are good scientists as well as bad, Tellers as well as Oppenheimers, and the difference between them is that the good scientists side with and defer to Hendry, instead of Carrington. Carrington's real crime, that is to say, worse than consorting with the enemy, is setting his own authority against that of the military. . . . Hendry's appearance at the base signals a change in command like the ones in *Twelve O'Clock High* and *Flying Leathernecks,* and the figurative one in *Clementine.* When he first arrives, he is warned that he is treading on alien territory. "Dr. Carrington is in charge here," says one of the scientists. Hendry's job is to seize control of the base and assert the authority of the soldiers over the scientists. Eventually confined to his quarters, Carrington shouts, . . . "You have no authority here," but when one of Hendry's men pokes a revolver in his face, Carrington learns that power grows out of the barrel of a gun.

And what about the people, the average Joes and plain Janes who are neither scientists nor soldiers? In *Them!,* it seems that they are almost as much of a problem as the ants themselves. They spend most of their time in films like this fleeing for their lives, obstructing the best efforts of the government to save them from themselves. Occasionally they pause long enough to riot, destroying valuable scientific equipment or medical supplies. Since the people are helpless to help themselves, the war against the ants has to be carried on by experts behind closed doors. In one scene, pilot Fess Parker, who has seen a queen in flight winging her way west to Los Angeles, has been thrown into a loony bin. The doctors and the local authorities, who have been kept in the dark by the scientists and soldiers, think he's crazy. When agent Graham questions him, it becomes clear that he isn't nuts—the pilot did see the flying queen—but nevertheless, he is not vindicated, as he would be in a radical film. On the contrary, Graham tells the doctors to keep him locked up in the hospital, his therapeutic prison: "Your government would appreciate it if you kept him here." Reporters . . . threaten official secrecy. Like their readers, they have to be kept in the dark. "Do you think all this hush-hush is necessary?" someone asks Dr. Medford. "I certainly do," he replies. "I don't think there's a police force in the world that could handle the panic of the people if they found out what the situation is." When it's no longer possible to cover up the facts, and the ants are strolling down Sunset Boulevard, the mayor of Los Angeles finally calls a press conference, but "there is no time for questions."

There is bad blood between the authorities and the press in *The Thing* too, but this conflict is resolved differently than it is in *Them!* A nosy reporter named Scotty (Douglas Spencer) realizes there's a big story afoot, and he wants to tag along. "This is Air Force information," says Hendry, refusing to let Scotty near the saucer. "The whole world wants to know," replies Scotty, sketching in the Big Picture for Hendry. But here, Big Picture-ism fails. "I work for the Air Force, not the world," snaps Hendry, voicing the conservative preference for the concrete and local over the abstract and general. But instead of the reporter being thrown in jail, an amiable arrangement is reached. Scotty is allowed to accompany Hendry to the Arctic base in exchange for agreeing to withhold the story until he gets permission from the authorities to release it. And at the end of the film, when he does tell part of the story in a broadcast to the world, he is allowed to speak for everyone, Hendry and Carrington, the soldiers and the scientists. As the voice of the center, he goes out of his way to pay special tribute to Carrington (who by this time has learned his lesson), papering over the differences that factionalized the group. . . . Once again, the center closes ranks before the world.

Scotty can be accommodated more easily than the reporters in . . . *Them!*, because *The Thing* is more populist. Within the community of soldiers and scientists at the base, relationships are more egalitarian than they are in similar communities in corporate-liberal films. When Tex, one of Hendry's men, enters a room and sees the group mobilizing against the Thing, he quips, "What's up? It looks like a lynching party." In corporate-liberal films that regard people acting on their own as mobs or would-be vigilantes, it would be; here, it's not. Hendry may give the orders, but a number of ideas bearing on the disposal of the Thing originate with others, are adopted by Hendry, and ultimately work. Even the best lines of what for sci-fi is an unusually talky script (by Charles Lederer) are democratically distributed among the officers, noncoms, civilians, and (one) woman alike. There is a good deal of overlapping dialogue; people continually interrupt one another with wisecracks and good-natured insults. There is a real sense of community, of people engaged in a common effort, which nevertheless doesn't prevent them from expressing their individuality.

If people in *Them!* obstruct authority, authority in *The Thing* frustrates people. The conflict between soldiers and scientists is complemented by another, this one between Hendry, his superior officer General Fogarty in Anchorage, and the brass back in Washington. Hendry begins his odyssey as the perfect Air Force organization man. He can't blow his nose without clearing it first with headquarters. Not only won't he allow Scotty to wire his paper without authorization from Fogarty, but Fogarty himself has to refer back to Washington. "That's what I like about the Air Force," quips Scotty, "smart all the way to the top."

The critique of bureaucracy, an obligatory preoccupation of conservative films, is given some new twists in science fiction. The absurdity of "going by the book," the limitations of "standard operating procedure," are never more apparent than when you're dealing with flying saucers and little green men. When Hendry goes by the book, it's a recipe for disaster. Using standard operating procedure to free the saucer from the ice, he accidentally blows it up with thermite. The film is filled with jokes about military bureaucracy. As the men stare at the frozen saucer, someone recalls that the Air Force dismissed UFOs as "a mild form of mass hysteria," but in *The Thing,* the masses aren't hysterical. On the contrary, the problem is the brass. Red tape, finally, immobilizes Hendry altogether. "Until I receive my instructions from my superior officers about what to do," he says, "we'll have to mark time."

When the orders finally do come, they are worthless. Although the Thing has been making Bloody Marys out of the boys at the base, Fogarty instructs Hendry to "avoid harming the alien at all costs.". . . Hendry is forced to disobey orders, even at the risk of court-martial. He can't go too far, like Carrington, but he has to do something, because the organization is out of touch with reality. And reality here is not national and abstract, but local and concrete. The problem has to be resolved on the spot. Like most conservative films, *The Thing* ultimately deals with the problem without calling in the federal government. The Thing is dispatched by means of a do-it-yourself electric chair, improvised out of the materials at hand. But what keeps this from being a right-wing execution is that although the men at the base do it themselves, they are still soldiers employed by the government, working ultimately in its interests. By this kind of sleight of hand, conservative films avoided having to make the either/or choice Whyte presented to his organization man. For all the ambivalence *The Thing* expresses toward the Air Force, Hendry's rebellion . . . is confined to the parameters of the organization. He remains an Air Force man to the last.

What about the Thing itself, and the ants? What do they "represent"? First, on a level so obvious that it is usually ignored, the ants represent an attack by nature on culture. Nature, for all mankind's technological expertise, is still a threat, red in tooth and claw. But the anthropomorphic gravity of American films is so strong that they have difficulty dramatizing genuine otherness. Aliens, no matter how seemingly strange and exotic, end up resembling humans in one way or another. It would be hard to imagine anything more Other than, say, giant ants, until Dr. Medford explains that "ants are savage, ruthless, and courageous fighters. They are the only creatures on earth aside from man who make war. Ants campaign, they are chronic aggressors, they make slaves of those they can't kill." In other words, the humans of *Them!* find that their adversaries are very much like Us.

If the ants are like humans, which humans are they like? In 1954, when *Them!* was made, those humans that Americans regarded as antlike, which is to say, behaved like a mass, loved war, and made slaves, were, of course, Communists, both the Yellow Hordes that had just swamped GIs with their human waves in Korea, and the Soviets, with their notorious slave-labor camps. Sci-fi films that presented Communists directly, like *Invasion U.S.A.* and *Red Planet Mars,* were rare. The analogy was usually oblique, but so close to the surface (in *The Naked Jungle,* also released in 1954, the ants that climbed all over Charlton Heston were actually red, and attacked private property to boot) as to be just below the level of consciousness. Presenting Reds as ants or aliens served to establish their Otherness. As Gerhart Niemeyer of Notre Dame put it, the Red mind "shares neither truth nor logic nor morality with the rest of mankind." They were *not* just like Us.

To corporate liberals, Russians in turn stood for the eruption of primitive aggressive behavior. Reds, in other words, were monsters from the id. If we press *Them!* a little further, it quickly becomes apparent that the ants are not only Reds, they're females. *Them!* has as much to do with the sex war as it does the cold war.

The film's attack on extremism becomes an attack on women in a man's world.

Centrist films, as we have seen, feared the eruption of nature within culture and were therefore afraid of sex and mistrusted women, particularly sexual women. . . .

Them! balances somewhat contradictory attitudes toward sex and sex roles. On the one hand, as we have seen, it explicitly presents an independent woman scientist, whose strong will prevails over agent Graham's this-is-no-place-for-a-woman conservatism. On the other hand, it implicitly presents, in slightly disguised form, a paranoid fantasy of a world dominated by predatory females. The ant society is, after all, a matriarchy presided over by a despotic queen. The queen, it seems, strikes only at patriarchy. Not only does she kill the male drones, but all her human victims are male (one man's phallic shotgun is bent like a paper clip), including two fathers. When the ants are finally cornered, they take cover in Los Angeles's womblike storm drains that conceal the queen's "egg chamber." "Burn 'em out," is the verdict of the male scientists and soldiers at the end of the film, as they perform a hysterectomy by flamethrower.

Them! examines on a fantasy level and on an apocalyptic scale what it leaves unexamined on the "realistic" level: the conflict between Pat Medford's independence and the chauvinism of the men. It conveys two complementary cautionary messages. To men the moral is: Better give an inch than lose a mile, better let Pat Medford assert herself, or face a far more serious challenge to male power in the future. To women: Don't be too assertive or you'll be punished for it. Centrist films often defined and negated the extremes, the limits of behavior, leaving it to the audience to negotiate an acceptable compromise within those limits.

Like *Them!*, *The Thing* in its most abstract aspect depicts nature's inhuman assault on civilization. The vast, bleak Arctic wastes play the same role here that the desert plays in *Them!* The film's final lines, the celebrated injunction to "watch the skies," ask us not only to fear that which comes from space, but space itself, absence, emptiness, the negation of culture. Like the expanse of ice, the sky is an image of Otherness, and that which is not-culture is dystopian. By contrast, enclosures, manufactured spaces, mean safety. The tiny Arctic base does not feel claustrophobic, nor is it experienced as a prison; rather it becomes a fortress of human warmth, albeit a fragile one, easily destroyed, like the trailer in *Them!*

Like the ants, the Thing bears multiple meanings. The Russians immediately come to mind. Hendry actually speculates early on that the puzzling occurrences in the Arctic "could be the Russians—they're all over the pole like flies." But Hendry finds out that the problem is *not* the Russians, but the Thing—or does he? What is the Thing? Despite the fact that it is apparently part of the natural world, more vegetable than mineral, the Thing is a robot. Some films rendered the distinction between nature and culture as one between animals and vegetables, where vegetables take on the characteristics usually associated with machines: they don't feel pain, have no emotions, and aren't retarded by moral scruples. In *Invasion of the Brain Eaters* (1958), for example, once the plantlike parasites have taken over, people become "like robots—machines taking orders." But the Thing, like the ants in *Them!*—like most film symbols—"depends on associations, not a consistent code," as critic Raymond Durgnat puts it. It slips and slides from one meaning to another. Although the Thing is supposed to be an entirely alien form of life, it looks like nothing more unusual than a large man. Which man is it like? Carrington, of course, the Thing's pal, the cold, unfeeling genius who is as superior to his colleagues as the Thing is smarter than garden-variety humans, and whose development has not been, as someone says of the Thing, "handicapped by emotional or sexual factors." (In one version of the script, Carrington is actually killed by the Thing, and Scotty says, "Both monsters are dead.") Carrington, as we have seen, is a pluralist mad scientist, but with his beard and Soviet-style fur hat, he is also a Russian, so we have come full circle. This film attacks pluralists by equating them with Reds. And if a film like *Them!*, through its linkage of nature, ants, women, and Russians, imagines Reds as monsters from the id, conservatives imagined them as emotionless veggies or robots, repressive, not eruptive. They represented reason run amok; they were monsters from the superego.

Finally, however, conservative films fell in line behind their corporate-liberal allies in time for the final fade-out. In *The Thing*, this means that although the blood-sucking carrot from another world is a head-over-heart veggie robot Red monster from the superego one minute, it is an extremist heart-over-head monster from the id the next.

When Hendry arrives at the Arctic base, before introducing himself to Carrington or investigating the strange "disturbances," he makes straight for the only woman, Nikki Nicholson (Margaret Sheridan).* First things first. It seems that the two are romantically involved, although Nikki is piqued because, on their last date, Hendry got drunk and took liberties. "You had moments of making like an octopus," she tells him. "I've never seen so many hands in all my life." If the head can get out of hand, hands can lose their heads, and Hendry has to learn to keep his to himself. "You can tie my hands, if you want to," he suggests, and in a bizarre scene, she does just that. As he sits in a chair, his hands safely tied behind his back, she pours a drink down his throat and then kisses him on the lips. In other words, she has to emasculate and infantilize him before he can become a safe and acceptable suitor. But the joke is on her. His hands aren't tied after all; he's just pretending, and at the end of the scene, he flings off the ropes and grabs her. Cut directly to a large block of ice bound with rope, just like Hendry. Inside the ice is the Thing, just as inside Hendry is the id. The ice accidentally melts, and the Thing gets loose, in the same way that Hendry escapes Nikki's bonds. At the end of the film, when the Thing is destroyed, the monster from Hendry's id is symbolically subdued, clearing the way for the union of Hendry and Nikki. The extremes of head (Carrington) and heart (Hendry's id), culture and nature, both represented by the Thing, have given way, once again, to the golden mean. But the denouement is a characteristically conservative one. As in *Forbidden Planet*, force, not therapy, is the solution to the problems of the self.

This confusing plurality of meanings is at least in part an expression of the center's inclination to reconcile contradictions, to be all things to all people. Conservative films, as we have seen, were torn between extremists on their right and corporate liberals

---

*Women in centrist sci-fi often had masculine names, like Nikki, here; Pat *(Them!)*; Steve *(Tarantula)*; and Terry. They were just one of the boys, part of the male group that restrained the monster from the id. Pat Medford, we recall, leads the expedition to torch the queen's egg chamber.

on their left. They fought against and borrowed from both in an attempt to achieve their own distinctive equilibrium. Both *Them!* and *The Thing* want soldiers and scientists to work together. The differences between the two films are those of emphasis. Each, in a slightly different way, equated the cold war with the sex war, politics with personality, the Russians with the id or superego or both. Each implied that not only did the Soviets pose an external threat and, worse, an internal one through unreliable, wrong-thinking elements like Carrington, but worst of all, they penetrated our very selves. We were all potentially extremists inside. As Schlesinger put it, "There is a Hitler, a Stalin in every breast."

VI

American Society
in the 1950s

An American family watches television. The prosperity of the 1950s enabled families to acquire television sets even more quickly than they had acquired radios in the 1920s. By 1956, 81% of American families had television. (Corbis-Bettman)

J. Ronald Oakley

GOOD TIMES: THE AMERICAN ECONOMY IN THE FIFTIES

J. Ronald Oakley's book *God's Country* presents an overview of America in the 1950s. In the following chapter Oakley, a professor of history at Davidson County Community College, discusses the American economy. His mention of conglomerates fails to note the distinguishing features of such organizations or the significance of the emergence of that business structure in the 1950s. Conglomerates are large corporations that engage in a variety of unrelated enterprises. In theory, at least, their diversity makes conglomerates less subject to the impact of economic downturns; if business is bad in one sector, conglomerates may compensate by doing well in another sector. In addition, conglomerates allow corporations to expand without bumping up against antitrust regulations. At the end of the chapter, Oakley attempts to assess the nature of the prosperity of the fifties. Despite the persistence of poverty and discrimination, most Americans were better off; as a group, they had a higher standard of living than any previous generation.

In the 1950s the United States enjoyed a period of unprecedented prosperity, consumerism, and economic optimism. Signs of the new prosperity were everywhere. At the middle of the decade, the United States, with 6 percent of the world's population and 7 percent of the area, produced almost half of the world's manufactured products and contained within its borders 75 percent of the automobiles, 60 percent of the telephones, and 30 percent of the televisions and radios. Not surprisingly, it also consumed almost half of the world's annual production of energy, 50 percent of the copper, 33 percent of the tin, 60 percent of the aluminum, and 65 percent of the newsprint. During the decade the Gross National Product climbed from $285 billion to $500 billion, per capita income rose by 48 percent, the median family income rose from $3,083 to

Reprinted from *God's Country: America in the Fifties* by J. Ronald Oakley. Copyright © 1986 by J. Ronald Oakley. Published by arrangement with Barricade Books, Inc., New York.

$5,657, and in spite of the inflation of the Korean War years, real wages rose by almost 30 percent. The number of stockholders jumped from 6.5 million in 1952 to almost 17 million by the early 1960s, and in that same time it was proudly pointed out that the number of millionaires rose from around 27,000 to almost 80,000. Although unemployment was a periodic problem and reached a decade high of 7.5 percent in 1958, the expanding economy continued to create jobs in record numbers: In 1960, when the unemployment rate was 6 percent, the number of working Americans had risen to a record level of 66.5 million.

No wonder many economists were declaring that the nation had become a great worker's paradise in which the old problems of poverty and inequality had been largely solved and superseded by the new, happy problem of what to do with the abundance of consumer goods that were pouring from the factories and farms. No wonder economists rhapsodized about "the affluent society," the "new era of capitalism," and the new "people's capitalism"—in America it was proudly proclaimed, everybody was a capitalist. Never, it seemed, had so many had it so good, and never had so many expected it to get better. To many observers of the American scene, the old adage, "The poor will always be with us," was a thing of the past. . . .

What were the causes of this prosperity? It was partly due to the consumer spending generated by the savings and deferred demand of the Second World War, when workers saved $150 billion that they would spend in the late 1940s and early 1950s. It was partly caused by the rapid population growth, which greatly expanded the market for homes, furniture, and goods and services for the growing army of young people. It was partly fed by the easy credit policies of banks, other lending institutions, and retail stores, which made it possible, even easy, to buy today and pay tomorrow. It was partly caused by increased productivity due to the introduction of computers, automation, and other labor-saving devices. It was promoted by the federal government, which pumped money into the economy through its welfare programs, subsidies for farmers, foreign-aid programs, and perhaps most of all, through its defense spending, which between 1946 and 1960 totaled over $500 billion and accounted for, on the average, about 10 percent of the annual GNP. By 1960, national defense and veterans' benefits had climbed to $51.3 billion, 55.6 percent of total federal spending, and 10.2 percent of the annual GNP. . . .

America's economic growth in the 1950s was also aided by an inexpensive, plentiful, and uninterrupted supply of energy. At the beginning of the decade, Eugene Holman, the president of Standard Oil, said that "I don't believe we'll run out of oil in the near or the foreseeable future" and predicted that oil reserves and new processes "will provide our requirements for hundreds of years." This optimistic assessment of energy supplies, made at a time when the nation exported oil and controlled, along with its European allies, most of the world's oil fields, prevailed throughout the decade. The nation went on an energy binge, as Americans filled their homes with new appliances, bought millions of big, gas-guzzling automobiles (averaging 12.7 miles per gallon), and turned away from coal to the more convenient fuel oil and natural gas to heat their homes and run their rapidly expanding industries. Energy use expanded by more than 30 percent during the decade. Gasoline use for passenger cars rose from 25 billion gallons of fuel in 1950 to 42 billion in 1960. In 1955 the country consumed, for the first time in its history, more energy than it produced, and by 1960 was importing 1.8 million barrels of oil a day, 19 percent of all domestic consumption. . . .

The prosperity of the decade was also promoted by a phenomenal rise in advertising—in fact, the economic health of the nation in the fifties was more dependent upon advertising than in any previous period in its history. Continuing a trend begun in the 1920s, the economy moved steadily away from a production economy trying to provide the basic needs of society to a consumption economy in which the essentials had already been met and emphasis was placed on consuming more and more luxury items. It was inevitable that the economy would become more and more dependent on advertising. The consumer had to be persuaded to buy not just what he needed, but what he simply wanted or could be convinced that he needed or wanted. As part of this convincing process, the amount of money spent on advertising was more than doubled during the decade, rising from about $6 billion in 1950 to $9 billion in 1955 and $13 billion in 1963. . . .

By stimulating consumption, Madison Avenue helped promote the rise of a credit society. So did the federal government's

Federal Reserve policies and low interest rates for GI housing, retail establishments' convenient charge plans, and the rise of credit card companies. The credit card business began in 1950 with the introduction of the Diner's Club card, which was initially honored only in a few restaurants in New York City but soon spread nationwide, rising to 750,000 card holders in 1958. The Diner's Club card had more holders than any other credit card in the 1950s, though the American Express card, founded in the mid-1950s, trailed not too far behind. Oil companies, motel and hotel chains, and many other companies introduced credit cards in the 1950s as well. Private debt jumped from $73 billion in 1950 to over $196 billion in 1960 as Americans used credit cards and easy installment plans to buy consumer goods, take vacations, and enjoy other pleasures of life offered by the prosperity of the time. By the middle of the decade, 60 percent of all new automobiles were bought on credit, often for as little as $100 down, and by 1960 over 10 million credit customers were shopping at Sears. Many older people, remembering the depression and other hard times of the past, were amazed at how easily and eagerly younger couples incurred thousands of dollars of debt in their search for the good life. A whole new type of consumer psychology was taking root in prosperous America.

The American economic system was not just growing, it was also undergoing some dramatic transformations. Some older industries—such as mining, iron and steel, lumber, textiles, and leather products—were declining or entering periods of slow growth, primarily because of the boom in synthetic products that had been stimulated by the Second World War. The plastics industry grew by 600 percent in the fifties, as chemical industries turned out a wide variety of plastics to take the place of wood, glass, and metals, and man-made fibers like rayon, Orlon, Dacron, and nylon to take the place of wool, cotton, linen, and silk. The electronics industry, also stimulated by the war, grew to become the nation's fifth largest industry (behind automobiles, steel, aircraft, and chemicals) as it tried to meet the demand for television, radios, hifis, tape recorders, home appliances, computers, testing and measuring devices for automation, and sophisticated controls for the complicated weaponry being purchased by the Defense Department. As another mark of the affluent age, it is not surprising that the automotive, home building, and oil and gas industries also grew rapidly in the fifties.

American capitalism was also moving into a new sophisticated era in industrial techniques, research, and information processing. Automation, viewed by more and more industries as a way to boost productivity and cut labor costs, spread rapidly, especially in the chemical, petroleum, automotive, and aircraft industries. Many of these same industries were also turning to the rapidly expanding field of research and development, for the economy was becoming too complex to depend on individual inventors or thinkers or even on small laboratories for new ideas and inventions. Between 1953 and 1964 the amount of money poured into research and development increased by 400 percent, and by the midfifties over 3,000 companies had established research facilities employing a total of almost a half million workers. As might be expected, the largest single funder of research and development was the federal government, which dispensed billions to universities and private think tanks all over the country in an effort to defeat the Russians in the race for development of destructive weapons. The advance of both automation and research and development was aided by the electronic computer, invented during World War II but not commercially marketed until the fifties. As late as 1954 the annual sales of these electronic marvels stood at only 20, but the number jumped to over 1,000 in 1957, over 2,000 in 1960, and over 3,000 in 1961. By the late fifties the computer was already being hailed as a revolutionary breakthrough in the processing and storage of information and as an essential tool for the functioning of complex industrial societies, though its major impact would not come until the 1970s and 1980s.

One of the most significant of all changes occurring in the economy was the rapid growth in the number, size, and power of the large corporations, which, in spite of sporadic governmental attempts at trust busting, had been on the rise ever since the time of their founding in the late nineteenth century. During the fifties the nation's economy became dominated by an economic oligarchy. Some 3,404 smaller companies were absorbed by about 500 larger ones, and by the end of the decade some 600 corporations, representing only one half of 1 percent of all corporations, were responsible for 53 percent of all corporate income, while the 200 largest corporations controlled over 50 percent of all the nation's business assets. The three major automakers produced 95 percent of all new cars, the three major aluminum companies provided 90 percent of all the aluminum, ten aircraft corporations employed 94 percent of all aircraft workers, and similar concentrations of production and workers could be found in the petroleum, steel, tire, office machine, and cigarette industries. Many of the conglomerates were international companies, with plants, investments, and workers all over the world and with annual budgets rivaling or surpassing those of many of the world's smaller countries. All of this was done with the tacit approval of the Department of Justice. . . . It was also done with the help of Congress, which promoted corporate profits and growth through generous tax policies on capital gains and depreciation and depletion allowances. In 1957, Humble Oil Company paid only $17 million on a pretax income of $193 million, and in some years some giant corporations paid no taxes at all.

The rise of the giant corporations had a profound effect on American life. A few hundred corporations controlled much of the nation's industrial and commercial assets and enjoyed a near monopoly in some areas. They dominated the seats of economic and political power. They employed millions of workers, a large percentage of whom populated the suburbs that were growing all across America and were helping to transform the country. They promoted a rise in the wage level, helped to make the middle class the largest class in the country, and helped to fight discrimination by adopting hiring practices that were often far ahead of smaller companies. Although their motives were self-serving, their foundations and other forms of charitable activities benefited many communities, organizations, and individuals. And finally, their recruitment and training of the much discussed "organization men" played a major role in the promotion of the conformity that characterized much of American life during the decade.

The changing American economy also experienced dramatic shifts in the composition of the work force. Fewer workers went into traditional fields such as manufacturing, agriculture, and mining, and more went into clerical, managerial, professional, and service fields. In 1956, for the first time in the nation's history, white collar workers outnumbered blue collar ones, and by the end of the decade blue collar workers constituted only 45 percent of the work force. The sexual composition of the work force also changed as more and more women entered the labor market. The influx of women into the work world that had been accelerated by the Second World War continued in the postwar period. By 1950, 16.5 million women were working outside the home, and by the end of 1956 this figure had grown to 22 million, almost a third of the labor force. For both sexes, the dramatic postwar rise in white collar jobs, wages, and college opportunities brought increased possibilities for entering the steadily widening middle class, which was enjoying the prosperity of the fifties and helping to mold the views, values, ideals, and beliefs of that decade. Most surveys showed that some 75 percent of adult Americans considered themselves part of the middle class, lending credence to the growing belief that the nation was becoming one large, prosperous, harmonious middle class.

The shifts in the composition of the work force inevitably affected the fortunes of organized labor. After making tremendous gains in the New Deal and World War II era, organized labor continued to prosper in the fifties, but it seemed to lose much of its vitality and public support. The labor movement was hurt by the changing economy, which was producing fewer jobs in manufacturing, where labor had always been the strongest, and more jobs in the white collar and service sectors, where labor generally made little headway. The labor movement also continued to suffer from antagonistic employers (especially in the South), right-to-work laws and other hostile state enactments, its own antagonism toward female and black workers, the Taft–Hartley Act (which, among other provisions, prohibited the closed shop), and occasional attempts by the government to ferret out supposed communists in unions. Finally, it was hurt by widespread charges of corruption and racketeering involving its leaders, allegations that eventually led in the late fifties to televised hearings of congressional investigating committees, the expulsion of the Teamsters Union from the AFL-CIO (united in 1955), the conviction and imprisonment of Teamster president Dave Beck, the investigation of James Hoffa and other labor leaders, and the passage in Congress of the Landrum–Griffin Act aimed at curbing union activity. . . .

Because of these problems, the number of unionized workers rose only from 14.3 million at the end of the Second World War to 18.5 million in 1957, then declined to around 17 million by the end of the decade. Big labor presented no real threat to big business's control of the economy or to the election or reelection of Eisenhower. In the probusiness atmosphere of the time, labor successfully concentrated on seeking improvements in wages (including a guaranteed annual wage and cost-of-living increases in the automotive industry), pensions, insurance, vacations, sick leave, and other fringe benefits. There were protracted strikes, like the steelworkers' strikes under Truman and again under Eisenhower in 1955 and 1959, but there were no big, pitched battles like those of earlier years. Generally relations were good between labor and management. Most labor leaders were highly paid executives who dressed and lived much like the managers they bargained with and were as conservative as Eisenhower Republicans on most political issues. Unions were strongly anticommunist and antisocialist, still discriminated against blacks and women, and generally opposed the civil rights movement and other emerging social causes of the fifties. . . .

Still another economic area undergoing vast changes was agriculture. From 1950 to 1960 agricultural productivity increased by over a third through the use of mechanization, better management, electrification, and the greater use of fertilizers and pesticides produced by the growing biochemical industry. As a result, the United States was in an unprecedented agricultural position, one that made her the envy of much of the rest of the world and would have been undreamed of by people of centuries past. The basic agricultural problem of the United States in the fifties was not how to relieve the scarcity of food, but what to do with all the agricultural surpluses that were piling up and how to arrest the corresponding drop in prices that was hurting so many farmers. Eisenhower dealt with the problems by establishing a flexible government price-support program, inaugurating a soil bank program that paid farmers for not growing food on a certain portion of their land, and shipping surpluses to schools, the military, and to people overseas in the form of charity, disaster relief, and foreign aid. Still, the surpluses accumulated, causing a decline in prices and serious political problems for the president who had entered office with hopes of returning agriculture to the free-market system. Like Roosevelt and Truman before him, Eisenhower never found the key to solving the problems of agricultural abundance.

These agricultural developments were bringing vast changes to the American farm belt. The number of farms declined from 6 million at the end of the Second World War to 3.9 million in 1960, and the number of farmers dropped from over 31 million (25 percent of the population) in 1939 to only 13.7 million (7.1 percent of the population) in the early 1960s. In the 1950s alone, the farm population declined by 17 percent, as 1.4 million people left the farms each year seeking better jobs in the city. More and more small farms disappeared, and farming became a big business run by farmers knowledgeable in the ways of modern business and technology. The average acreage of farms grew from 191 in 1945 to 297 in 1960, while the number of people one farmer could feed rose from 14.6 to 25.8. Those who remained on the farm steadily became more like urban dwellers, as the extension of roads, television, and electricity into rural areas ended the historical isolation of farmers and their differences from city dwellers.

What were Americans doing with their newfound prosperity in a land that was producing over half of the world's manufactured products? They bought automobiles, on the order of 5 to 7 million a year. They also bought new houses. By 1960 there were almost 10 million more homeowners than there had been in 1950, 58 percent of all nonfarm families owned their own homes, and 25 percent of all the nation's homes had been built in the previous ten years. . . .

Americans filled the insides of their homes with all the labor-saving appliances and gadgets they could afford to buy with cash or credit. By 1959, 98 percent of electrically wired homes had a refrigerator, 90 percent had a television, 93 percent had an electric washing machine, 37 percent had a vacuum cleaner, 22 percent had a freezer, 18 percent had an electric or gas dryer, and 13 percent had an air-conditioner. . . . In 1954, in "The Pushbutton Way to Leisure," *House and Garden* used pictures and text to rhapsodize about eighteen new or relatively new devices that were making life more convenient for Americans. "These 18 mechanical servants work part-or-full time," it wrote, and "combine the talents of caretaker, gardener, cook, maid." Among the eighteen servants were electric serving carts to keep food hot, electric dishwashers, automatic incinerators "far more reliable than the local trash collector," food freezers that were the "next best thing to a cook in the kitchen," washers and dryers to "do all the blue jeans, bed linens and beach towels you can toss into them," electric blenders "so easy to operate that children can have a soda fountain at home," automatic coffee percolators, electric lawn trimmers, baby tractors for lawn and garden work, and portable barbecues.

It seemed in the midfifties that convenience products were flooding the market. In 1956, in an article lauding the new products of the previous ten years, *Newsweek* marveled that "hundreds of brand-new goods have become commonplace overnight: TV and hi-fi, frozen, low-calorie, and instant foods, aerosol containers and electronic garbage disposals, power steering and power transmission, the entire field of synthetic chemistry—from plastic squeeze bottles to synthetic textiles." Some consumers had trouble accepting the new products—many were still wary of electric blankets, for example—but for most the biggest problem was not one of acceptance but of keeping the new products in good working order. Americans frequently complained of how often their new gadgets broke down and how difficult and expensive it was to get them repaired. In 1957, there were an estimated 1.8 million repairmen in the country doing $16.6 billion worth of business every year. One appliance that was never allowed to be out of order for long was the television; polls of the decade consistently showed that consumers would pay to have their television repaired even if they had to use rent or house payment money to pay for it. In 1956, television repairs cost some $2 billion, more than the total cost of all new sets sold that year.

Americans also spent more on foods, and as the decade progressed, more and more of it went into convenience foods like TV dinners, instant coffee, frozen orange juice, and frozen and canned foods. The growth of suburbia brought an explosion in outdoor barbecuing, creating a large market for barbecue grills, cooking utensils, beef, pork, poultry, soft drinks, beer, and potato chips. Hot dog production jumped from 750 million pounds in 1950 to 1,050 million pounds in 1960, while potato chip production rose from 320 million pounds to 532 million pounds in that same length of time. As the decade progressed, more and more food and other products were bought in convenient disposable packages. In 1960,

for example, the average American family discarded 750 cans. Affluent America was becoming a wasteful, throwaway society.

Americans also began to eat out more, both at traditional
restaurants and at the fast-food chains that sprang up across the
country in the second half of the decade. Hamburger and hot dog
eateries had long been part of the American scene, of course, and
even before the fifties began, a few entrepreneurs had built regional chains of fast-food restaurants. But a big change came in
1954 when Ray Kroc, a fifty-two-year-old businessman who had
been engaged in several business ventures over the years, paid the
McDonald brothers, Maurice and Richard, $2.7 million for the
franchise rights to their hamburger diner in San Bernardino, California. Kroc adapted and refined their very successful assembly-line
process for making hamburgers, and after opening his own first
diner, complete with the soon to be famous golden arches, in Des
Plaines, Illinois, in 1955, he established a chain of McDonald
restaurants, all offering a highly standardized burger that was 1.6
ounces in weight, 3.9 inches in diameter, and served on a 3.5-inch
wide bun with a quarter ounce of onions.

Each McDonald's featured well-dressed employees, clean
kitchens and rest rooms, standardized food, and standardized
prices. Recognizing that Americans were people on the move, that
they wanted a dependable and clean place to eat, and that a fortune
could be made from serving whole families, Kroc banned juke-
boxes, pinball machines, telephone booths, and other features that
would have made his restaurants teen hangouts. In the beginning
he even refused to hire young girls, fearing they would attract too
many teenage boys. The McDonald's restaurants spread rapidly all
across the country, and before the decade was out, in 1959, Kroc
opened his one-hundredth restaurant. At that time his famous
hamburger still sold for fifteen cents, just as it had under the
McDonald brothers and just as it would until 1967, when it went
to eighteen cents. In 1959 the average franchise grossed $204,000
a year, and all the restaurants combined had sold a total of 50 million burgers. Kroc's success spawned dozens of imitators, and fast-
food chains began to spread across the land.

The affluent nation spent millions on clothing, both for work
and school wear and for the faddish, casual clothing that was

becoming so popular in an age when large numbers of Americans had so much disposable income and so much leisure time. Over this ten-year period, women's clothes showed a wide range of styles: full skirts worn over crinolines, strapless evening gowns, A-line skirts, tube dresses, sack dresses, short shorts, two-piece bathing suits, bikinis, blue jeans, bobby sox, penny loafers, baggy and tight sweaters—just to mention a few. Some styles had a short life span—the sack dress (also called the chemise, the bag, the loose look, and the Moslem look) lasted less than a year before it was hung in the back of the closet, where, according to some critics, it looked far better on a rack than it ever had on a woman's body. And some fashions caused some women to run into legal problems. Short shorts, which became the rage among teenage girls and even older women in 1956, were widely applauded by males, but in White Plains, New York, and a few other cities women were occasionally fined for violating "indecent exposure" laws. In Southampton, Long Island, several women were fined $10 for violating an ordinance declaring that "no person shall walk or ride in any vehicle upon or along the public streets . . . in any bathing suit, shorts, trunks, or other apparel which does not cover properly the body and limbs from midway between the knees and hips to and including the shoulders."

Clothes for men, who in the past were restricted by convention and designers to drab styles, showed a greater variety than ever before. Conservative types still wore gray flannel suits, blue pinstripes, or tweeds to the office, but more and more men were wearing bolder clothing to work and acquiring a large leisure wardrobe that they often wore to work as well. There was an almost endless range of clothing to fit every age, need, and pocketbook: colorful (even checkered) sports jackets, tuxedos (now in red, yellow, blue, and other colors), white and colored dress shirts, sports and dress shirts with button-down collars, dress shirts with large French cuffs, polo shirts with a crocodile insignia stitched on the breast (given a big sales boost when Eisenhower showed up at the golf course wearing such a shirt), oversize Madras plaid sport shirts, gaudy Hawaiian sports shirts like those sported by President Truman on his vacations, baggy pegged pants, rogue trousers with a white side stripe, slacks with a belt in the back, Bermuda shorts of all colors, canvas shoes, car coats, mohair alpaca sweaters, wing tip shoes, Bass Weejuns, sports caps with a buckle in the back, blue jeans, and leather jackets. In 1955, the male species stunned the world—and perhaps himself—by emerging dressed in pink—pink shirts, Bermuda shorts, slacks, and colonel string ties. Whether he was in the office, in the classroom, or on a motorcycle with the rest of the gang, the male in the fifties came out in all his sartorial splendor.

For both sexes, the trend was toward the casual, convenient, and colorful. In the midfifties, for example, men were buying fewer suits and more separates (different colored slacks and sports coats), 8 million sports jackets (ten times the number they had in the early forties), 62 million pairs of slacks (about five times what they had in the early forties), and 60 percent more sports shirts than dress shirts. Reflecting on these figures, social critic Russell Lynes said that "one would think from this that American men did nothing but hang around country clubs." . . . As the decade progressed, more and more of the clothing for both sexes was made from the increasing number of synthetic fibers bearing labels promising that they would "drip dry" and required "little or no ironing."

One of the central elements of the prosperity of the fifties was the automobile, which Americans bought in record numbers. Spurred by the growth of the population, suburbs, disposable incomes, easy credit, and advertising, annual sales of passenger cars rose steadily from 6.7 million in 1950 to a record 7.9 million in 1955, then hovered around 5 to 6 million for the rest of the decade. Nearly 58 million automobiles were manufactured during the decade. By 1960, 80 percent of American families owned at least one automobile, and the number of families owning two or more had grown to 15 percent. There were more automobiles in Los Angeles County alone that year than in all of South America or Asia. . . .

Meanwhile, a network of good roads was being built throughout the country as the nation went on a road-building binge to handle the growing number of cars that were taking to the highways. Existing dirt roads were paved, new roads were constructed, thousands of miles of toll roads (like the 837-mile series of state turnpikes between New York and Chicago) were built, and the new Interstate system was initiated by the Eisenhower administration.

Eisenhower had mounted a strong campaign for federal development and partial financing of a nationwide network of modern four-lane roads to make travel easier and safer, to relieve traffic congestion on the open road and in the cities, to make the cities more accessible while permitting through traffic to bypass them, and to provide for the rapid mobilization of military troops and supplies and the evacuation of urban civilians during an atomic attack. Backed by almost everyone—the politicians, the military, city planners, truckers, oil companies, automakers, road builders, and drivers—the Interstate Highway Act of 1956 provided for the construction of 41,000 miles of freeways to be built over a ten-year period at a cost of $26 billion, to be shared by federal and state governments. It was the largest public works project in American history and the most ambitious road-building plan attempted since the 50,000-mile road system of the Roman Empire. Despite its size, few anticipated that a quarter of a century later the system would still not be completed and that costs would have risen to over $100 billion.

The national Interstate system, along with the toll roads and other road networks, made travel easier, safer, faster, and more convenient and helped to unify the nation as it had never been unified before. It accelerated the growth of the suburbs, contributed to urban flight and the decline of the inner city, accelerated the decline of the railroad and other forms of mass transit, contributed to atmospheric pollution and other environmental problems, and precluded the discussion and development of viable alternatives to the nation's transportation problems. The national Interstate system also committed the nation to a system of transportation based on the private automobile for traveling and on trucks for shipping. The automobile reigned supreme as it never had before, and the nation entered the 1960s with over 3 million miles of roads, almost three fourths of them paved. Total miles traveled by automobile, which had stood at 458 billion miles in 1950, had risen to 800 billion by 1963, when 90 percent of all travel between cities was by private automobile.

It would be difficult to exaggerate the importance of the automobile in the 1950s. It had become an integral part of American life by 1930, when there were some 26 million cars in the country, and the importance of it had steadily increased ever since then. By the early fifties, the automobile was directly or indirectly responsible for one sixth of the GNP, providing jobs for millions in the automotive manufacturing industry, the petroleum industry, all the many companies that made materials that went into the manufacture of new cars, the tourist and travel industry, service stations, drive-in movies and restaurants, advertising, repair shops, and highway construction and maintenance. The automobile was helping to bring rural areas into the mainstream of American life and, along with television and other technological advancements, was helping to make the United States a more homogeneous nation. It was contributing to the growth of suburbia, shopping centers, drive-in movies, drive-in banks, and fast-food chains. It was also promoting the decay of the metropolitan areas, the decline of railway passenger traffic, air pollution (smog was reaching dangerous levels in Los Angeles as early as the 1940s), and traffic jams, traffic accidents, and massive chain-reaction smashups—like the record seventy-four-vehicle collision in Los Angeles in 1955. Ironically, because of the congestion, new highways and powerful automotive engines did not always mean faster travel. Traffic jams in major cities became a way of life.

In spite of the disadvantages of the growth of an automotive society, the average American was convinced that his automobile was a part of his life that he could not live without. It gave him mobility, status, freedom, privacy, and the ability to get to his job and other destinations far easier than ever before. It allowed him to live outside the city while working inside and enjoying all the other amenities of city life without its problems. It made his life easier, more interesting, and more varied, opening up new places to go and new things to do. It was more important even than that other great necessity of the fifties, the television set. . . .

In their celebration of the heavenly benefits of American capitalism, the high priests of the prosperity of the fifties suffered from a severe case of economic myopia. In spite of the widening prosperity, the old inequalities in wealth remained. After all the economic gains of the decade, Americans entered the sixties with the top 1 percent of the population holding 33 percent of the national wealth, the top 5 percent holding 53 percent, and the top 20 percent holding 77 percent. The bottom 20 percent held only 5 percent of the wealth, about the same as at the end of the Second World War. Most Americans were better off than ever before, and the middle class was becoming the largest class, but a small group at the top still got the largest slice of the economic pie. In spite of all the talk about "people's capitalism," over half of Americans throughout the fifties had no savings accounts and over 96 percent held no corporate stock. The Rockefeller family alone owned more stock than all the nation's wage earners combined. There was also a stark contrast in income and life-style between the average American and the corporate rich, like the presidents of General Motors and Du Pont, making close to $500,000 a year in salaries and bonuses in the early fifties, and the board chairmen of the big oil companies with annual salaries between $175,000 and $250,000. The nation's wealthiest citizen, oilman J. Paul Getty, made close to a billion dollars in 1957 alone, yet throughout the decade was known to complain that "a billion dollars isn't what it used to be." Generous tax loopholes allowed wealthy Americans to keep much of what they made, leaving most of the national tax burden to the less fortunate members of the middle and lower classes. In 1959, five Americans with incomes over $5 million paid no taxes at all at a time when private and government studies were beginning to "discover" that millions of Americans lived in poverty.

Little attention was given to the poor in the fifties, but they were there. Poverty was a hard condition to define, but throughout the decade most governmental and private studies of poverty set the poverty-level income at $3,000 annually for a family of four and $4,000 for a family of six. Using these criteria, most studies of poverty showed that from 20 to 25 percent of the population lived in poverty, with perhaps another 10 percent living on the poverty line and struggling desperately to avoid falling below it. If these figures are correct, then in any given year in the fifties something like 40 to 50 million people lived on the edge of poverty or below it.

The existence of such chronic poverty in the midst of plenty was overlooked by most contemporary observers of the economic scene. One reason why it was overlooked was that most Americans believed that it was being eradicated by the prosperity of the times

and that soon everybody would become a full member of the affluent society. Another reason was that the poor were largely invisible
to those on the economic and social ladder above them and had no
influential spokesmen to plead their cause. The poor were the
blacks living in the core cities that most Americans were able to
avoid as they sped to other destinations on the new expressways
being built around the slums. They were the poor whites in the
troubled farming and mining industries in the isolated Appalachian
areas that stretched from Pennsylvania to Georgia. They were the
rural people of both races in the South, left behind by the others
who migrated to the North to escape the agricultural and industrial stagnation of these southern regions. They were minorities,
like the blacks in urban and rural areas in the North or South, the
Puerto Ricans who crowded into New York and other northern
cities in the post-World War II period, the Chicanos in rural and
urban areas in the Southwest, and the Indians living in squalid conditions on backward reservations or in urban slums. They were the
elderly, most of whom had nothing to fall back on after retirement
except Social Security checks that almost automatically put them
below the poverty line. And they were single, divorced, or wid-
owed mothers with dependent children.

Everyday, when they turned on their television sets, America's poor were reminded they lived in an affluent and consumer-
oriented society that had long ago passed the production levels required to meet the basic needs of its citizens and was now pouring
out a superabundance of consumer goods that added extras to life.
But every day their meager incomes reminded them that they were
not full participants in this affluent society—even as their expectations were being raised. It was true, as many analysts said, that
America's poor had higher living standards than most of the
world's population, an incontrovertible fact that led some defenders in Eisenhower's America to proclaim that the poor should be
grateful for what they had and should not complain. But the poor
judged their living standards by comparing them with those of
middle- and upper-class Americans, not to the peasants of Latin
America or China. It was inevitable that they should become envious, frustrated, and resentful. How envious, frustrated, and resentful would not become fully clear until the 1960s, but these feelings

existed long before poverty was publicized by Michael Harrington (in *The Other America*) and other social analysts.

But except for the poor, poverty was not an issue in the 1950s, and most Americans felt that the disparities in wealth were more than offset by the low unemployment rate (an average of 4.6 percent throughout the decade), the steady rise in real wages, the low inflation rate (an annual average of 1.5 percent during Eisenhower's two terms), and the plethora of consumer goods that rising wages and easy credit were enabling them to buy. Some economists were disturbed by the periodic recessions of the period and by the slow growth rate. The economy grew rapidly from 1950 to 1952 (spurred by the Korean War), slumped into a recession from 1953 to 1954, entered a period of rapid growth from 1954 through 1957, entered another recession in the middle of 1957 that lasted through the early part of 1958, and then picked up again in late 1958 and performed well until it lapsed into another recession in 1960. After an average annual growth rate of 4.3 percent between 1947 and 1952, the growth rate leveled off for the rest of the fifties and actually ended up with an annual average for the decade of only 2.9 percent, considerably below the 4.5 percent range for most years of the prosperous 1920s.

But poverty, periodic recessions, a slow growth rate, and other economic problems did not detract from the general public belief that the nation had never had it so good. More Americans were working than ever before, and the typical worker was drawing more pay, working fewer hours, and enjoying more of the necessities and luxuries of life than any generation of workers in American history. For white, middle-class males and their white, middle-class families, these were, indeed, good times.

Elaine Tyler May

COLD WAR—WARM HEARTH

Elaine Tyler May, a social historian and professor of American Studies at the University of Minnesota, examines the relationship between the cold war, domestic politics, and the emphasis on family and home so characteristic of the 1950s. May argues that in a tense international situation, made more dangerous by atomic weapons, and facing threats to individual identity from pressures to conform, young couples turned to family life for security and identity. She further argues that family life served to "contain" threats to social stability, much as the United States sought to contain the Soviet Union and the spread of communism. The nuclear family channeled potentially disruptive forces such as women's sexuality, greater educational opportunities for women, and widespread affluence into wholesome family life, rather than into decadence.

In the summer of 1959, a young couple married and spent their honeymoon in a bomb shelter. *Life* magazine featured the "sheltered honeymoon," with photographs of the duo smiling on their lawn, surrounded by canned goods and supplies. Another photo showed them descending twelve feet underground into the twenty-two-ton, eight-by-eleven-foot shelter of steel and concrete where they would spend the next two weeks. The article quipped that "fallout can be fun," and described the newlyweds' adventure—with obviously erotic undertones—as fourteen days of "unbroken togetherness." As the couple embarked on family life, all they had to enhance their honeymoon were some consumer goods, their sexuality, and total privacy. This is a powerful image of the nuclear family in the nuclear age: isolated, sexually charged, cushioned by abundance, and protected against impending doom by the wonders of modern technology.

Children engage in a "duck and cover" drill intended to prepare them for a nuclear attack. Fear of nuclear annihilation helped shape the attitudes of the baby boom generation. (© Sondak/FPG International)

The stunt itself was little more than a publicity device; yet seen in retrospect it takes on symbolic significance. For in the early years of the cold war, amid a world of uncertainties brought about by World War II and its aftermath, the home seemed to offer a secure, private nest removed from the dangers of the outside world. The message was ambivalent, however, for the family also seemed particularly vulnerable. It needed heavy protection against the intrusions of forces outside itself. The image of family togetherness within the safety of the thick-walled shelter may have been a reassuring one to Americans at the time, for along with prosperity, World War II left new unsettling realities in its wake. The self-contained home held out the promise of security in an insecure world. At the same time, it also offered a vision of abundance and fulfillment. As the cold war began, young postwar Americans were homeward bound.

Demographic indicators show that Americans were more eager than ever to establish families. The bomb-shelter honeymooners were part of a cohort of Americans who brought down the age at marriage for both men and women, and quickly brought the birth rate to a twentieth-century high after more than a hundred years of steady decline, producing the "baby boom." These young adults established a trend of early marriage and relatively large families that lasted for more than two decades and caused a major but temporary reversal of long-term demographic patterns. From the 1940s through the early 1960s, Americans married at a higher rate and at a younger age than their European counterparts. Less noted but equally significant, the men and women who formed families between 1940 and 1960 also reduced the divorce rate after a postwar peak; their marriages remained intact to a greater extent than did those of couples who married in earlier as well as later decades. Although the United States maintained its dubious distinction of having the highest divorce rate in the world, the temporary decline in divorce did not occur to the same extent in Europe. Contrary to fears of the experts, the roles of breadwinner and homemaker were not abandoned; they were embraced.

Why did postwar Americans turn to marriage and parenthood with such enthusiasm and commitment? Scholars and observers frequently point to the postwar family boom as the inevitable result of a return to peace and prosperity. They argue that depression-weary

Americans were eager to "return to normalcy" by turning the fruits of abundance toward home and hearth. There is, of course, some truth to this point; Americans were indeed eager to put the disruptions of hardship and war behind them. But prosperity followed other wars in our history, notably World War I, with no similar rush into marriage and childbearing. Peace and affluence alone are inadequate to explain the many complexities of the postwar domestic explosion. The demographic trends went far beyond what was expected from a return to peace. Indeed, nothing on the surface of postwar America explains the rush of young Americans into marriage, parenthood, and traditional gender roles.

It might have been otherwise. The depression had brought about widespread challenges to traditional gender roles that could have led to a restructured home. The war intensified these challenges, and pointed the way toward radical alterations in the institutions of work and family life. Wartime brought thousands of women into the paid labor force as men left to enter the armed forces. After the war, expanding job and educational opportunities, as well as the increasing availability of birth control, might well have led to delayed marriages, fewer children, or individuals opting out of family life altogether. Indeed, many moralists, social scientists, educators, and other professionals at the time feared that these changes would pose serious threats to the continuation of the American family. Yet the evidence overwhelmingly indicates that postwar American society experienced a surge in family life and a reaffirmation of domesticity resting on distinct roles for women and men in the home.

The rush began in the early 1940s and continued for two decades. But then it stopped. The family explosion represented a temporary disruption of long-term trends. . . .

Observers often point to the 1950s as the last gasp of time-honored family life before the sixties generation made a major break from the past. But the comparison is shortsighted. In many ways, the youth of the sixties resembled their grandparents more than they did their parents. Their grandparents had come of age in the first decades of the twentieth century; like many of their baby-boom grandchildren, they challenged the sexual norms of their day, pushed the divorce rate up and the birth rate down, and created a unique youth culture, complete with music, dancing, movies, and other new forms of urban amusements. They also behaved in similar ways politically, developing a powerful feminist movement, strong grass-roots activism on behalf of social justice, and a proliferation of radical movements to challenge the status quo. Against the backdrop of their grandparents, then, the baby boomers provide some historical continuity. The generation in between—with its strong domestic ideology, pervasive consensus politics, and peculiar demographic behavior—stands out as different.

It is important to note that observers normally explain the political activism and the demographic behavior of the baby-boom generation as the effects of affluence and the result of expanding opportunities for women in education and employment. Yet precisely those conditions obtained twenty years earlier, at the peak of the domestic revival. The circumstances are similar, yet the responses are quite different. What accounts for this time lag? How can we explain the endorsement of "traditional" family roles by young adults in the postwar years and the widespread challenge to those roles when their children, the baby boomers, came of age? Answering these questions requires entering the minds of the women and men who married and raised children during these years. The families they formed were shaped by the historical and political circumstances that framed their lives.

The context of the cold war points to previously unrecognized connections between political and familial values. Diplomatic historians paint one portrait of a world torn by strife, and a standoff between two superpowers who seem to hold the fate of the globe in their hands. Sociologists and demographers provide a different picture of a private world of affluence, suburban sprawl, and the baby boom. These visions rarely connect, and we are left with a peculiar notion of domestic tranquility in the midst of the cold war that has not been fully explained or fully challenged. In this exploration, public policy and political ideology are brought to bear on the study of private life, allowing us to see the family as existing within the larger political culture, not outside of it. The approach enables us to see the cold war ideology *and* the domestic revival as two sides of the same coin: postwar Americans' intense need to feel liberated from the past as well as secure in the future.

The power of this ideological duality, as well as its fundamental irony, are most apparent in the anti-Communist hysteria that swept the nation in the postwar years. It is well to recall that McCarthyism was directed against perceived internal dangers, not external enemies. The Soviet Union loomed in the distance as an abstract symbol of what we might become if we became "soft." Anti-Communist crusaders called upon Americans to strengthen their moral fiber in order to preserve both freedom and security. The paradox of anticommunism, however, was precisely in that double-edged goal, for the freedom of modern life itself seemed to undermine security. McCarthyism was fueled in large measure by suspicion of the new secularism, materialism, bureaucratic collectivism, and consumerism that represented not only the achievement but also the potential "decadence" of New Deal liberalism.

Cosmopolitan urban culture represented a threat to national security akin to the danger of communism itself; indeed, the two were often conflated in anti-Communist rhetoric. If American democracy resided in adherence to a deeply rooted work ethic tied to a belief in upward mobility as the reward for the frugal and virtuous, then the appeal of mass purchasing, sexual temptations in the world of amusements, and even the "cushion" of the welfare state could serve to unravel that essential virtue. Many feared that the restraints imposed by the watchful eyes of small-town neighbors would dissolve in the anonymous cities. The domestic ideology emerged as a buffer against those disturbing tendencies. Rootless Americans struggled against what they perceived as internal decay; the family seemed to offer a psychological fortress that would, presumably, protect them against themselves. Family life, bolstered by scientific expertise and wholesome abundance, might ward off the hazards of the age.

This challenge prompted Americans to create a family-centered culture that took shape in the early years of the cold war. This "cold war culture" was more than the internal reverberations of foreign policy, and it went beyond the explicit manifestations of anti-Communist hysteria such as McCarthyism and the Red Scare. It took shape amid the legacy of depression and war and the anxieties surrounding the development of atomic weapons. It reflected the aspirations as well as the fears of the era, as Americans faced the promises as well as the perils of postwar life. Prosperity had returned, but would there be a postwar slump that would lead to another depression, as there had been after World War I? Would men returning from war be able to find secure positions in the postwar economy? Women such as the proverbial "Rosie the Riveter" had proved themselves competent in previously all-male blue-collar jobs, but what would happen to their families if they continued to work? Science had brought us atomic energy, but would it ultimately serve humanity or destroy it? The family was at the center of these concerns, and the domestic ideology taking shape at the time provided a major response to them. The legendary fifties family, complete with appliances, a station wagon, a backyard bar-b-que, and tricycles scattered along the sidewalk, represented something new. It was not, as common wisdom tells us, the last gasp of "traditional" family life with roots deep in the past. Rather, it was the first wholehearted effort to create a home that would fulfill virtually all of its members' personal needs through an energized and expressive personal life.

One of the most explicit descriptions of this modern domestic ideal was articulated, significantly, by a major politician in an international forum at the peak of the cold war. In 1959, Vice-President Richard M. Nixon traveled to the Soviet Union to engage in what would become one of the most noted verbal sparring matches of the century. In a lengthy and often heated debate with Soviet premier Nikita Khrushchev at the opening of the American National Exhibition in Moscow, Nixon extolled the virtues of the American way of life, as his opponent promoted the Communist system. What is remarkable about this exchange is its focus. The two leaders did not discuss missiles, bombs, or even modes of government. Rather, they argued over the relative merits of American and Soviet washing machines, televisions, and electric ranges. According to the American vice-president, the essence of the good life provided by democracy was contained within the walls of the suburban home.

For Nixon, American superiority rested on a utopian ideal of the home, complete with modern appliances and distinct gender roles. He proclaimed that the "model home," with a male breadwinner and a full-time female homemaker, and adorned with a wide array of consumer goods, represented the essence of American freedom. Nixon insisted that American superiority in the cold war rested not on weapons but on the secure, abundant family life available in modern suburban homes, "within the price range of the average U.S. worker." Houses became almost sacred structures, adorned and worshiped by their inhabitants. Here women would achieve their glory, and men would display their success. Consumerism was not an end in itself, but rather the means for achieving a classless ideal of individuality, leisure, and upward mobility.

With such sentiments about gender and politics widely shared, Nixon's remarks in Moscow struck a responsive chord among Americans at the time. He returned from Moscow a national hero. The visit was hailed as a major political triumph; popular journals extolled his diplomatic skills in this face-to-face confrontation with the Russian leader. Many observers credit this trip with establishing Nixon's political future. Clearly, Americans did not find the kitchen debate trivial. The appliance-laden ranch-style home epitomized the expansive, secure life-style postwar Americans wanted. Within the protective walls of the modern home, worrisome developments like sexual liberalism, women's emancipation, and affluence would lead not to decadence but to wholesome family life. Sex would enhance marriage; emancipated women would professionalize homemaking; affluence would put an end to material deprivation. Suburbia would serve as a bulwark against communism and class conflict, for, according to the widely shared belief articulated by Nixon, it offered a piece of the American dream for everyone. Although Nixon vastly exaggerated the availability of the suburban home, one cannot deny the fact that he described a particular type of domestic life that had become a reality for many Americans, and a viable aspiration for many more.

What gave rise to the widespread endorsement of this familial consensus in the cold war era? The depression and war laid the foundations for a commitment to a stable home life, but they also opened the way for what might have become a radical restructuring of the family. The yearning for family stability gained momentum and reached fruition after the war; but the potential for restructuring did not. Instead, that potential withered, as a powerful ideology of domesticity became imprinted on the fabric of everyday life. Traditional gender roles revived just when they might have died a natural death, and became, ironically, a central feature of the "modern" middle-class home.

Since the 1960s, much attention has focused on the plight of women in the fifties. But at the time, critical observers of middle-class life considered homemakers to be emancipated and men to be oppressed. Much of the most insightful writing examined the dehumanizing situation that forced middle-class men, at least in their public roles, to be "other-directed" "organization men," caught in a mass, impersonal white-collar world. The loss of autonomy was real. As large corporations grew, swallowing smaller enterprises, the numbers of self-employed men in small businesses shrank dramatically. David Riesman recognized that the corporate structure forced middle-class men into deadening, highly structured peer interactions; he argued that only in the intimate aspects of life could a man truly be free. Industrial laborers were even less likely to derive intrinsic satisfactions from the job itself; blue-collar and white-collar employees shared a sense of alienation and subordination in the postwar corporate work force. Both Reisman and William Whyte saw the suburbs as extensions of the corporate world, with their emphasis on conformity. Yet at the same time, suburban home ownership and consumerism offered compensations for organized work life.

For women, who held jobs in greater numbers than ever before, employment was likely to be even more menial and subordinate. Surveys of full-time homemakers indicated that they appreciated their independence from supervision and control over their work, and had no desire to give up their autonomy in the home for wage labor. Educated middle-class women whose career opportunities were severely limited hoped that the home would become not a confining place of drudgery, but a liberating arena of fulfillment through professionalized homemaking, meaningful child-rearing, and satisfying sexuality.

While the home seemed to offer the best hope for freedom, it also appeared to be a fragile institution, in many ways subject to forces beyond its control. Economic hardship had torn families asunder, and war had scattered men far from home and thrust women into the public world of work. The postwar years did little to alleviate fears that similar disruptions might occur again. In spite of widespread affluence, many believed that reconversion to a peacetime economy would lead to another depression. Peace itself was also problematic, since international tension was a palpable reality. The explosion of the first atomic bombs over Hiroshima and Nagasaki marked not only the end of World War II but also the beginning of the cold war. At any moment, the cold war could turn hot. The policy of containment abroad faced its first major challenge in 1949 with the Chinese revolution. That same year, the Russians exploded their first atomic bomb. The nation was again jolted out of its sense of fragile security when the Korean War broke out in 1950, sending American men abroad to fight once again. Many shared President Truman's belief that World War III was at hand.

Insightful analysts of the nuclear age, such as Paul Boyer and Robert J. Lifton, have explored the psychic impact of the atomic bomb. Boyer's study of the first five years after Hiroshima shows that American responses went through dramatic shifts. Initial reactions juxtaposed the thrill of atomic empowerment and the terror of annihilation. The atomic scientists were among the first to organize against the bomb, calling for international control of atomic energy. Others followed suit in expressing their moral qualms. But by the end of the 1940s, opposition had given way to proclamations of faith in the bomb as the protector of American security. As support grew for more and bigger bombs, arguments for international control waned, and the country prepared for the possibility of nuclear war. Psychologists were strangely silent on the issue of atomic fear, and by the early fifties the nation seemed to be almost apathetic. Boyer suggests that nuclear fear did not evaporate, but may well have been buried in the national consciousness. Boyer echoes Robert J. Lifton in suggesting that denial and silence may have reflected deep-seated horror rather than complacence; indeed, in 1959 two out of three Americans listed the possibility of nuclear war as the nation's most urgent problem.

Lifton argues that the atomic bomb forced people to question one of their most deeply held beliefs: that scientific discoveries would yield progress. Atomic energy presented a fundamental contradiction: science had developed the potential for total technological mastery as well as total technological devastation. Lifton describes "nuclear numbing" as the result of the overwhelming reality of the bomb's existence. He points to unrealistic but reassuring civil defense strategies as efforts on the part of government officials to tame the fear, or "domesticate" the threat. Lifton does not see this numbing, or domestication, as evidence of indifference, but rather of the powerful psychic hold the fear of nuclear annihilation had on the nation's subconscious.

Americans were well poised to embrace domesticity in the midst of the terrors of the atomic age. A home filled with children would provide a feeling of warmth and security against the cold forces of disruption and alienation. Children would also provide a connection to the future, and a means to replenish a world depleted by war deaths. Although baby-boom parents were not likely to express conscious desires to repopulate the country, the deaths of hundreds of thousands of GIs in World War II could not have been far below the surface of postwar consciousness. The view of childbearing as a duty was painfully true for Jewish parents, after six million of their kin were snuffed out in Europe. But they were not alone. As one Jewish woman recalled of her conscious decision to bear four children, "After the Holocaust, we felt obligated to have lots of babies. But it was easy because everyone was doing it— non-Jews, too." In secure postwar homes with plenty of children, American women and men might be able to ward off their nightmares and live out their dreams.

In the face of prevailing fears, Americans moved toward the promise of the good life with an awareness of its vulnerability. The family seemed to be one place left where people could control their own destinies, and maybe even shape the future. Of course, nobody actually argued that stable family life could prevent nuclear annihilation. But the home did represent a source of meaning and security in a world run amok. If atomic bombs threatened life, marriage and reproduction affirmed life. Young marriage and lots of babies offered one way for Americans to thumb their noses at doomsday predictions. . . .

Thoughts of the family rooted in time-honored traditions may have allayed fears of vulnerability. Nevertheless, the "traditional" family was quickly becoming a relic of the past. Much of what had previously provided family security became unhinged. For many Americans, the postwar years brought rootlessness. Those who moved from farms to cities lost a way of life familiar to them and rooted in the land itself. Children of immigrants moved from familiar ethnic neighborhoods with extended kin and community ties in order to form nuclear families in the homogeneous suburbs, and invested them with extremely high hopes. Suburban homes offered freedom from kinship obligations, along with material comforts that had not been available on the farm or in the ethnic urban ghetto. . . . But consumer goods would not replace community, and young mobile nuclear families could easily find themselves adrift. Whyte noted the "rootlessness" of the new suburban residents. Newcomers devoted themselves to creating communities out of neighborhoods comprised largely of transients. . . .

Young adults aged twenty-five to thirty-five were among the most mobile members of the society, comprising 12.4 percent of all migrants but only 7.5 percent of the population. Higher education also prompted mobility; fully 45.5 percent of those who had one year of college or more lived outside their home states, compared with 27.3 percent of high school graduates. Overwhelmingly, these young, educated migrants worked for large organizations: three-fourths of all clients of long-distance movers—those affluent enough to afford the service—worked for corporations, the government, or the armed services, with corporate employees the most numerous. In their new communities, they immediately forged ties with other young transients. As Whyte noted, "The fact that they all left home can be more important in bonding them than the kind of home they left is in separating them." In the new community, they endeavored to forge ties that would be as rewarding and secure as the ones left behind, without the restraints of the old neighborhood.

Postwar Americans struggled with this transition. The popular culture was filled with stories about young adults shifting their allegiances from the old ethnic ties to the new nuclear family ideal. When working-class situation comedies shifted from radio to television, ethnic kin networks and multigenerational households faded as the stories increasingly revolved around the nuclear family. One of the most successful films of the 1950s was *Marty*, winner of the Academy Award for Best Motion Picture. In this enormously popular film, the main character, a young man living with his mother, sustains a deep commitment to the ethnic family in which he was reared. The sympathy of the audience stays with Marty as he first demonstrates tremendous family loyalty, allowing his mother to bring her cranky aging sister to live with them and doing his filial duty as the good son. As the story unfolds, Marty falls in love, and to the horror of his mother and his aunt, decides to marry his sweetheart and move away from the old neighborhood. Far from his family and their obligations, the young couple can embark upon a new life freed from the constraints of the older generation. By the film's end, the audience has made the transition, along with the main character, from loyalty to the community of ethnic kinship to the suburban ideal of the emancipated nuclear family.

The film ends there, providing no clues as to what would replace the loving kinship network portrayed so favorably at the beginning of the story. New suburbanites would need to figure that out for themselves. One way this could be achieved was through conformity to a new, modern, consumer-oriented way of life. William Whyte called the suburbs the "new melting pot" where migrants from ethnic neighborhoods in the cities moved up into the middle class. Kin and ethnic ties were often forsaken as suburban residents formed new communities grounded in shared experiences of home ownership and childrearing.

Young suburbanites were great joiners, forging new ties and creating new institutions to replace the old. . . . Church and synagogue membership reached new heights in the postwar years, expanding its functions from prayer and charity to include recreation, youth programs, and social events. Church membership rose from 64.5 million in 1940 to 114.5 million in 1960—from 50 percent to 63 percent of the entire population (a hundred years earlier only 20 percent of all Americans belonged to churches). In 1958, 97 percent of all those polled said they believed in God. Religious affiliation became associated with the "American way of life." Although many observers have commented upon the superficiality and lack of spiritual depth in much of this religious activity, there is no question that churches and synagogues provided social arenas for suburbanites, replacing to some extent the communal life previously supplied by kin or neighborhood.

Still, these were tenuous alliances among uprooted people. As William Whyte observed, suburbs offered shallow roots rather than deep ones. With so much mobility in and out of neighborhoods, and with success associated with moving on to something better, middle-class nuclear families could not depend upon the stability of their communities. Much as they endeavored to form ties with their neighbors and conform to each other's life-styles, they were still largely on their own. So the nuclear family, ultimately, relied upon itself. As promising as the new vision of home life appeared, it depended heavily on the staunch commitment of its members to sustain it. The world could not be trusted to provide security, nor could the newly forged suburban community. What mattered was that family members remained bound to each other, and to the modern, emancipated home they intended to create.

To help them in this effort, increasing numbers of women and men turned to scientific expertise. Inherited folkways would be of little help to young people looking toward a radically new vision of family life. The wisdom of earlier generations seemed to be increasingly irrelevant for young adults trying self-consciously to avoid the paths of their parents. As they turned away from "old-fashioned" ways, they embraced the advice of experts in the rapidly expanding fields of social science, medicine, and psychology. After all, science was changing the world. Was it not reasonable to expect it to change the home as well?

Postwar America was the era of the expert. Armed with scientific techniques and presumably inhabiting a world above popular passions, the experts had brought the country into the atomic age. Physicists developed the bomb; strategists created the cold war; scientific managers built the military-industrial complex. It was now up to the experts to make the unmanageable manageable. As the readers of *Look* magazine were assured, there was no reason to worry about radioactivity, for if ever it became necessary to understand its dangers, "the experts will be ready to tell you." Science and technology seemed to have invaded virtually every aspect of life, from the most public to the most private. Americans were looking to professionals to tell them how to manage their lives. The tremendous popularity of treatises such as Dr. Benjamin Spock's *Baby and Child Care* reflects a reluctance to trust the shared wisdom of kin and community. Norman Vincent Peale's *The Power of Positive Thinking* provided readers with religiously inspired scientific formulas for success. Both of these bestselling authors stressed the centrality of the family in their prescriptions for a better future.

The popularity of these kinds of books attests to the faith in expertise that prevailed at the time. One recent study by a team of sociologists examined the attitudes and habits of over four thousand Americans in 1957 and found that reliance on expertise was one of the most striking developments of the postwar years. Long-term individual therapy reached unprecedented popularity in the mid-1950s; 14 percent of the population said they had sought the help of professionals—counselors, social workers, psychiatrists, and the like—at some point in their lives. The authors concluded,

> Experts took over the role of psychic healer, but they also assumed a much broader and more important role in directing the behavior, goals, and ideals of normal people. They became the teachers and norm setters who would tell people how to approach and live life. . . . They would provide advice and counsel about raising and responding to children, how to behave in marriage, and what to see in that relationship. . . . Science moved in because people needed and wanted guidance.

A survey taken in the mid-fifties confirms these findings. Respondents frequently mentioned the experts they had read, used therapeutic jargon in their answers to questions, and even footnoted authorities in anonymous questionnaires. One out of six had consulted a professional for marital or emotional problems. Yet fewer than one-third that number considered their personal problems to be severe. It seems evident that people were quick to seek professional help. Clearly, when the experts spoke, postwar Americans listened.

In spite of public perceptions of aloofness and objectivity, professionals themselves were not far removed from the uncertainties of the day, and they groped for appropriate ways to conceptualize and resolve them. Like other postwar Americans, experts feared the possibility of social disintegration during the cold war era. As participants in the cold war consensus, they offered solutions to the difficulties of the age that would not disrupt the status quo. Professionals helped to focus and formulate the domestic ideology. For these experts, public dangers merged with private ones, and the family appeared besieged as never before. The noted anthropologist Margaret Mead articulated this problem in a 1949 article addressed to social workers. The methods of the past, she wrote, offered "an inadequate model on which to build procedures in the atomic age." Children were now born into a world unfamiliar even to their parents, "a world suddenly shrunk into one unit, in which radio and television and comics and the threat of the atomic bomb are everyday realities." For the coming generation, she wrote, "our miracles are commonplace." The task for the helping professions—psychologists, family counselors, social workers—would be especially complicated, because conditions had changed so drastically. For each adult in the new age faced "the task of trying to keep a world he [*sic*] never knew and never dreamed steady until we can rear a generation at home in it."

Political activism was not likely to keep the world steady. Instead of resistance, the experts advocated adaptation as a means of feeling "at home." The solution they offered was a new vision of family life. The modern home would offer the best means of making the inherited values of the past relevant to the uncertainties of the present and future. Experts fostered an individualist approach to family life that would appeal to postwar Americans who felt cut off from the past as they forged into a world both promising and threatening. The new home had to be fortified largely from within. Couples embarking on marriage were determined to strengthen the nuclear family through "togetherness." With the guidance of experts, successful breadwinners would provide economic support for professionalized homemakers, and together they would create the home of their dreams.

Testimonies drawn from a survey of six hundred husbands and wives during the 1950s reveal the rewards as well as the disappointments resulting from these fervent efforts to create the ideal home. The respondents were among the cohort of Americans who began their families during the early 1940s, establishing the patterns and setting the trends that were to take hold of the nation for the next two decades. Their hopes for happy and stable marriages took shape during the depression, while many couples among their parents' peers struggled with disruption and hardship. They entered marriage as World War II thrust the nation into another major crisis, wreaking further havoc upon families. They raised children as the cold war took shape, with its cloud of international tension and impending doom. Yet at the same time, they were fiercely committed to the families they formed, determined to weather the storms of crises.

These women and men were hopeful that family life in the postwar era would be secure and liberated from the hardships of the past. They believed that affluence, consumer goods, satisfying sex, and children would enhance and strengthen their families, enabling them to steer clear of potential disruptions. As they pursued their quest for the good life at home, they adhered to traditional gender roles and prized marital stability highly. Very few of them divorced. They represented a segment of the predominantly Protestant white population that was relatively well-educated and generally lived a comfortable middle-class life. In other words, they were among those Americans who would be most likely to fit the normative patterns. If any Americans had the ability to achieve the dream of a secure, affluent, and happy domestic life, it would have been these prosperous young adults.

These women and men were among the first to establish families according to the domestic ideology taking shape at the time. Their children would be among the oldest of the baby-boom generation. By the time their families were well established in the 1950s, they easily could have been the models for the American way of life Nixon extolled in Moscow. Relatively affluent, more highly educated than the average, they were among those Americans who were best able to take advantage of postwar prosperity. They looked toward the home, rather than the public world, for personal fulfillment. No wonder that when they were asked what they felt they sacrificed in life as a result of their decision to marry and raise a family, a decision that required an enormous investment of time, energy, and resources, an overwhelming majority of both men and women replied "nothing." Their priorities were clear.

One of the most striking characteristics of these respondents was their apparent willingness to give up autonomy and independence for the sake of marriage and family. Although the 1950s marked the beginning of the glamorization of bachelorhood, most of the men expressed a remarkable lack of nostalgia for the unencumbered freedom of a single life. . . .

Women were equally quick to dismiss any sacrifices they may have made when they married. Few expressed any regret at having devoted themselves to the homemaker role—a choice that effectively ruled out other lifelong occupational avenues. Although 13 percent mentioned a "career" as something sacrificed, most claimed that they gained rather than lost in the bargain. . . .

Many of the wives who said they abandoned a career were quick to minimize its importance. One said she gave up a "career—but much preferred marriage," suggesting that pursuing both at the same time was not a viable option. Many defined their domestic role as a career in itself. As one woman wrote of her choice to relinquish an outside profession: "I think I have probably contributed more to the world in the life I have lived." Another mentioned her sacrifices of "financial independence. Freedom to choose a career. However, these have been replaced by the experience of being a mother and a help to other parents and children. Therefore the new career is equally as good or better than the old." Both men and women stressed the responsibilities of married life as a source of personal fulfillment rather than sacrifice. One man remarked that "a few fishing trips and hunting trips are about all I have given up. These not to keep peace in the family, but because the time was better (and more profitably) spent at home."

Further evidence of the enormous commitment to family life appears in response to the question, "What has marriage brought you that you could not have gained without your marriage?" While the most common responses of both men and women included family, children, love, and companionship, other typical answers included a sense of purpose, success, and security. It is interesting to note that respondents claimed that these elements of life would not have been possible without marriage. . . .

Men were equally emphatic about the satisfactions brought about by family responsibility. Responding in their own words to an open-ended question, nearly one-fourth of all the men in the sample claimed that their marriages gave them a sense of purpose in life and a reason for striving. Aside from love and children, no other single reward of marriage was mentioned by so many of the husbands. . . .

Others linked family life to civic virtues by claiming that marriage strengthened their patriotism and morals, instilling in them "responsibility, community spirit, respect for children and family life, reverence for a Supreme Being, humility, love of country." Summing up the feelings of many in his generation, one husband said that marriage "increased my horizons, defined my goals and purposes in life, strengthened my convictions, raised my intellectual standards and stimulated my incentive to provide moral, spiritual, and material support; it has rewarded me with a realistic sense of family and security I never experienced during the first 24 years of my life."

The modern home would provide not only virtue and security, but also liberation and expressiveness. Most of the survey respondents agreed with the widely expressed belief that "wholesome sex relations are the cornerstone of marriage." Sexual expertise was one of several skills required of modern marital partners; as one historian has noted, by the 1940s experts had fully articulated the "cult of mutual orgasm." The respondents repeatedly noted that sexual attraction was a major reason they married their particular partners, while sexual compatibility and satisfaction were deemed essential elements in a marriage. One man wrote about his future wife, "I like particularly her size and form. . . . She attracts me strongly, physically." Others wrote about the centrality of "sex desire" in their relationships, and how important it was that they were "passionately attracted to each other." Women as well as men were likely to mention the "great appeal physically" of their partners. In essence, sexual liberation was expected to occur *within* marriage, along with shared leisure, affluence, and recreation. The modern home was a place to feel good.

These comments express a strong commitment to a new and expanded vision of family life, one focused inwardly on parents and children, and bolstered by affluence and sex. The respondents claimed to have found their personal identities and achieved their individual goals largely through their families. Yet on some level the superlatives ring a bit hollow—as if these women and men were trying to convince themselves that the families they had created fulfilled all their deepest wishes. For the extensive responses they provided to other questions in the survey reveal evidence of disappointment, dashed hopes, and lowered expectations. Many of the respondents who gave their marriages high ratings had actually resigned themselves to a great deal of misery.

As postwar Americans endeavored to live in tune with the prevailing domestic ideology, they found that there were costs involved in the effort. The dividends required a heavy investment of self. For some, the costs were well worth the benefits; for others, the costs turned out to be too high. . . .

. . . Even if the result did not fully live up to the hopes brought to it, these husbands and wives never seriously considered bailing out. Keeping in mind the fact that this generation brought down the divorce rate, it is important to consider the limited options and alternatives these men and women faced. It was not a perfect life, but it was secure and predictable. Forging an independent life outside the home carried enormous risks of emotional and economic bankruptcy, along with social ostracism. As each of these couples sealed the psychological boundary around their family, they also in large measure sealed their fates within it. No wonder it was their deepest wish to build a warm hearth against the cold war.

SUGGESTIONS FOR FURTHER READING

The last decade has seen the publication of a number of overviews of the 1950s. Among the best are William L. O'Neill, *American High: The Years of Confidence, 1945–1960* (1986); David Halberstam, *The Fifties* (1993); J. Ronald Oakley, *God's Country: America in the Fifties* (1986); and John Patrick Diggins, *The Proud Decades: America in War and Peace, 1941–1960* (1988). Still worth reading is Eric Goldman's *The Crucial Decade—and After: America, 1945–1960* (1955, 1960). See also Robert H. Bremner and Gary Reichard, eds., *Reshaping America: Society and Institutions, 1945–1960* (1982).

The Eisenhower Presidency

There is now a voluminous scholarship on the Eisenhower presidency. Some good general studies are Stephen E. Ambrose, *Eisenhower: The President* (1984); Gary Reichard, *Politics as Usual: The Age of Truman and Eisenhower* (1988); Chester J. Pach, Jr., and Elmo Richardson, *The Presidency of Dwight D. Eisenhower* (1979, 1991); William Bragg Ewald, Jr., *Eisenhower the President: Crucial Days, 1951–1960* (1981); Fred I. Greenstein, *The Hidden-Hand Presidency: Eisenhower as Leader* (1982); Charles C. Alexander, *Holding the Line: The Eisenhower Era, 1952–1961* (1975); Herbert S. Parmet, *Eisenhower and the American Crusades* (1972); R. Alton Lee, *Dwight D. Eisenhower: Soldier and Statesman* (1981); and Peter Lyon, *Eisenhower: Portrait of the Hero* (1974). Robert Griffith's important article "Dwight D. Eisenhower and the Corporate Commonwealth," *American Historical Review,* vol. 77 (February 1982), pp. 87–122, argues that Eisenhower held a well-developed political philosophy that rejected both the traditional conservatism of his own party and the federal statism of the Democrats. Yet, Griffith concludes, Eisenhower's vision "was no match for the vast and powerful forces of modern America."

Several anthologies capture the scope of Eisenhower revisionism. Perhaps the best is Shirley Anne Warshaw, ed., *Reexamining the Eisenhower Presidency* (1993). See also Joann P. Krieg, ed., *Dwight D. Eisenhower: Soldier, President, Statesman* (1987) and Gunter Bischoff and Stephen E. Ambrose, eds., *Eisenhower: A Centenary Assessment* (1995).

William V. Shannon's article "Eisenhower as President," *Commentary,* vol. 26 (November 1958), pp. 390–398, summed up the once-traditional view of the Eisenhower presidency when it described Eisenhower's two terms as "the time of the great postponement." Other traditional accounts of Eisenhower's presidency include Marquis Childs, *Eisenhower: Captive Hero: A Critical Study of the General and the President* (1958); Richard Neustadt, *Presidential Power: The Politics of Leadership* (1960); and William F. Buckley, "The Tranquil World of Dwight D. Eisenhower," *National Review,* vol. 5 (January 18, 1958), pp. 57–59.

A landmark article by Murray Kempton, "The Underestimation of Dwight D. Eisenhower," *Esquire,* vol. 68 (September 1967), pp. 108–109, 156, argued for a reappraisal of Eisenhower. In *Nixon Agonistes* (1969), Gary Wills insisted that "Eisenhower was not a political sophisticate; he was a political genius." Richard H. Rovere, "Eisenhower Revisited—A Political Genius? A Brilliant Man?" *New York Times Magazine,* February 1971, pp. 14, 15, 54, 58, 59, 62, criticized the enthusiasm shown by writers like Kempton and Wills but nevertheless arrived at a more favorable evaluation of Eisenhower than Rovere himself had done almost a decade earlier in "Eisenhower Over the Shoulder," *American Scholar,* vol. 31 (Spring 1962), pp. 176–179.

Parmet's *Eisenhower and the American Crusades* set the tone for a scholarly reappraisal of the Eisenhower presidency in the early 1970s. It was joined by Alexander's *Holding the Line;* Lyon's more critical *Portrait of a Hero;* Gary W. Reichard's *The Reaffirmation of Republicanism: Eisenhower and the Eighty-Third Congress* (1975); and Cornelius P. Cotter, "Eisenhower as Party Leader," *Political Science Quarterly,* vol. 98 (Summer 1983), pp. 255–283.

Review essays of scholarship on the Eisenhower presidency include Vincent P. De Santis, "Eisenhower Revisionism," *Review of Politics,* vol. 38 (April 1976), pp. 190–208; Mary S. MacAuliffe, "Eisenhower, the President," *Journal of American History,* vol. 68 (December 1981), pp. 625–632; and Anthony James Joes, "Eisenhower Revisionism: The Tide Comes In," *Presidential Studies Quarterly,* vol. 15 (Summer 1985), pp. 561–571.

Published documents include Alfred Chandler's massive and ongoing project, *Papers of Dwight D. Eisenhower* (1970–); Robert H. Ferrell, ed., *The Eisenhower Diaries* (1981); Robert Griffith, ed., *Ike's Letters to a Friend: 1941–1958* (1984); and Robert Ferrell, ed., *The Diary of James C. Hagerty* (1983).

A number of major figures of the Eisenhower years published memoirs. Eisenhower's own two-volume presidential memoirs, *Mandate for Change, 1953–1956* (1963) and *Waging Peace, 1956–1961* (1965), are quite well done and informative. Among those in Eisenhower's official or personal circle who published memoirs are Sherman Adams, *First Hand Report: The Inside Story of the Eisenhower Administration* (1961); Arthur Larson, *Eisenhower: The President Nobody Knew* (1968); Emmet John Hughes, *The Ordeal of Power: A Political Memoir of the Eisenhower Years* (1963); Richard M. Nixon, *Six Crises* (1962); Ezra Taft Benson, *Cross Fire: The Eight Years with Eisenhower* (1962); Robert Cutler, *No Time for Rest* (1965); and Milton S. Eisenhower, *The President Is Calling* (1974). Robert J. Donovan, a journalist, was given extraordinary access to the first Eisenhower administration and produced a useful account, *Eisenhower: The Inside Story* (1956).

Biographies

Biographies of Eisenhower are too numerous to list. A good place to begin is Ambrose's two-volume *Eisenhower* (1983, 1984), which is also available in a condensed one-volume version (1990). See also William B. Pickett, *Dwight David Eisenhower and American Power* (1995); Piers Brendon, *Ike: His Life and Times* (1986); Robert F. Burk, *Dwight D. Eisenhower: Hero and Politician* (1986); and Steve Neal's *The Eisenhowers* (1984). Biographies of other important political figures of the fifties include Wills, *Nixon Agonistes;* Roger Morris, *Richard Milhous Nixon* (1989); Herbert S. Parmet, *Nixon and His America* (1990); Stephen E. Ambrose, *Nixon* (3 vols., 1987–1991); John Bartlow Martin, *Adlai Stevenson and the World* (2 vols., 1979); Rodney M. Sievers, *The Last Puritan: Adlai Stevenson in American Politics* (1983); Richard Norton Smith, *Thomas E. Dewey and His Times* (1982); Robert Dallek, *Lone Star Rising: Lyndon Johnson and His Times, 1908–1960* (1991); Rowland Evans and Robert Novak, *Lyndon B. Johnson: The Exercise of Power* (1966); James T. Patterson, *Mr. Republican: A Biography of Robert A. Taft* (1972); D. B. Hardeman and Donald C. Bacon, *Rayburn* (1987); Anthony Champagne, *Congressman Sam Rayburn* (1984); Carl Solberg, *Hubert Humphrey* (1984); and Charles L. Fontenay, *Estes Kefauver* (1980).

Joseph McCarthy and the Red Scare

Among the many studies of Joseph McCarthy and the red scare, see Richard M. Fried, *Nightmare in Red: The McCarthy Era in Perspective* (1990); Robert Griffith, *The Politics of Fear: Joseph R. McCarthy and the Senate* (1970; revised 2nd edition, 1987); Athan G. Theoharis, *Seeds of Repression: Harry S. Truman and the Origins of McCarthyism* (1971); David Caute, *The Great Fear: The Anti-Communist Purge under Truman and Eisenhower* (1978); Richard M. Fried, *Men Against McCarthy* (1976); Ellen W. Schrecker, *No Ivory Tower: McCarthyism and the Universities* (1986); Thomas C. Reeves, *The Life and Times of Joe McCarthy* (1982); David Oshinsky, *A Conspiracy So Immense: The World of Joe McCarthy* (1983); Richard H. Rovere, *Senator Joe McCarthy* (1959); and Edwin Blayley, *Joe McCarthy and the Press* (1988). Studies of Eisenhower's response to McCarthy are William Bragg Ewald, *Who Killed Joe McCarthy?* (1984); Jeff Broadwater, *Eisenhower and the Anti-Communist Crusade* (1992); John G. Adams, *Without Precedent: The Story of the Death of McCarthyism* (1983); and Allan Yarnell, "Eisenhower and McCarthy: An Appraisal of Presidential Strategy," *Presidential Studies Quarterly*, vol. 10 (Winter 1980), pp. 90–97.

Civil Rights

For Eisenhower's civil rights policies, see Robert F. Burk, *The Eisenhower Administration and Black Civil Rights* (1984) and several articles by Michael S. Mayer, "Eisenhower and the Southern Federal Judiciary: The Sobeloff Nomination," in Warshaw, *Reexamining the Eisenhower Presidency* (1993) pp. 57–83; "The Eisenhower Administration and the Desegregation of Washington, D.C.," *Journal of Policy History*, vol. 3 (1991), pp. 24–41; "The Eisenhower Administration and the Civil Rights Act of 1957," *Congress and the Presidency*, vol. 16 (Autumn 1989), pp. 137–154; "With Much Deliberation and Some Speed: Eisenhower and the *Brown* Decision," *Journal of Southern History*, vol. 52 (February 1986), pp. 43–76; and "Regardless of Station, Race, or Calling: Eisenhower and Race" in Krieg, *Dwight D. Eisenhower* (1987) pp. 33–41. James C. Duram, *A Moderate among Extremists: Dwight D. Eisenhower and the School Segregation Crisis* (1981) is not especially well done. An early account of the Civil Rights Act of 1957 is J. W. Anderson, *Eisenhower,*

Brownell, and the Congress (1964). E. Frederic Morrow was the first black man to hold an executive position in the White House. He produced two memoirs, *Black Man in the White House* (1963) and the somewhat more angry *Forty Years a Guinea Pig* (1980).

For the civil rights movement in general, see Steven F. Lawson, *Running for Freedom: Civil Rights and Black Politics in America Since 1941* (1991); Robert Weisbrot, *Freedom Bound: A History of America's Civil Rights Movement* (1990); Taylor Branch, *Parting the Waters: America in the King Years, 1954–1963* (1988); David Garrow, *Bearing the Cross: Martin Luther King, Jr., and the Southern Christian Leadership Conference* (1986); Aldon Morris, *The Origins of the Civil Rights Movement: Black Communities Organizing for Change* (1984); and August Meier and Elliott Rudwick, *CORE: A Study in the Civil Rights Movement* (1975).

Policy Issues

Iwan Morgan has asserted that the budget "touched in some way or other" virtually every issue during the Eisenhower years except McCarthyism and civil rights. William O'Neill has suggested that Eisenhower's budgets are his greatest achievements. For information on the budget, see John W. Sloan, *Eisenhower and the Management of Prosperity* (1991); Iwan W. Morgan, *Eisenhower versus "The Spenders": The Eisenhower Administration, the Democrats, and the Budget, 1953–1960* (1990); Raymond Saulnier, *Constructive Years: The U. S. Economy Under Eisenhower* (1991); and Maurice H. Stans, *One of the President's Men: Twenty Years with Eisenhower and Nixon* (1995).

Other monographs dealing with specific policy issues are Alan McAdams, *Power and Politics in Labor Legislation* (1964); Aaron Wildavsky, *Dixon-Yates: A Study in Power Politics* (1962); Mark Rose, *Interstate: Express Highway Politics, 1941–1956* (1979); and David Frier, *Conflict of Interest in the Eisenhower Administration* (1969).

The Warren Court

Eisenhower is often quoted as having made a remark to the effect that appointing Earl Warren as chief justice of the Supreme Court was the greatest mistake of his presidency. There is no evidence that he ever made any such statement and much evidence to contradict it. Certainly, however, the appointment of Warren, along with those of justices Potter Stewart, William Brennan, and John Marshall Harlan rank among Eisenhower's most significant legacies. For information on the Warren Court, see Mark Tushnet, ed., *The Warren Court in Historical and Political Perspective* (1993); Philip B. Kurland, *Politics, the Constitution, and the Warren Court* (1970); Paul L. Murphy, *The Constitution in Crisis Times, 1918–1969* (1972); and Kermit Hall, "The Warren Court," *Indiana Law Review*, vol. 28 (1995), pp. 309–328. Biographies of Earl Warren include Bernard Schwartz, *Super Chief: Earl Warren and His Supreme Court—A Judicial Biography* (1983) and G. Edward White, *Earl Warren: A Public Life* (1982). See also Earl Warren, *The Memoirs of Chief Justice Earl Warren* (1977).

Foreign Policy

Eisenhower's foreign policy has been the source of sometimes heated debate among historians. One would have to search hard to find a historian who still holds on to the notion that Eisenhower ineptly bumbled through eight years of the cold war and, in any case, delegated the formulation conduct of foreign policy to John Foster Dulles. Robert Divine, *Eisenhower and the Cold War* (1981) provides a brief, mildly revisionist overview. Other overviews include Ambrose, *Eisenhower: The President* (vol. 2); Piers Brendon, *Ike: His Life and Times* (1987); Virgil Pinkley with James F. Scheer, *Eisenhower Declassified* (1979); and Richardson and Pach, *The Presidency of Dwight D. Eisenhower.* More critical is Blanche Wiessen Cook, *The Declassified Eisenhower* (1980). The postrevisionist view is put forth in Robert J. McMahon, "Eisenhower and Third World Nationalism: A Critique of the Revisionists," *Political Science Quarterly*, vol. 101 (1986), pp. 453–473. Richard H. Immerman's thoughtful "Confessions of an Eisenhower Revisionist: An Agonizing Reappraisal," *Diplomatic History*, vol. 14 (Summer 1990), pp. 319–342, balances revisionist and postrevisionist perspectives through a discussion of the New Look. See also Richard A. Melanson and David Mayers, eds., *Reevaluating Eisenhower: American Foreign Policy in the Fifties* (1987).

Nuclear Policy

For nuclear policy, consult David Alan Rosenberg, "The Origins of Overkill: Nuclear Weapons and American Strategy," in Norman A. Graebner, ed., *The National Security: Its Theory and Practice* (1986); Samuel F. Wells, Jr., "The Origins of Massive Retaliation," *Political Science Quarterly*, vol. 96 (Spring 1981), pp. 31–52; and H. W. Brands, "The Age of Vulnerability: Eisenhower and the National Insecurity State," *American Historical Review*, vol. 94 (October 1989), pp. 963–989. Burton Kaufman, *Trade and Aid: Eisenhower's Foreign Economic Policy, 1953–61* (1982) covers economic diplomacy. Covert operations under Eisenhower have drawn a good deal of attention. See Stephen E. Ambrose with Richard H. Immerman, *Ike's Spies: Eisenhower and the Espionage Establishment* (1981). Studies of specific covert operations include Richard H. Immerman, *The CIA and Guatemala: The Foreign Policy of Intervention* (1982); Stephen Schlesinger and Stephen Kinzer, *Bitter Fruit: The Untold Story of the American Coup in Guatemala* (1981); Barry Rubin, *Paved with Good Intentions: The American Experience and Iran* (1980); James A. Bill, *The Eagle and the Lion: The Tragedy of American-Iranian Relations* (1983); and Michael R. Bechloss, *Mayday: Eisenhower, Khrushchev and the U-2 Affair* (1986). Anna Kasten Nelson has studied Eisenhower's management of the national security structure in "The Top of the Policy Hill: President and the National Security Council," *Diplomatic History*, vol. 7 (Fall 1983), pp. 307–326.

Specific foreign policy episodes have also received excellent treatment. On the CIA-backed coup in Guatemala, see Immerman, *The CIA and Guatemala* and Schlesinger and Kinzer, *Bitter Fruit*. For a different perspective, consult Frederick W. Marks III, "The CIA and Castillo Armas in Guatemala, 1954," *Diplomatic History*, vol. 14 (Winter 1990), pp. 67–86. The overthrow of the Mossadegh government is covered by Bill, *The Eagle and the Lion* and Rubin, *Paved with Good Intentions*. On Eisenhower's dealings with the Cuban revolution, consult Richard E. Welch, Jr., *Response to Revolution: The United States and the Cuban Revolution, 1959–1961* (1985) and Trumball Higgins, *The Perfect Failure: Kennedy, Eisenhower, and the CIA at the Bay of Pigs* (1987). A more general study of Latin America is Stephen Rabe, *Eisen-*

hower and Latin America: The Foreign Policy of Anticommunism (1988).

Eisenhower's policy in Indochina has been the subject of several excellent scholarly treatments. Melanie Billings Yun, *Decision Against War: Eisenhower and Dien Bien Phu, 1954* (1988) praises Eisenhower's decision not to intervene in Indochina. David Anderson, *Trapped by Success: The Eisenhower Administration and Vietnam, 1953–61* (1991) argues that Eisenhower "postponed the day of reckoning" in Indochina and made decisions that deepened the American commitment to South Vietnam. See also James R. Arnold, *The First Domino: Eisenhower, the Military, and America's Intervention in Vietnam* (1991) and George C. Herring and Richard H. Immerman, "Eisenhower, Dulles, and Dienbienphu: 'The Day We Didn't Go to War' Revisited," *Journal of American History*, vol. 71 (September 1984), pp. 343–363.

For Eisenhower's policy toward the Middle East, particularly with respect to the Suez crisis, see Isaac Alteras, *Eisenhower and Israel: U.S.-Israeli Relations, 1953–1960* (1993); Cole C. Kingseed, *Eisenhower and the Suez Crisis of 1956* (1995); and Donald Neff, *Warriors at Suez: Eisenhower Takes America into the Middle East* (1980).

A pioneering discussion of Eisenhower's relationship with John Foster Dulles is Richard H. Immerman, "Eisenhower and Dulles: Who Made the Decisions?", *Political Psychology* vol. 1 (Autumn 1979), pp. 3–20. See also Richard H. Immerman, ed., *John Foster Dulles and the Diplomacy of the Cold War* (1990) and Townsend Hoopes, *The Devil and John Foster Dulles* (1973).

Foreign policy plays itself out in the domestic political arena as well. Consult, for example, Duane Tananbaum, *The Bricker Amendment Controversy: A Test of Eisenhower's Political Leadership* (1988). The space race began in the 1950s, as related by Robert A. Divine, *The Sputnik Challenge: Eisenhower's Response to the Soviet Satellite* (1993); James R. Killian, *Sputnik, Scientists, and Eisenhower* (1977); and Walter A. McDougall, *The Heavens and Earth: A Political History of the Space Age* (1985).

Postwar American Culture

Studies of postwar American culture and society have abounded in recent years. A good place to begin an examination of American society is Robert H. Brenner and Gary W. Reichard, eds., *Reshaping America: Society and Institutions, 1945–1960* (1982).

Education Issues

Studies of education include Diane Ravitch, *The Troubled Crusade: American Education, 1945–1980* (1983); Fred M. Hechinger, *The Big Red Schoolhouse* (1968); Robert Hampel, *The Last Little Citadel: American High Schools Since 1940* (1986); Lawrence A. Cremin, *American Education: The Metropolitan Experience, 1876–1980* (1988). See also Arthur Bestor, *Educational Wastelands: The Retreat from Learning in Our Public Schools* (1954), a powerful critique of progressive theories of education.

Labor Issues

On labor, consult Foster Rhea Dulles and Melvyn Dubofsky, *Labor in America* (1984); James R. Green, *The World of the Worker* (1980); David Brody, *Workers in Industrial America* (1980); and R. Alton Lee, *Eisenhower and Landrum-Griffin: A Study in Labor-Management Politics* (1990).

Postwar Women's Issues

Works on women include William Chafe, *The American Woman: Her Changing Social, Economic, and Political Roles, 1920–1970* (1972); Susan Lynn, *Progressive Women in Conservative Times: Racial Justice, Peace, and Feminism 1945 to the 1960s* (1992); Leila J. Rupp and Verta Taylor, *Survival in the Doldrums: The American Women's Rights Movement, 1945 to the 1960s* (1987); and Eugenia Kaledin, *Mothers and More: American Women in the 1950s* (1984). Elaine Tyler May's *Homeward Bound: American Families in the Cold War Era* (1988) relates the revival of domesticity to themes of the cold war. See also Ricky Solinger, *Wake Up, Little Susie: Single Pregnancy and Race before Roe v. Wade* (1992).

James Gilbert's *A Cycle of Outrage: America's Reaction to the Juvenile Delinquent in the 1950s* (1986) considers why juvenile delinquency became almost a national obsession in the absence of reliable evidence that there was an increase in the rate of juvenile offenders.

The fifties were a time of significant demographic change. The population shifted from the North and East to the South and

West; it also shifted from urban to suburban areas. For information on suburbs, see Kenneth T. Jackson, *Crabgrass Frontier: The Suburbanization of the United States* (1985) and Zane Miller, *Suburb: Neighborhood and Community in Forest Park, Ohio, 1935–1976* (1981). Richard M. Bernard and Bradley R. Rice, *Sunbelt Cities: Politics and Growth Since World War II* (1983) deals with the growth of cities in the South and West.

Economic Issues

For economic issues, consult Harold G. Vatter, *The U.S. Economy in the 1950s* (1963) and W. Elliot Brownlee, *Dynamics of Ascent: A History of the American Economy* (1974).

Historical Inquiry

American culture of the postwar era has been one of the richest areas of historical inquiry in the last decade. Among the most useful works are W. T. Lhamon, *Deliberate Speed: The Origins of a Cultural Style in the American 1950s* (1990); William S. Graebner, *The Age of Doubt: American Thought and Culture in the 1940s* (1991); Stephen J. Whitfield, *The Culture of the Cold War* (1991); and Paul Carter, *Another Part of the Fifties* (1983). A more specialized study is Paul Boyer, *By the Bomb's Early Light: American Thought and Culture at the Dawn of the Atomic Age* (1985).

The 1950s

The fifties produced outstanding intellectual achievement in a wide variety of areas. Richard Pells, *The Liberal Mind in a Conservative Age: American Intellectuals in the 1940s and 1950s* (1985) deals with political intellectuals. Two influential groups receive attention in Alexander Bloom, *Prodigal Sons: The New York Intellectuals and Their World* (1986) and Zoltan Tar, *The Frankfurt School: The Critical Theories of Max Horkheimer and Theodor W. Adorno* (1985). Studies of individuals include Richard Fox, *Reinhold Niebuhr* (1985); George Kateb, *Hannah Arendt: Politics, Conscience, Evil* (1984); Irving Louis Horowitz, *C. Wright Mills: An American Utopian* (1983); and Stephen Whitfield, *A Critical American: The Politics of Dwight Macdonald* (1984).

American intellectuals of the 1950s produced a number of works of great consequence. Their work remains well worth reading. A brief sample includes Hannah Arendt, *The Origins of Totalitarianism* (1951); David Riesman, Nathan Glazier, and Reuel Denney, *The Lonely Crowd* (1950); William Whyte, Jr., *The Organization Man* (1956); Daniel Bell, *The End of Ideology* (1960); Reinhold Niebuhr, *Moral Man and Immoral Society* (1952) and *Children of Light, Children of Darkness* (1944); and C. Wright Mills, *White Collar* (1951) and *The Power Elite* (1956).

Until recently, conservative intellectuals have received relatively little attention. That gap has been filled by George Nash, *The Conservative Intellectual Movement in America Since 1945* (1976); Michael W. Miles, *The Odyssey of the American Right* (1980); and Paul Gottfried, *The Conservative Movement* (1993). Influential works by postwar conservative thinkers include Friedrich A. Hayek, *The Road to Serfdom* (1944); Leo Strauss, *What Is Political Philosophy? and Other Studies* (1959); and Russell Kirk, *The Conservative Mind* (1953).

The 1950s and Popular Culture

Popular culture has received even more attention than high culture. For information on television, consult James L. Baughman, *The Republic of Mass Culture: Journalism, Filmmaking, and Broadcasting in America Since 1941* (1992); Leo Bogart, *The Age of Television* (1956, 1972); and Erik Barnouw, *Tube of Plenty: The Evolution of American Television* (1975, 1990). The history of rock-and-roll is chronicled in Charlie Gillett, *The Sound of the City: The Rise of Rock and Roll* (1970, 1983) and David P. Szatmary, *Rockin' in Time: A Social History of Rock-and-Roll* (1987, 1991). Studies of film include Nora Sayre, *Running Time: Films of the Cold War* (1982); Peter Biskind, *Seeing Is Believing: How Hollywood Taught Us to Stop Worrying and Love the Fifties* (1983); and Andrew Dowdy, *The Films of the Fifties: The American State of Mind* (1973).

The 1950s and Religion

Some studies of religion include Henry May, *Ideas, Faiths, and Feelings: Essays on American Intellectual and Religious History,*

1952–1982 (1983); Robert Wuthnow, *The Restructuring of American Religion: Society and Faith Since World War II* (1988); Carol V. R. George, *God's Salesman: Norman Vincent Peale and the Power of Positive Thinking* (1993); William G. McLoughlin, Jr., *Billy Graham: Revivalist in a Secular Age* (1960); William Martin, *A Prophet with Honor: The Billy Graham Story* (1991); and Fox, *Reinhold Niebuhr.* Will Herberg's classic study, *Protestant, Catholic, Jew* (1955), remains an insightful look into American religion of the fifties.